THE
GRAMOPHONE
GUIDE TO HI-FI

John Borwick
Audio Editor of
GRAMOPHONE

D1349930

DAVID & CHARLES
Newton Abbot   London

British Library Cataloguing in Publication Data

Borwick, John
  The Gramophone guide to hi-fi.
  1. High-fidelity sound systems—
  Catalogs
  I. Title
  621.389′3   TK7881.7

  ISBN 0–7153–8231–4

Typeset by Keyspools Ltd,
Golborne, Warrington, WA3 3QA
and printed in Great Britain
by Butler & Tanner Limited,
Frome and London
for David & Charles (Publishers) Limited
Brunel House Newton Abbot Devon

Contents

1
Pleasures in Store

I have just been listening to Elisabeth Schwarzkopf singing Schubert's *An die Musik* (To Music) to get myself into a suitably relaxed mood to write about music in the home. I entirely agree with the song's sentiment, which I roughly translate as 'Blessed art, how often in grey hours you have transported me to a better world and better days.'

Astute readers, who know that Miss Schwarzkopf retired from the concert platform in the late 1970s, will have realised that I could not actually have been listening to the celebrated soprano 'live' but on one of her many recordings (HMV ALP 3843). However, the recording balance is admirably clear, with the singer and the piano (played by Edwin Fischer) positioned at a natural distance in a pleasant acoustic ambience. Also my record playing equipment has been chosen with care and well looked after, with the loudspeakers located for best results in my particular room and in proper relation to my armchair. It therefore needs only a little effort on my part to *imagine* that I am listening to a live recital.

To the extent that we have only an illusion to listen to, reproduced music must always be less accurate and emotionally absorbing than the real thing. Yet the ability to hear music of our own choice at any hour of the day or night is a blessing indeed, and there are other advantages too. Without having to dress up, brave the weather and the barrage of rustling programmes, wait until an appointed hour, or travel across a crowded city, we can choose whole symphonies or snippets, opera or old-time dance music. At the touch of a switch we can conjure up star performers that a king's ransom could not gather together. As well as for serious or at least deliberate listening to music, a home system is a perfect source of background music for relaxation, entertaining, reminiscing and making light of domestic chores. We can dance to it, hum, sing, study and work to it.

A further bonus is the possibility of making immediate comparisons of performances by different artists, including voices from the past. For example my collection contains several performances of Schubert's *An die Musik*. Just a week

ago, as I write, I was present at a talk on 'The performance of
the German Lied' given by Elisabeth Schwarzkopf in the
Queen Elizabeth Hall. She played recordings of various
singers, including the famous German baritone Gerhard
Hüsch. Lo and behold, though his eightieth birthday was only
a few days away, he was there in the audience and rose to
acknowledge the applause. I have his 1938 recording of *An die
Musik* (transcribed on World Records SHB 65) and, though the
recording quality shows its age, I am happy to 'suspend my
disbelief' and succumb to the illusion of hearing him in person.

Each reader will no doubt have his own list of favourite
contemporary and former-age musicians, and a record collection can both provide a dose of nostalgia when we feel like it,
and keep us bang up to date with the latest rock musicians or
the music from a show or concert we have just attended. The
radio too can expand our knowledge of music, with talks and
magazine programmes as well as relays of music in all its
variety. Thus a collection of records or tapes, and a decent
home sound system including a radio receiver, can be at the
centre of a whole world of musical enjoyment.

Infinite variety

The pleasures we derive from listening to music are many and
varied. They range from the cerebral and intellectual to the
emotional and ephemeral. They have their origins in prehis-
tory and therefore defy exact analysis. This gives music a
certain aura of mystery, and has caused it to be associated with
various therapeutic or even mystical powers—as 'Music hath
charms to soothe a savage breast' (Congreve). Again, the old
legend of 'The Pied Piper of Hamelin' as retold by Robert
Browning ascribes strange powers indeed to music.

From small beginnings (see next chapter) music and
entertainment on tap are now a commonplace in nearly every
home and in most countries of the world. Radio and television
offer a wide choice of programmes, though the timing and
precise selection of items is outside the consumer's hands.
Records and cassettes can be played whenever the mood takes
you, and you can skip or repeat pieces to your heart's content.
You pay the piper and *you* call the tune. By adding a tape
recorder, you can get the best of both worlds by taping radio or
TV programmes for later listening or viewing. A taste for any
particular type of music can be indulged and developed, as you
build up a collection of your favourite music performed by your
favourite artists.

However, with so much music to choose from, it does pay to

be a bit selective. A browse in your local record shop will soon show you the infinite range of recorded music available. The *Gramophone Classical Catalogue*, for example, has about 200 pages in its composers section alone, with 160 records on average to a page—about 32,000 classical albums in total! And there are companion catalogues for *Popular Music* and *The Spoken Word*. One fairly recent development has been a greater spirit of adventure on the part of the record companies. So, while continuing to bring out new recordings of all the old favourites like Tchaikovsky, Beethoven and Mozart, they now explore less well charted musical territory. Early music and ultra-modern music are now readily available. Appendix 1 provides a basic collection of recommended records and tapes.

The quest for quality

Perhaps the most obvious change which has taken place in home music equipment has been in the quality of sound reproduction. Edison's first phonograph produced a barely recognisable croaking imitation of his voice, with the musical pitch very much at the mercy of the speed at which he cranked the handle. However, as the years went by, the faithfulness or 'fidelity' of reproduction became progressively better. The expression 'high fidelity', abbreviated to 'hi-fi', came into universal currency around 1950 to denote sound equipment of above average quality.

Hi-fi remains a relative, rather than an absolute, term despite many attempts to give it a precise definition. Our ultimate aim is clear enough: to achieve the reproduction of music with such accuracy that the sounds heard are an exact replica, ie they cannot be distinguished from the original. An analogy would be a high quality reproduction of a famous painting. Yet reproducing music is a complex business, with the acoustics of the listening-room itself influencing the sounds we hear, and clearly limiting the 'scale' of the reproduced sound. Also, our ability to detect small imperfections in the sound constantly develops so that we soon become dissatisfied with a standard of quality that once seemed perfectly adequate.

All that can be achieved is a specification for the *minimum* requirements for the units in a hi-fi system, and even this will need to be revised as the 'state of the art' progresses. Here are just two of the main headings which such a specification might include (for a more technical explanation see Chapter 12).

(a) *Frequency range* This refers to the equipment's ability to reproduce all the sounds of the musical spectrum, from the deepest organ pedal notes and double basses up to the top overtones which characterise the sounds of a trumpet, violin or piccolo. Human hearing is generally taken to extend from 20 to 20,000Hz (Hertz) but a practical minimum range for equipment deserving to be labelled 'hi-fi' might be 35–15,000Hz. Within this range, the equipment must respond evenly, and so we should qualify the range by indicating the extent (in decibels) by which the response is allowed to vary, eg 35–15,000Hz ±2dB.

The most usual frequency range deficiency is a lack of bass. This, as might be expected, makes the music sound thin or lacking in body and is a characteristic of small loudspeakers. Conversely, some systems peak up in loudness at or around some low frequency and this produces a tiring one-note-bass effect. We associate this problem with the resonating cabinets of old-fashioned radiograms, but it can occur in a modern system too—perhaps because the loudspeakers are awkwardly placed close to a wall or the floor. A falling response at the high frequency end of the spectrum can be tolerated but of course it robs the music of much of its brightness and life. On the other hand, a rising treble response gives an unwelcome edge to the music and will emphasise any surface noise or harshness on records.

(b) *Dynamic range*   Just as there is a prescribed range of frequencies to which the human ear will respond, so there is a definite maximum level of sound intensity which the ear can withstand without damage. Also, at the other end of the loudness scale, we find a more or less definable lower threshold below which sounds become inaudible. The range of sound intensities to which the ear can respond is almost unbelievably wide, with the upper limit measuring about 1,000,000,000,000 times greater than the lower. To avoid dealing in such large numbers, and to accord more accurately with the way in which the brain assesses the level of stimuli to all five of our senses, namely by estimating the *ratio* between stimuli, sound levels are expressed in logarithmic rather than linear units. The dynamic range is divided into twelve steps called Bels (after Alexander Graham Bell). Each step represents a tenfold increase and is further subdivided into ten smaller ratios called decibels (dB).

Fortunately, perhaps, music does not utilise the full 120dB range of human hearing. It stops some way short of the full +120dB level, which would correspond to the noise of a pneumatic road-drill. At the low end of the intensity scale, music also runs into a barrier which limits how quiet the players can go. The fact is that we are always immersed in ambient noise of some kind or another, compounded of distant traffic noise, people breathing, central heating or ventilation machinery. Therefore, in a concert hall, though less so perhaps in a well sound-proofed recording studio, players find that their quietest pianissimo must level out at the prevailing ambient noise level if it is to remain just audible.

In practice, the dynamic range in a Beethoven symphony, for example, might be about 75dB between a solo violin pianissimo passage and a full orchestral fortissimo. If we add a few dB for the excesses of some twentieth-century scoring, and the fact that recording engineers place their microphones at varying distances from the performers, it might be thought that we are asking our reproducing equipment to handle 85dB overall. However, records and broadcasts are more restricted than this. Studio tape machines can handle up to about 65dB, LP records perhaps 55dB and AM radio transmissions tend to be compressed to a mere 30dB. For an audio system to reproduce all these music sources adequately, therefore, it should possess a minimum dynamic range capability of, say, 70dB. This, for an amplifier, for example, will usually be quoted in terms of the 'signal-to-noise ratio', ie the ratio of the rated maximum output power level to that of the residual inherent noise.

What you need

LP gramophone records continue to be the foremost source of music in the home. This is the format in which the widest choice of music is already encapsulated and the way that most new recordings still come on to the market. So a record player is essential, with the 33⅓ revolutions per minute speed used for 12in LPs and the 45rpm speed too if you will want to play 7in 'single' discs. The old 78rpm speed is useful only for enthusiasts who still have collections of the old, brittle, shellac records, and there are in fact very few turntables made nowadays which can be switched to that speed.

Musicassettes, that is prerecorded tape cassettes sold as alternatives to discs, are to be found in increasing numbers in the shops. Though cassettes are a long way from catching up with disc records in the choice of repertoire in the catalogues, most record companies now issue a cassette equivalent either simultaneously or soon after the release of the LP album. The added mobility of a cassette deck therefore makes it worth considering as well as a record player. The big advantage is, of course, that a cassette machine allows you to record as well as play back. This opens out a number of creative possibilities, such as combining recording with hobbies or education.

Finally, no home audio system should omit a good radio receiver. There are very real advantages in including the VHF/FM band, both in terms of sound quality and the avoidance of interference from unwanted stations. However, some broadcasts of interest may be available on the medium, long or short wavebands only and so this point should be checked before making a final choice.

Apart from equipment to take care of these three sound sources—disc, tape and radio—the remaining requirements include an amplifier which will act as a control centre and provide the necessary boosting of levels to drive the loud-speakers. Stereophonic reproduction, involving two channels instead of the old-fashioned single-channel mono, is now so well established as the norm that you should budget for a stereo amplifier and a pair of matching loudspeakers. Chapter 6 describes in detail the various shapes and combinations available, from the humble one-piece record-player or portable radio-cassette recorder to the most ambitious component hi-fi system beloved of 'audiophiles'.

Besides the main music installation, many people like to be able to switch the music through to remote loudspeakers in other rooms, or set up less complex systems in bedrooms, etc. This is discussed in Chapter 10, along with ideas for enjoying audio on the move—in cars, boats or even on headphones while you jog or play golf. In short, music can now be enjoyed anywhere—and to standards of sonic fidelity once thought impossible. Even as I write, plans are well advanced for launching laser-beam disc players (see Chapter 15), to add yet another sound source to our home systems.

2
The Evolution of Sound Recording

Equipment for recording and reproducing sounds has been with us for more than 100 years. This means that every one of us has grown up to expect music of our own choosing at the touch of a switch. It is therefore difficult for us to imagine a world in which recorded sound was only a subject for fanciful fables: like the story of a Chinese prince of ancient times who possessed a box with magical powers. He would whisper messages into this box and send it to distant parts. When the recipient opened the box, out would come the spoken message.

In the event, sound recording as a practical reality had to await the upsurge of inventive genius in the latter half of the nineteenth century which heralded the arrival of the electric light, the telephone, the wireless, the motor car and the aeroplane.

1877: the birth of recording

Audio historians are now arguing over the rival claims of the Frenchman, Charles Cros (1842–88), and the American, Thomas Alva Edison (1847–1931), as the true inventor of sound recording. With the advantage of hindsight, we might be tempted to ask why nobody got it to work sooner. After all it is a common experience that we can produce sounds by running a fingernail across the grain of a piece of wood (an analogy in miniature of running a stick along a line of railings). It does not seem such a far cry to inscribe or emboss patterns on some suitably pliant surface and retrace these with a needle coupled to some sound amplifying device such as a stretched paper diaphragm.

Much preliminary work had been done by earlier scientists, including Thomas Young who showed that a vibrating tuning fork could be made to inscribe a wavy line on a rotating cylinder (1807), Duhamel who recorded the vibrations of a stretched cord (1840) and Leon Scott the French typesetter whose Phonautograph (1857) can be seen as the direct inspiration for all that followed. This device had a flared horn to collect the sound, with a parchment diaphragm at the narrow end. A long bristle was fixed to the diaphragm with sealing wax and held against a lamp-blacked cylinder which could be rotated by hand. As the diaphragm vibrated in response to changing air pressures caused by speech or music directed into the horn, the bristle would transcribe the vibrations as a clear waveform on the cylinder. After the Phonautograph was demonstrated in London in 1859, Prince Albert is said to have diverted Queen Victoria with it.

In an improvement developed by Scott's associate Koenig, a threaded rod caused the cylinder to track laterally so that the bristle centre line traced a plain helix on the cylinder surface. Sound recording was therefore an accomplished fact; what was now needed was a method of reproducing the original sounds by retracing the waveform.

Charles Cros was directly inspired by Scott's Phonautograph and applied to the problem some techniques he had worked out in developing a system of three-colour photography (where ironically he was pre-empted by a rival inventor, Ducos du Hauron, just as he was to be by Edison). In April 1877, Cros set down his ideas for reproducing the wavy spiral traced as a transparent line on a lamp-blacked cylinder. The waveform would first be converted into a relief trace in a hard material such as steel by 'currently well known photographic processes'. A metal point, if the trace were etched as a groove, or a notched finger, if the trace were formed in etched relief, could subsequently be caused to follow the undulations and set up equivalent vibrations in a diaphragm. Surprisingly, though it is presumed that he was short of the necessary funds to take out proper patent papers, Cros deposited his ideas with the French Académie des Sciences in a sealed packet (receipted on 30 April 1877) with instructions that it should remain unopened until December. The relevance of all this attention to precise dates will appear when we look at Edison's story.

It seems certain that Edison also knew all about Scott's Phonautograph. We may assume that he knew nothing of the Cros manuscript but it is possible that he could have seen an article dated 10 October 1877 by L'Abbé Lenoir, a friend of Cros, proposing the etching and reproducing of a sound trace, and using the term 'phonograph' for the first time.

However, Edison's own account of the events leading up to his invention attributes his success more to the process of serendipity (making happy and unexpected discoveries by accident). In the summer of 1877, Edison was working on improvements to the Bell telephone, or 'speaking telegraph' as it was then called (for which he was granted about forty patents over a period of ten years). The device he was developing was designed to speed up the sending of telegrams. A paper tape carried the telegram messages, transcribed by indented Morse code dots and dashes, and could be run at high speed to economise in wire usage time. Edison noticed that the indented dots and dashes made a humming noise as they passed the guide spring at high speed. Still with the telephone in mind, he began to see the possibility of indenting and reproducing speech sounds—as an extension of the telegraph dot buzzing.

In later years, when Edison had become a celebrated figure, he was often asked to describe these early inventive days. He would even be persuaded to reconstruct the prototype laboratory models and let himself be photographed as if in the process of inventing the phonograph for the first time. In addition, his early notebooks almost became public property and, just as his story no doubt became embellished in the retelling, there is more than a suggestion that some of the dated entries in the notebooks, including some countersigned by his working associates, may have actually been written over at a later date. Mindful of these reservations, the notebooks nevertheless make fascinating reading. Thus, on some of the key dates we read:

18 July 1877 'Just tried experiment with diaphragm having an embossing point and held against paraffin paper moving rapidly. The speaking vibrations are indented nicely, and there's no doubt that I shall be able to store up and reproduce automatically at any future time the human voice perfectly.'

12 August 1877 Famous sketch of prototype with words 'Kruesi— Make this.'

So the story goes, Edison's assistant Kruesi built the prototype in a mere 30 hours and Edison shouted the nursery rhyme 'Mary had a little lamb' into the mouthpiece. Then, having put on the reproducing needle, he cranked the handle and 'was never so taken aback in my life' to hear a recognisable reproduction of his own voice. Sound recording was born, and other important dates were:

22 December 1877 Article in *Scientific American* described a demonstration of the machine by Edison in their offices.

24 December 1877 Patent application filed.

19 February 1878 US Patent 200521 issued.

This first machine (Plate 1) was based on a solid metal cylinder mounted on a threaded rod, like the Phonautograph, so that it moved sideways when rotated. Two diaphragm and needle devices were provided, one for recording and one for playing back. The medium used was a sheet of tin-foil wrapped around the cylinder. Guided by the spiral, the recording needle indented its trace vertically ('hill-and-dale') into the foil. On replay, the second needle could similarly follow the spiral trace and, in riding up and down, transmit vibrations to the diaphragm.

1877–1925: cylinder progress

The tin-foil phonograph was an overnight wonder, even though it was primitive in action and the foil track itself would stand up to only a few playings. The Edison Speaking Phonograph Company was formed as early as 24 January 1878 and agents took models all over the United States giving evening entertainments to packed houses. Edison worked on various improvements for about six months, and even tried a flat disc version, but his attention was then diverted to the incandescent lamp and other projects. Public interest also waned after a while and the phonograph practically disappeared.

A new lease of life for the cylinder was heralded about eight years later by a much improved model jointly promoted by Chichester Bell (a cousin of the telephone's Alexander Graham Bell) and Charles Sumner Tainter. They filed a patent on 27 June 1885 which actually specified a flat disc, but was eventually manufactured as a cylinder machine. They replaced the tin-foil with a removable cardboard tube coated with beeswax and designed a 'floating' stylus mounting which was capable of more sensitive recording and playback. Other improvements included the production of more steady pitch by the use of a foot-treadle or electric motor instead of cranking by hand. The sound volume was lower than on Edison's machine, however, and ear tubes had to be used. The new machine was called the Graphophone, a name hardly likely to please Edison. Indeed, when Bell and Tainter sought Edison's cooperation prior to their commercial launch, he refused. Instead, he worked energetically on an improved phonograph—it is said that at one stage he worked for 72 hours without stopping. The famous photograph taken on 16 June 1888 shows him all but exhausted alongside his new battery-powered phonograph with its all-wax cylinders.

Unedifying wrangles over claims and counter-claims kept the courts and lawyers busy for years, which is an unfortunate feature throughout the history of recording and radio in the USA. The immediate cylinder commercialisation got off to a reasonable start due to the clever intervention of Jesse H. Lippincott, a Pittsburgh businessman who secured the distribution rights for both the Graphophone and the improved Phonograph. Both systems were therefore kept viable, but it was unfortunate that Lippincott concentrated on promoting the machines for office dictation work only. When Edison took over control, after Lippincott's health, and profits, began to decline, he too failed to realise the cylinder's potential as a home entertainment medium. Coin-in-the-slot machines did well, however, and produced decent profits for a while.

Changes in the diaphragm material brought about small improvements in sound quality. Paper first of all gave way to mica or celluloid, or even 0.17mm- (0.007in)-thick glass. The wax cylinders were a definite improvement over tin-foil. They could be indented deeper, and shaved smooth to allow them to be recorded on more than once. Also the pitch of the screw could be made narrower to give increased playing time.

The principal drawback to commercial exploitation was the absence of any satisfactory method for duplicating recordings in large quantities. One early device made copies by replaying the master machine alongside a second machine set to record on to a blank cylinder. By simply coupling, the second machine would cut a copy cylinder by sympathetic vibration. This device could produce up to about twenty copies an hour, but was eventually replaced by an electroplating process not unlike that used for modern gramophone records. The Crystal Palace exhibition in 1888 was the very first to show a range of recording machines and the Paris Exhibition in the following year featured no fewer than forty-five different models.

Cylinder versus disc

Already the cylinder found itself in direct competition with machines which could play flat prerecorded discs. The first viable disc recording and playback system to use discs was introduced in the USA by Emile Berliner (1851–1921), an immigrant from Germany. He called his machine the Gramophone (Plate 2) to differentiate it from the recently launched Graphophone and Edison Phonograph. It is a curiosity of history that 'phonograph' has continued as the generic term for any player—cylinder or disc—in the USA, while most other countries use 'gramophone' for all disc players.

Berliner applied for his first patent on 28 September 1887. This described a photo-engraved disc embodying ideas carried over from both the Scott Phonautograph and the writings of Charles Cros. By the next year he was demonstrating a workable technique using a zinc disc coated with a fatty film. This film was highly suitable for the cutting process and was also impervious to the dilute acid (hydrochloric or hydrofluoric) used for etching the cut groove into the zinc. This original system was impressive but showed no vital advantages over the cylinders of the time. Then, six years later, Berliner arrived at a process for making a metal reverse matrix copy of his master disc and then using this as a mould or 'stamper' to press out records in quantity. The process can be visualised as first depositing a thin metal film on the master disc by electroplating, then peeling off the metal and pressing it down on to some suitable soft material—like using a metal seal to press insignia on softened sealing wax.

Though Edison and others could soon duplicate their cylinders at a useful rate, employing a centrifuge, the much greater ease of pressing out flat discs gave them a practical advantage which would eventually kill off the cylinder completely. At first the discs were made of hard rubber or ebonite but these were found to produce recordings which were only semi-permanent. Berliner therefore approached the Durinoid Button Company and obtained from them a new button material based on shellac which proved much more suitable. Indeed, shellac continued to be the basic material for all gramophone records for nearly fifty years (until vinyl plastics came along during the Second World War). Perhaps we should not forget the more exotic disc materials used on occasion such as edible chocolate and celluloid-faced postcards. Record diameters began at only 125mm (5in) but soon progressed to 175mm (7in) and eventually the standard 250mm (10in) and 300mm (12in) sizes. Record speeds hovered around 74–82 revolutions before settling down at an agreed 78rpm and this, with the groove pitch of about 100 grooves to the inch, gave playing times that began down around 1 minute, and increased to 3 and $4\frac{1}{2}$ minutes respectively for the 250mm and 300mm standard record sizes.

Not for the last time, if we think of the various incompatible video recording systems on the present market, the buying public found themselves having to choose between rival formats whose records could not be interchanged. There were three basic systems on offer:

(a) cylinders with hill-and-dale cut (ie varying depth but almost constant width);
(b) discs with lateral cut (ie constant depth but varying side-to-side amplitude);
(c) discs with hill-and-dale cut (eg Pathé).

System (b) had established a clear lead in volume of sales by 1910 and the others, though attempting to compete for about fifteen years more, eventually disappeared. Both cylinders and discs benefited from a number of equipment advances, notably in the construction of soundboxes and motors. It was an Italian immigrant in New York, Gianni Bettini (1860–1903), who first incorporated a 'spider' connection between the needle and the diaphragm. This contacted the diaphragm at several points and gave smoother sound quality. Bettini called his machine the Micro-Phonograph and he also raised the status of the phonograph generally by persuading top opera singers to record for him so that the public had a chance to hear something more than the novelty numbers and music-hall artists which were the only fare on offer up till then.

The Berliner Gramophone Company were very successful too with their Improved Gramophone, introduced in 1897. This had an updated soundbox and has acquired perennial fame as the subject of the well-known *His Master's Voice* painting featuring the dog 'Nipper'. In fact, Francis Barraud (1856–1924), a Frenchman living in England, had originally painted his pet dog listening quizzically to a cylinder machine, the Edison Commercial Phonograph dating from around 1893. He offered the painting to Edison-Bell who were not interested. In 1899 he called at the offices of the Gramophone Company Limited, the London subsidiary of the Berliner company, who offered him £50 for the painting and a further £50 for the copyright provided he painted out the cylinder player and substituted their disc gramophone. The painting was handed over on 17 October and still hangs in the boardroom of EMI Limited. It is said that traces of the cylinder phonograph can still be detected if the painting is viewed from the left-hand side.

Reproductions of the painting were hung in Gramophone Company shops by December, and Barraud indeed supplied many copies over a period of years, being paid an annual pension for his work. The public response was so favourable that the company changed its name to HMV (His Master's Voice) and the dog trademark has spread everywhere, being owned by RCA in America, the Japanese Victor Company (JVC) in Japan, as well as EMI in most of Europe and Australasia.

As the designers' understanding of the principles of acoustic horns developed, both the available volume of sound and its quality increased dramatically. Some models used such large horns that extra supports were needed, while others went in for floral decorations and fanciful shapes (Plate 3). The Lumière design took the form of a large shallow-pleated cone with the needle carried at the apex, so that the cone acted as both soundbox and horn. A domestically more practicable version of this idea reappeared as late as 1926, using a horn bent round (re-entrant) into the cabinet itself. The needle-cum-soundbox was coupled to a small length of expanding tube to form the horn apex. This had advantages over most contemporary systems in which the playing end had to support quite massive horn structures.

Prices of records began to fall, while the choice of musical repertoire increased rapidly. New issues reached the shops every month, until catalogues listing several hundred titles were built up. By the early 1920s the gramophone record had established itself as a major medium of entertainment for very large numbers of homes. In April 1923, Compton Mackenzie brought out the first issue of a monthly magazine, *The Gramophone*, containing articles on music and reviews of the latest records. His aim, as expressed in his first editorial, was 'to encourage the recording companies to build up for generations to come a great library of good music'. Publication of the magazine has continued without interruption to the present day, and it remains the only publication anywhere in the world which sets out to print critical reviews of every classical record to be issued in Britain in the month of publication.

Broadcasting begins

The popularity of the now ubiquitous gramophone suffered a setback when radio broadcasts first spread into people's homes offering entertainment, news and information without the need to buy records. Record sales did indeed fall off steeply for a while, and the large Columbia Record Company in the USA, for example, was reputedly in financial difficulties. Before long, however, the new technology which made radio broadcasting possible was being adapted to improve the quality of both records and record-players. Therefore what had at first seemed a very real threat turned out to be a benefit in disguise, enabling the gramophone to leap forward in sound quality and universal popularity.

The early evolution of radio proceeded concurrently with the birth of sound recording. Edison himself filed a patent relating to 'wireless' communications as early as 1885, and the German Heinrich Hertz (1857–94) made pioneering advances in the theory and practice of causing electromagnetic signals to be radiated outwards from a 'transmitter' and picked up by a distant 'receiver'. It was the Italian Guglielmo Marconi (1874–1937) who first brought wireless transmissions out of the laboratory environment to a successful translantic link-up between Poldhu in Cornwall and Newfoundland on 12 December 1901. American pioneers included Reginald Fessenden, who first demonstrated voice transmissions (instead of Morse code) in 1900; Lee de Forest, who invented the Audion three-element thermionic valve in 1905; and Edwin H. Armstrong (1890–1954) whose 'feedback' patent of 1913 and super-heterodyne receiver circuit of 1918 were only the first of many contributions he was to make over the years (to be followed by frequency modulation in 1933, and multiplex two-channel transmission a year later).

The world's first licensed radio station was KDKA in Pittsburgh, which began broadcasting for 1 hour a day on 360m in 1920. In Britain, informal semi-amateur transmissions gave way to regular scheduled programmes in 1922 when the British Broadcasting Company was formed. This became a public corporation in January 1927, by which time over 500 local radio stations were licensed in the USA.

Early radio reception was subject to all sorts of spurious noise and interference, yet already listeners could recognise that the sound quality was potentially superior to that of acoustic (soundbox and horn) gramophones. With the exception of a few top class acoustic models, gramophone sound was severely limited in frequency response and smoothness. These limitations were inherent at both ends of the recording and reproducing chain where acoustical/mechanical transformations were employed first to collect and transcribe the sound information, and then to reconvert the groove undulations into audible sounds. In radio broadcasting, the acoustic recording horns were replaced by relatively more sensitive microphones which converted the sound signals into an electric current. This could be amplified by the new thermionic valves and drive new types of electromagnetic cutting machines. The valves in the radio receiver could similarly produce a sound output of any required volume.

Descriptions of early acoustic recording procedures underline the miracles of advancement which just a few years have brought about. Background noises could enter at every stage of the process, so that only loud speech or music had any chance of being audible on the finished record. At first, therefore, brass instruments, loud patter songs and occasionally operatic arias formed the main diet. String instruments were generally too faint, even when brought up very close to the recording horn. This explains the invention of the Stroh violin which became popular briefly because it had its own attached horn to boost its sound. Resonance peaks in the middle-frequency region of the ear's greatest sensitivity gave a harsh edge to many instruments and voices, which was not helped by the almost total absence of the lower and upper octaves.

Originally the musicians and recording machine were in the same room and grouped together for maximum ability to project sounds into the recording horn. Problems arose over the musical balance between soloists and accompaniment so that the musicians had often to move back and forth as the music proceeded. An upright piano was usually preferred to the larger grand piano because of its compactness and sometimes raised several feet above the floor so that its sounds could more effectively enter the horn which had been placed to line up with the singer's mouth. Later studios were built with the horn projecting through a communicating wall into the control room. Here the engineers could make ready their wax discs and cutting needles without mutual interference with the performers. However, the fixed horn positions and the absolute necessity of cutting as loud a musical signal as possible into the wax, free from extraneous noises, must have been very limiting and frustrating for everyone involved.

The microphone suddenly freed the recording session from many of these restrictions. Even though early microphones were primitive and very large by modern standards, they could be placed at any desired position or height. The connecting cable led to an amplifier and so the musicians found to their delight that they could perform more or less naturally both in terms of their physical grouping and their individual loudness balance. It even became possible to set up additional microphones and mix their separate signals together to correct errors of balance or perspective brought about by awkwardly shaped rooms or insufficient numbers of players. Of course the engineer's responsibility was then even greater than before since his ideas on musical balance might be at variance with those of the conductor and other musicians, so that musically trained engineer/producers were needed, as was proper consultation on specific balance points or problems.

The freedom made possible by the use of microphones enabled the recording (and radio) companies to set up their equipment in concert halls, opera houses and other locations with at least the promise of results technically the equal of studio productions. In fact a number of ambitious location recordings of this type helped to alert the public to the greater potential of the new 'electric' recordings. One of these

(Columbia 9084) was recorded in the Metropolitan Opera House, New York, on 31 March 1925. It featured 850 glee-club voices singing 'D'ye ken John Peel' on one side and the audience joining in to swell the number of singers to an alleged 4,500 in a rendering of 'Adeste Fideles' on the other.

To anyone prepared to make a proper comparison, records like this were audibly better than the acoustically recorded discs in a number of ways. The loudness range was increased. The frequency range was similarly extended downwards and upwards to something like 100–5,000Hz, giving extra solidity to the bass and clarity to the treble which acoustic discs sadly lacked. There was also more spaciousness because the microphones, having the benefit of electrical amplification, could be set back at greater distances from the performers.

Inevitably the new electrical records had to be played on the existing acoustic gramophones to begin with. This led to problems in tracking the more 'difficult' groove undulations of the wider response discs, so that, far from revealing the capabilities of the new records, the machines often produced a disappointing screeching sound. It also took the engineers some time to become familiar with the new microphones and techniques, therefore quality remained uneven for a while.

New types of player

As radio sets began to enter people's homes in increasing numbers, it was a natural consequence that acoustic gramophones would soon fall into disuse (except for a few wind-up portables to take on a picnic in these pre-transistor days). Electric motors had already become popular, and the acoustic soundbox soon gave way to an electromagnetic pickup head in which the needle vibrations, instead of directly activating a diaphragm, generated an electric current. This could be fed to a valve amplifier driving a loudspeaker, the outfit forming an electric gramophone. Various groupings competed for popularity. A simple record-player with electric pickup could be plugged into a separate radio receiver, to save on cost by utilising the radio's built-in amplifier and loudspeaker. Alternatively the turntable unit and radio could be integrated into a single cabinet, the 'radiogram', with a selector switch to change over from radio to record-player at will.

The first all-electric record-player was the Brunswick 'Panatrope' which appeared in 1925 in versions with or without combined radio. Other models soon followed in numerous shapes and sizes. Over the next twenty years, these changes in appearance were more spectacular than any improvements in the achievable sound quality. Record changers were launched by Victor in America in 1927 and Garrard in England in 1932. Several short-lived novelties also appeared, including constant linear speed systems intended to avoid end-of-side distortion and a Garrard turntable (1938) which could play both sides of a disc without turning it over.

Some improvements in quality did take place, for example in regard to the need for equalisation. This is the technique of choosing a particular frequency response characteristic during recording and matching this with a mirror-image response on replay—with the aim of eliminating noise or distortion products inherent in the process. Electrical recording began with the granting of a patent in 1924 to H. C. Harrison of Western Electric. From the outset, the cutter was an electromagnetic device, giving a constant velocity characteristic (of which more in Chapter 7), that is, a rising amplitude at low frequencies. It was necessary to restrict the bass amplitude to adhere to a viable groove pitch of around 100 grooves per inch, and it became standard practice to boost treble frequencies at the same time. The replay equalisation curve reversed the process, restoring the bass to its original relative level and, in similarly bringing back the treble to normal level, provided a useful degree of reduction in record surface noise. For a while, different record companies used an assortment of equalisation curves so that some records would sound over-bright and others bass-heavy unless played through the proper equalisation network.

By the middle 1930s, these small differences were enough to worry enthusiasts for high quality sound ('high fidelity') who would take pains to construct switchable equalisation networks, labelled 'HMV', 'Columbia', etc, to try to get the very best results from each record in their collection. A greater awareness of the importance of recorded sound quality could be detected in individual record companies too, as shown by the Decca Record Company's 'ffrr' (full frequency range recording) project in 1944. However, just as electrical recording had completely overthrown the acoustic record twenty years earlier, the 78rpm shellac disc was about to be delivered a fatal blow.

The 'long play' microgroove disc

In a now famous, well stage-managed press demonstration in June 1946, Columbia Records introduced a new record format which overcame many of the limitations of 78rpm discs. Principal amongst these was the playing time of only about $4\frac{1}{2}$

minutes per side, which made it impossible to enjoy a continuous performance of works longer than this. At the press demonstration, the Columbia engineers, headed by the inventor of the new format, Peter Goldmark, highlighted their increased time capability by showing an 8ft- (2.44m)-high pile of 78rpm records alongside a mere 15in (38cm) stack of the new records containing the same amount of music.

The new LP ('Long Playing') records had achieved about a sixfold extension of playing time, to give about 23 minutes on each side of a 30cm (12in) disc. Part of the extension was obtained by making the grooves thinner and packing them closer together, about 240 grooves to the inch instead of the old 100. Of course this new 'fine groove' or 'microgroove' format demanded new stylus dimensions, basically a tip radius of only 25μm (0.001in) instead of the previous 63μm (0.0025in). The remainder of the time extension was secured by adopting a slower turntable speed, $33\frac{1}{3}$rpm instead of 78rpm. On the face of it, this might restrict the high frequency performance since slowing down the recording rate of any medium—disc, cylinder or tape—has the effect of compressing the recorded waveform and making it difficult to reproduce the upper frequencies. However, the demonstration left no one in doubt that the proposed finer stylus tip more than made up for the speed reduction. Of course it was necessary not to record too far in towards the label area, where the linear speed is at its lowest, but, with this proviso, the new LP seemed easily able to match the 78rpm disc for frequency range.

Even more spectacular, however, was the enormous reduction in record surface noise. The 78rpm record, apart from being brittle and easily broken, was characterised by a continuous frying noise during playing. This was caused by the mixing into the shellac of emery powder or other abrasive fillers in order to give a reasonable resistance to wear from the heavy pickups then in use, averaging about 5oz (140g) in tracking force, and incidentally to grind the soft steel or thorn needles into a neat fit for the groove contour. The new LP records were made of quiet, soft, practically unbreakable vinyl plastics. No abrasive fillers were added and quiet passages in the music could be heard and appreciated as never before. A new attitude was needed of course for the stylus/disc relationship. Instead of having hard records and soft throw-away needles, it became necessary with these new soft records to employ a stylus of carefully ground and polished dimensions and make it of some very hard material so that these dimensions would be practically unchanged after playing a large number of LP sides. Pickup tracking forces also had to be drastically reduced to avoid the risk of exceeding the elastic limits of the vinyl material. At the CBS launch, a prototype pickup was used tracking at 6–7g, but 3g soon became commonplace and the better-class modern pickups track at about 1g.

There had been other, less successful, attempts to introduce long playing records. Neophone had produced a 50cm- (20in)- diameter record as early as 1904 and Edison himself had managed to record up to 40 minutes on a single disc in 1927. However the CBS microgroove LP had been based on intensive research not only into the best use of the new vinyl materials but also into market requirements. It was therefore an immediate success from the first appearance of commercial records in June 1948 (two years after the famous press demonstration) by which time both the record companies and record-player manufacturers had assembled suitable products. The days of the 78rpm record were over.

Columbia's traditional antagonist, RCA, did launch a rival disc format in 1949. This used a similar vinyl material and microgroove contour but was based on discs measuring only 18cm (7in) in diameter running at a new compromise speed of 45rpm. At first, RCA promoted the use of a special high-speed autochange turntable to give longer playing times than the 4 minutes per side maximum of their new disc. However, the feared 'war of the speeds' was resolved fairly quickly with the $33\frac{1}{3}$ and 45rpm speeds complementing each other rather than being in direct conflict. Record-players were manufactured with a switch to run at either of the speeds (plus 78rpm to begin with, though this eventually began to be regarded as obsolete). The $33\frac{1}{3}$rpm LP was obviously better suited to longer compositions or selections, while the 45rpm 'single' was convenient for short popular repertoire.

There was an inevitable teething period during which sound quality tended to vary but, once the studio and cutting-room techniques had been mastered and home equipment improved to take advantage of the microgroove's potential, new levels of fidelity were achieved. Frequency range was extended almost to the limits of audibility, and dynamic range, while still restricted, could reach more realistic proportions than ever before.

The arrival of stereo

Evolution towards greater realism had now to depend on finding some method of recreating the spatial effect of being present at a live performance. Early attempts had been spasmodic and rendered non-viable by other limitations in the recording chain. Yet many inventors had dreamed of incorporating the directional effect bestowed on our hearing faculties by the use of two spaced ears. The very first was the French engineer Clément Ader, who achieved a sort of directional effect more than 100 years ago. As a special demonstration at the Paris Exposition of 1881, he set up primitive carbon-rod 'microphones' to left and right of the stage at the Paris Opéra and connected them by separate telephone lines to ranks of earpieces at the exhibition pavilion. By holding an earpiece to each ear, visitors were astonished to find that they could follow the left/right movements of singers and enjoy a sense of spatial ambience.

Other novelty experiments followed, but it is about fifty years later before we come to the definitive British patent number 394,325 (1931) in which A. D. Blumlein (1903–42) described all-embracing theories and practical designs for recording and reproducing two-channel sound on discs. He had solved the basic problems of dual-microphone techniques and of inscribing two mutually independent channels of information in a single record groove. One of his suggested microphone arrangements has come to be called the 'Blumlein method' and consists of a pair of bi-directional microphones at right angles to each other and placed as nearly together as possible (Fig. 2.1). This eliminates any time-of-arrival differences at the two microphone diaphragms (of which more when we discuss directional hearing in Chapter 3) but

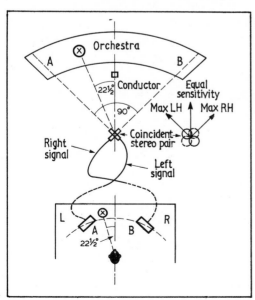

Fig. 2.1 Stereo recording using a coincident pair of directional microphones presents the listener with a horizontal spread of sound. The source X, for example, appears at an angle of $22\frac{1}{2}°$ from the centre line both in the concert hall and the listener's home

produces intensity differences because each microphone has its maximum sensitivity in different directions. Therefore a sound source X at the left of centre, for example, will produce a greater signal level from the left microphone than the right. Then, when these signals are reproduced from a pair of suitably spaced loudspeakers, the listener will hear a 'phantom image' similarly spaced to the left of centre. An orchestra or other group of performers can therefore be made to sound spread out in their natural layout.

This kind of recording and reproduction has come to be called stereophony (or 'stereo' for short, after the Greek *stereos*—'solid'). Another approach to directional recording was researched at Bell Laboratories in America. They sought to recreate the binaural (two ears) listening situation by fitting microphones into the ears of a tailor's dummy, affectionately called Oscar. In fact the action of the dummy-head did create a naturalistic spread of sound, particularly when the signals were listened to on headphones. This form of dummy-head (or *Künstkopf*) stereo recording has been revived quite recently, and a number of radio plays and documentaries have been very successful. With the best modern equipment a three-dimensional soundfield can be recreated, with height directivity as well as left/right.

The Blumlein patent suggested that the left/right signals could be inscribed in the groove at right angles to each other and at $\pm 45°$ to the record surface (see Fig. 2.2). However, the very first public demonstration of a two-channel disc system given by Arnold Sugden at the London Audio Fair and British Sound Recording Association in 1956 used the more obvious

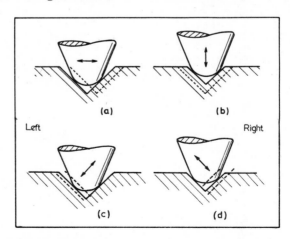

Fig. 2.2 How record grooves are modulated: (a) mono lateral; (b) mono hill-and-dale; (c) and (d) stereo left and right channels at $\pm 45°$ to the record surface

combination of lateral and hill-and-dale groove modulations. A year later, a worldwide agreement was reached by industry chiefs, including Arthur Haddy of Decca and Westrex in America, to fix on 45°/45° as a universal standard. This, combined with the greater capabilities of the, now established, LP disc and the large sales of records and record-players now taking place, led to a ready market for stereo discs from their launch around 1958.

The appearance of stereo discs caught some companies unawares and it took a year or two before consistent standards began to be achieved either in terms of the recordings or the record-players. However most record companies had begun stockpiling stereo recordings in anticipation of an agreed disc standard. Indeed, stereophonic reproduction was already available to the few enthusiasts who could afford the expensive two-track open-reel tape decks being made by EMI and others to play the small numbers of 'Stereosonic' tapes marketed since 1955.

Magnetic recording

Running parallel with the evolution of, first, acoustic recording and, later, electrical/mechanical recording can be traced an equally interesting though slower-to-develop progress in magnetic recording. As a matter of history, Edison had foreseen the possibility of storing sound signals as a magnetic pattern in a steel sheet at the time of his original 1878 patent. However, the acknowledged pioneer of a viable method for magnetic recording is Valdemar Poulsen, a Dane settled in America. His 1897 patent described a Telegraphone which had steel wire wound in a single layer on a stationary drum. An electromagnet was tracked along the wire during recording and had the effect of leaving the wire in a state of local magnetisation which corresponded to the rise and fall of the original sound waveform (see more detailed description in Chapter 8). When the electromagnet was lifted back to the beginning and passed along the wire once more, the field surrounding the wire induced a tiny electrical current into the coil of the electromagnet and so reproduced the sounds. Developments of this idea included the Stille machine (1900) which drew steel wire from one reel to another past a stationary head, and the Blattnerphone (1927) which used flat steel ribbon and improvements such as high frequency bias and erasure. However, these were bulky and expensive machines and found only a few applications in broadcasting studios.

By 1935, however, AEG in Germany were manufacturing

Magnetophon recorders which used new types of coated tape just developed by BASF. The magnetic coating, based on iron oxide particles, was at first applied on to paper tape, but a change to plastic film around the time of the Second World War brought dramatic improvements in both sound quality and tape durability. German radio stations had exclusive use of the new tape recording medium from 1938 to the end of the war but, after 1945, magnetic tape recording spread very rapidly to every corner of the professional and amateur world.

Tapes carying prerecorded music were first marketed in 1954, mainly on 18cm (7in) spools recorded at the most common speed on domestic machines, namely 18cm (7½in) per second. Prices were prohibitive, however, and though the appearance of Stereosonic tapes in 1955, as already mentioned, produced a wave of interest, the gramophone record remained supreme as the medium for recorded music in the home. Successive moves towards reducing tape costs involved slower tape running speeds and interleaved narrower tracks (as described in Chapter 8), but there was still some opposition to the tape format because of the need to thread the loose end of tape from one spool to the other. Various solutions to this problem came along in the shape of tape magazines or containers. These included the RCA cartridge (1958), the Fidelipac cartridge (1962) and the Eart Muntz cartridge (1962) but all of these were eclipsed by the Philips Compact Cassette first introduced in 1963.

As will be described later, prerecorded cassettes in the Philips format—called Musicassettes—have gradually grown in popularity and become more refined in quality, until they can be regarded as comparable to LP records in most aspects.

Subsequent developments, such as digital recording and four-channel 'surround sound' techniques will be outlined in Chapter 15, 'Future Developments'.

3
Let's Go to a Concert

Before we tackle the equipment and procedures which we hope will produce for us the *illusion* of a live musical performance, it might be helpful to consider what happens at a real concert. Imagine that we have gone along to the Wigmore Hall to hear a piano recital. The business of getting through the London traffic and disposing of tickets, overcoats and the like all completed, we take our seats in eager anticipation. We are naturally eager; after all, our coming to the recital was a deliberate decision involving some expenditure of cash, time and effort. It follows that this music, or this player, or both are to our liking. To a round of welcoming applause, the pianist walks on to the platform and, with a bow to acknowledge the applause, he sits down and begins to play. Immediately the piano comes to life, radiating musical sounds which travel out through the air to reach our ears and work their magic on our emotions. Let us take a slightly more scientific look at how the sounds are physically produced, and then follow them on their way to our brains.

How the sounds are made

Like other keyboard instruments, but unlike the violin for instance, the piano has strings pre-tuned to every note on the scale. The player has only to press down any given key and a lever action propels a felt-covered hammer at high speed to strike the appropriate string. In the standard grand piano there are eighty-eight keys to encompass the twelve semitones in each octave over a range of about seven-and-a-third octaves. The player can control the initial loudness of each note by varying the force with which he strikes the key. Hence the full name of the instrument, pianoforte (which literally translates 'soft-loud'). However he has only limited control over the rate of decay of sound—and cannot, for instance, produce a sustained tone as on the orchestral string and wind instruments. So the piano is effectively a percussion instrument with each note starting at full power and immediately commencing its steady decay to silence as the string vibrations die out. If the player lifts his finger promptly from the key, the hammer action falls back and a damping pad contacts the string, silencing it quite quickly. Alternatively, the player may hold the key down, and thus extend the duration of the note by keeping the pad off the string. Foot pedals give him a further measure of control. Pressing the right-hand pedal, called the 'loud' or more accurately 'sustaining' pedal, removes the dampers from all the strings and allows maximum sympathetic vibration and slowest decay. The left-hand 'soft' pedal reduces the maximum loudness either by restricting the length of stroke of the hammers or by some other means.

In practice, there are usually three strings to each note for the upper five octaves, to reinforce the available sound power, then two per note for the next octave or so, and one string for the remainder. The pitch of the note emitted by a stretched string depends on three factors: (a) its *length*, so piano strings are graduated in length from the full available length of the instrument for bass notes to quite short strings in the treble; (b) its *tension*, so one end of each string is fixed in a pin which is turned by small amounts to effect fine tuning; (c) its *weight per unit length*, so the bass strings are thicker and wrapped around with coiled wire.

Musical pitch and frequency

A digression may be permitted here on the question of pitch. If we had visited the hall say an hour before the recital, it is quite likely that we would have found a piano tuner at work. His job is to correct any drifting in string tension, and therefore pitch, due to temperature changes, etc. He begins by returning the note A in the treble clef to International Concert Pitch, as sounded by his standard tuning fork. This has a vibration rate or *frequency* of 440 cycles per second (440 Hertz) and he tunes the string by ear, listening for a true unison between string and fork, when the pulsations or 'beats' will disappear. Once A has been corrected, he can move to all other notes in turn, using his knowledge of their frequency ratios and counting beats as necessary until all the notes and frequencies correspond as nearly as possible to the values shown in Fig. 3.1. It will be seen that the notes an octave apart have frequencies in the ratio 2:1 and that the piano covers a range from 27.5 to 4,186Hz. However, it must not be thought that these are the only frequencies sounded by the piano. These nominal frequencies for each note are merely the *fundamental* tones, which determine the basic pitch on the musical scale. The string vibrations are in fact very complex so that numerous overtones

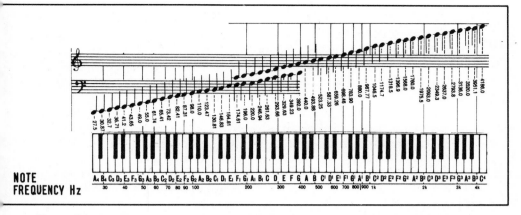

Fig. 3.1 Diagram showing the frequency and musical notation for all the white notes of the piano when the treble clef A is tuned to 440Hz, and equal temperament tuning is used

are produced having frequencies which are, for the most part, exact multiples of the fundamental. These *harmonics* enrich the tone or timbre of musical notes, and their numbers and relative strengths vary with different instruments. Thus quiet notes from the flute possess only the first few harmonics, while notes from the violin and piano are amazingly rich in harmonics extending all the way up to the limits of human hearing (20,000Hz) and beyond.

As our concert pianist varies the loudness of his playing in accordance with the composer's dynamic markings from *ppp* all the way up to *fff*, the timbre of the notes also changes. The hammer makes a greater initial kink in the string at the moment of impact when it is struck more forcibly, and this throws a higher proportion of the player's energy into the upper harmonics. Thus the louder notes are also brighter and more clangorous. This is one of the reasons why reproduced music may sound disappointing if it is not played back at a level corresponding approximately with the original. By the same token, any interference with levels by the engineers may spoil the realism of a recording. And it follows as an even more basic corollary that the chain of equipment all the way through from the microphone to our speakers at home must be capable of reproducing the full range of audible frequencies. Otherwise the harmonics which help us to distinguish the timbre of the various instruments, and which incidentally convey much of the interest and excitement of music, will be lost.

The initial attack or *transient* of piano notes is also a vitally characteristic ingredient in their overall sound, and will all too easily disappear if any component in the recording and playback chain cannot respond quickly enough. This is easily enough demonstrated by making a tape recording of a piano note, or that of an oboe or trumpet, say, and then cutting out the first few millimetres of tape. When the remainder is played back, it becomes much more difficult to identify the instruments. The vital part played by the initial transient also explains the inability of electronic organs to imitate other instruments convincingly. The stops labelled 'piano', 'oboe', etc, do introduce harmonics mixed according to known recipes for the individual timbres but, lacking the characteristic attack, the notes sound only vaguely like the instrument intended.

Resonance and reverberation

To get back to our piano, it is clear that a vibrating string would not produce a very loud sound without some assistance. It would tend to cut through the air, whereas what we want is to set a sizeable amount of air into imitative vibration. This is where the body of the instrument comes into prominence. The string vibrations pass down through a bridge or support to the soundboard. This is a large wooden panel forming the underside of the piano and it is the soundboard vibrations over a large area which more effectively radiate sound energy into the surrounding air. Each particle of air close to the soundboard is alternately pushed outwards and pulled inwards during each cycle of the soundboard's movement. And this to and fro motion is imitated successively by more and more layers of air particles as the sound spreads outwards.

Eventually the travelling wavefront will reach the air close to our ears and this will set our eardrums into tiny movements which the brain will recognise as having been caused by musical sounds. Notice that the air itself does not travel outwards from the guitar; rather it is a wavefront of vibratory energy like the shock-wave that travels along a line of railway trucks during shunting, or the ripples on a pond when a stone is thrown into the water. The speed with which sound travels in air is about 340m (1,115ft) per second, which is relatively pedestrian compared with the speed of light (and radio waves)—300,000,000m (186,000 miles) per second. So we are actually hearing our pianist playing each note a fraction of a second after we see him striking it.

In fact, we hear each note many times over. This is because the ever-widening wavefront is continually being bounced or reflected from the walls, floor, ceiling and large obstacles such as pillars (see Fig. 3.2). So a multitude of imitative wavefronts

1 An early example of the Edison tin-foil 'Phonograph' (*Photo Conservatoire National*)

2 The very first 'Gramophone', patented by Emile Berliner in 1887 (*Photo DGG*)

3 Gramophone horns could be decorative as well as enhancing the sound from acoustic gramophones (*Photo Thorens*)

4 A live performance in the concert hall will always be a unique experience, which reproduced music can only seek to imitate in sonic terms. (Royal Liverpool Philharmonic Orchestra) (*Photo Carl Fox*)

5 A pop concert relies on complex lighting and amplified sound from arrays of loudspeakers (*Photo Electro-Voice*)

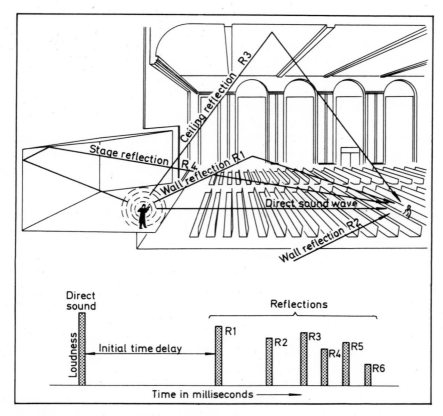

Fig. 3.2 Diagram showing how sounds from the platform reach the audience by an infinite number of routes. The reflected rays *R1* etc follow the direct sound after a time delay and are progressively attenuated (*after Beranek*)

reaches our ears and the initial sound, which came to us by the shortest direct route, is followed by a reverberant tail. This has the effect of prolonging the sounds, each contributing 'echo' having been delayed by an amount proportional to the extra distance travelled, and diminished in strength as the wavefront expanded and lost some of its energy at each reflection.

The length of time that it takes for sounds to die away to silence (officially to fall to -60dB, or one millionth of its original intensity) is called the *reverberation time*. Very reverberant enclosures like cathedrals might have a reverberation time of several seconds. The Royal Albert Hall reverberates for about 2.5 seconds, and smaller halls like the Wigmore Hall where we have come for our imaginary piano recital have reverberation times in the range 1.2–1.6 seconds. It comes as no surprise that the largest enclosures have the longest reverberation times. This is because the sound waves travel greater distances between each reflection, and suffer less scattering and absorption as a result.

However, there are two other important factors which influence the character as well as the amount of the reverberation. The first of these relates to the materials used in the construction of the building, the furnishings, etc. Porous materials make quite efficient sound absorbers. The incident sound waves cause the air particles in the interstices of the material to oscillate and energy is lost, or technically converted into heat, due to friction. This form of absorption is more effective at high frequencies, so that this kind of absorption robs the music of some of its brightness as well as reducing the overall reverberation. The precise band of frequencies most effectively absorbed also varies with different materials and even with their thickness, so the balance of frequencies may be upset. Audiences cannot be ignored in this context, as each member of the audience acts as a sound absorber. The result is that a concert hall which has been designed to have a suitable reverberation time when the audience is present may be unpleasantly over-reverberant during rehearsals and, as a secondary consideration, too reverberant for leasing by the recording companies. In some modern halls this problem has been reduced by designing upholstered audience seats which will absorb about the same amount of sound energy when empty as when occupied.

The word 'suitable' was used above, and it is clear that different amounts of reverberation have come to be regarded as suitable for different kinds of music. Church music has always been written to suit large, reverberant enclosures and can sound quite disappointing if the warmth and ambience of a church-like acoustic is missing. Chamber music, as its name implies, was intended in the baroque and classical periods for performance by small groups of players to a small audience in fairly small rooms. Only moderate reverberation is therefore desirable if the details in the music are not to become blurred. Perhaps unfortunately it has now become a commercial necessity often to put on chamber music recitals in large concert halls, with resulting difficulties in terms of both reverberation and audibility. The modern symphony orchestra has evolved in several stages of increased complexity and sheer weight of numbers since its origins in the preclassical age. Up until about 1800, an orchestra might contain anything from just a single player on each instrument to a maximum ensemble comprising 8 first violins, 6 second violins, 4 violas, 2 cellos, 2 basses, 2 flutes, 2 oboes, 2 clarinets, 2 bassoons, 2 French horns, 2 trumpets and timpani. Contrast this with the score of *Ein Heldenleben* by Richard Strauss (1898) which demands 62 string players, 3 each of flute, oboe, clarinet and bassoon plus piccolo, cor anglais and double bassoon, 8 horns, 5 trumpets, 3 trombones, tenor and bass tuba, timpani, bass drum, side drum, military drum and cymbals. Not surprisingly, the growth in the size of orchestras has been paralleled by a similar increase in the dimensions of modern concert halls.

Wavelength and directivity

The second factor affecting the behaviour of sound waves at a concert relates to directional effects, which may produce a variable balance of sound in different parts of the auditorium. The key property of a sound wave in this context is the *wavelength*. This is defined as the distance travelled by a wave during one cycle of the originating vibration. But we have already defined the *speed of sound* as the distance travelled per second and so, since *frequency* is the number of cycles (and therefore wavelengths travelled) per second, we arrive at the universal formula, true of all forms of travelling wave:

$$speed = frequency \times wavelength.$$

Taking the speed of sound as 340m per second, a simple calculation produces the results listed in Table 3.1.

Table 3.1 Sound wavelengths in air

Frequency (Hz)	Wavelength (metres)
20	17
34	10
340	1
1,000	0.34
3,400	0.1
10,000	0.034
20,000	0.017

The wavelength of a given sound, and in particular its length in relation to the dimensions of the source, has an important bearing on the way the sound is radiated outwards. If the source is small compared with the wavelength, the sound energy tends to be radiated equally in all directions, like the light from a bare electric light bulb. It follows that this non-directional type of radiation, while useful for giving equal loudness to listeners over a wide arc, does not carry efficiently over long distances. This is because the available sound energy is spread over a wavefront which is rapidly expanding. Therefore the loudness falls off steeply for more remote listeners. By contrast, if a source is large compared with the wavelength, or has a large reflector surface nearby, it has the ability to beam the sound energy in one or more specific directions, like the action of a car headlamp.

In practice, as is shown by Table 3.1, musical instruments are intermediary in size compared with the range of wavelengths which they are required to radiate. The result is that they tend to radiate low notes fairly equally in all directions but with only moderate carrying power. Then, as we move up the scale of fundamental notes and even further into the realm of overtones or harmonics, the instruments become more directional. This is why the tonal quality becomes brighter as well as subjectively louder when we listen on the radiation axis of a trumpet or a violin, for example. It also explains why the instruments of the string family—violin, viola, cello and double bass—are graduated in dimensions to match their lower frequency ranges (longer wavelength) and keep them roughly equivalent in radiating efficiency.

We also begin to see why the layout of instrumental ensembles has an important bearing on the balance of sounds which will reach the audience. The forward beaming effect of the reflector splay mounted above and behind the platform in some concert halls is also explained.

Note, however, that the relative size of an obstacle in the path of a soundwave and the wavelength of the latter has an important bearing on the reflection effect. It turns out that sounds reaching an obstacle which is much smaller than the wavelength are able to bend round the obstacle and continue as if it were not there. At higher frequencies (shorter wavelengths) the obstacle does bounce the waves back and so the frequency distribution is altered, with high frequencies made more prominent in front of the obstacle and deficient at the rear, where a kind of high frequency 'sound shadow' is cast. A particular case would affect any member of the audience who was unlucky enough to sit behind a wide pillar.

The human head is itself an effective obstacle at high frequencies, and this has an effect on our ability to locate the direction of sounds, as we shall see in the next section.

How we hear

Returning to our piano recital, we have now reached the point where the sound wavefront has reached the air in the neighbourhood of our ears, with each note followed quickly afterwards by a procession of reflected waves forming the reverberation or ambience. While the direct sound arrives by the shortest route straight from the piano, the others will be coming at us from all sides. By some miracle, all these vibrations are combined into one complex dance movement performed by each and every air particle. The sound energy enters the canal in our outer ears and imparts an imitative vibration to our eardrums—the thin, stretched membranes situated at the end of the ear canal.

This is not the place to embark on a lengthy treatise on the anatomy and psychology of hearing. Suffice it to say that motion of the eardrums acts through a system of tiny bone levers and a frequency selective resonator/generator mechanism to convey electrochemical messages to the brain. These signals contain clues as to the sound frequencies present, their relative strengths and their times of arrival to an incredible degree of accuracy. Despite centuries of research, there are still aspects of the ear/brain relationship which cannot be explained—for instance, the phenomenon of 'absolute' or 'perfect' pitch whereby a few people so gifted can immediately ascribe to any note its proper place on the musical scale.

Much of what we know about the basic limits of human hearing was established in researches carried out by Fletcher and Munson in America in 1933. They used test tones at various frequencies to check the hearing acuity of large numbers of people and produced a series of 'equal loudness curves' which were soon used as a standard. Figure 3.3 is based on more recent research in England by Robinson and Dadson and differs only in detail from the Fletcher–Munson results.

The broken line shows the lower 'threshold of hearing', that is the lowest sound intensity level at each frequency which could just be heard by an average listener. The fact that this is

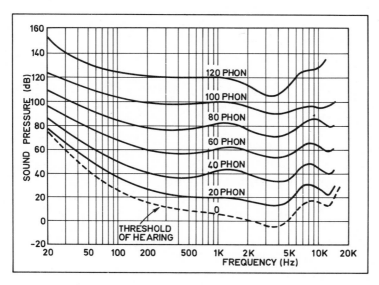

Fig. 3.3 Equal loudness contours for an average listener (*After Robinson and Dadson*)

not a straight line demonstrates that we are not equally sensitive to sounds at all frequencies. We tend to be best able to hear sounds in the middle frequency register and become less sensitive at low and high frequencies. The family of 'equal loudness' curves was built up by increasing the sound level at the 1,000Hz reference frequency in fixed steps (20dB) and asking the observers to state the level at other frequencies for which the sound seemed equally loud. Both the horizontal (frequency) and vertical (intensity) scales are logarithmic, to accord with the ear's method of assessing changes in pitch and loudness, namely in terms of the *ratio* rather than the difference between two frequencies or intensity levels.

The range of audible frequencies is seen to be about 20 to 20,000Hz, as we mentioned in Chapter 1, or a total ratio of 1,000:1, about ten octaves. The range of sound intensities to which the ear can respond is even more impressive. Down at the threshold of hearing the level is about one billionth of a watt per square metre. At the other extreme, the top curve in Fig. 3.3 when we are approaching a 'threshold of pain', we are withstanding a full 1 watt per square metre—a ratio of 1,000,000,000,000:1. This corresponds to 120dB, as was also mentioned in Chapter 1.

Directional hearing

In addition to being able to respond to a wide spectrum of frequencies and a fantastic range of intensity levels, the human ear/brain combination can identify the specific direction of a sound source, even in the presence of competing sounds. This direction-finding and selection ability— sometimes called the 'cocktail party effect' because it enables us to choose which of a jumble of voices we will listen to—owes its existence to our having two ears instead of just one. While some details remain unexplained, it is clear that the brain compares the signals transmitted to it from the two ears and deduces from the clues supplied whether a given sound has arrived from straight ahead, or the left or right.

Pretty obviously, if I am looking straight towards the pianist in the Wigmore Hall, the direct sounds from the piano will reach both my ears at the same instant and with the same intensity. The brain, ignoring any difference between the sensitivities of my two ears which would in any case be a permanent bias and therefore easily allowed for, would accordingly deduce that the sound source is straight ahead. To be exact, if I had my eyes closed, I might be in some doubts whether the piano was in front of me or directly behind, but forward bias due to the shape of my outer ears and a quick, unconscious movement of the head are usually enough to remove this doubt. If I now deliberately turn my head to the left, the sounds will reach my right ear earlier than the left, giving the brain a useful clue to its direction. They will also be slightly louder in my right ear, partly because of the extra distance travelled but also because of the 'sound shadow' effect previously described due to the obstacle effect of my head.

Research has shown that both the time difference and intensity difference play their part in directional hearing, with a third aural clue in the form of timbre difference. This arises from the frequency filtering effect which takes place as the obstacle effect of the head becomes progressively greater at high frequencies (shorter wavelengths). Time difference is more important at frequencies below about 1,000Hz, with intensity difference predominant above 4,000Hz. Errors in location can occur at middle frequencies. As we might expect, sound location is more accurate in the horizontal plane and less so in the vertical plane.

It might be thought that directional hearing would contribute very little to our enjoyment of a solo piano recital, but this would be to underestimate the brain's activity. There is a continual assessment of the volume and quality of random reverberant sound, so that the total listening experience is one of appreciating the given music in a given acoustic ambience. For example, the sound in a long, narrow hall would be noticeably different from that in a wide, fan-shaped one. These subtleties have an important bearing on the problems of recording and reproducing music with true high fidelity and we shall return to them later.

When numbers of players are involved, as at an orchestral concert (Plate 4), it seems likely that directional hearing enhances our ability to separate out the strands in the musical score. We soon accustom ourselves to the sounds of the woodwind coming from the middle of the orchestra, with the french horns, percussion and brass grouped in an arc behind them. Certainly the controversy which surrounds the different layouts of orchestral strings—first and second violins on the left of the conductor, cellos on his right (American system); violins divided, firsts on the left, seconds on the right with cellos in the centre (German system)—suggests that positioning and hence directivity has musical importance. And yet for listeners at some considerable distance from the platform, the orchestra is condensed into a very small arc subtending an angle of perhaps less than 15°. So for them the ability to locate individual instruments must be limited.

At a pop concert the acoustic effects can be very different indeed (Plate 5). Instruments and voices are almost always amplified. Not only does this mean that they can be very much louder than the real thing, they can also be fed through numerous electronic processors which change their character completely before sending them to arrays of loudspeakers. In directional terms the sound reinforcement engineers have quite a difficult problem of balance if each member of the audience is to be left with the impression that the sounds are coming from the artists he can see on the stage. While there will be loudspeakers in the stage area, a large auditorium will almost certainly need further loudspeakers arranged down the sides or over the heads of the audience. Unless special steps were taken, the audience would hear the sounds as coming from the nearest loudspeaker since this is louder than the direct stage sound and actually reaches them earlier because the electrical signals travel along the cables faster than the speed of sound through the air. Therefore the engineers introduce electronic delay by progressively greater amounts in the feeds to the more remote loudspeakers. Then, by what is called the 'precedence' effect, the audience still associate the sounds with the artists on stage.

There is a further complication with regard to loudspeakers in that electronic musical instruments like the electric guitar and organ actually emit no acoustic sounds but rely on amplifiers and loudspeakers of their own. Each player must therefore have a loudspeaker near him so that he can hear himself playing, and he will often require additional loud-speakers or headphones to enable him to hear the others in the group. The electronic processing can be very exotic and include shimmering echc effects, pitch wobbling, deliberate distortion and 'space' tones or extra voices from synthesisers or prerecorded tapes.

Ironically much of this complexity is necessitated by the need for the performers to get as close as they can to the sound of their gramophone records. The public get to know their performances on record, which will have been assembled on multi-track tape machines in the studio perhaps over a period of weeks (see next chapter) and they come along to a concert expecting to hear the same mixture of sounds that was captured on disc. This is in direct contrast to the situation in so-called 'classical' music where we traditionally regard the live concert as the real thing and hope that the recording will recreate that experience as closely as possible.

The importance of vision

It is difficult to assess the importance of being able to see as well as hear at a concert, but it is certainly considerable. Of course the eye reinforces the impressions of direction and space gained by the ear, and indeed takes command in circumstances where the ear may impart only vague evidence to the brain. Having seen the general dimensions of the auditorium, and his position in it relative to the stage area, the listener can sublimate his aural curiosity in these regards and concentrate more easily on the music. Similarly he can let his eye wander over the orchestra, perhaps to look at the flute during a solo passage or take his cue from the conductor as to the mood or the pace of the passage coming up next. Even the mundane sight of a percussion player getting to his feet warns of a clash of cymbals or a thwack on the bass drum.

These visual cues are all lost to us when we listen to a sound recording or broadcast. So to some extent, except where we are already familiar with the music in question, we are at a disadvantage. Also, the dominance of eye over ear means that we can accept errors of balance at a live concert, such as a soloist being masked by too loud an accompaniment, because the fact that we can see him playing or singing enables the brain to focus attention on that particular source of sound. Arguments such as these place a special responsibility on the recording engineer. He must be experienced in estimating which aspects of the sound balance, hall reverberation and perhaps stage movements or offstage effects in an opera will need to be underlined or diminished in purely sonic terms if the unseeing listener is to receive as satisfying a succession of impressions as would have a member of the audience.

It might be thought that television relays of musical events, and the pre-recorded video programmes now being promoted as the natural successors to the sound-only gramophone record, could restore to us all the visual cues available to the members of the audience. Yet there remain numerous difficulties. The small screen size means that a fixed view of the whole orchestra would not allow the viewer to direct his attention to individual players very easily. The television producer therefore feels obliged to switch to close-up views of different instruments or sections of the orchestra as the music proceeds. Inevitably his choice of viewpoint may conflict with the viewer's aspirations. Also, as we shall explore in the next chapter, the sound balance must remain a musically correct overview and so the changing camera close-ups must necessarily introduce a degree of conflict between the impressions received by eye and ear.

4

The Concert Hall in Your Home

Certainly so far as serious music is concerned, it would seem to be a principal objective of high quality sound reproduction to recreate the sounds and sensations that we experience at a live concert. However, it could be argued that this objective might be reached in two different ways: the home listening experience could be one of apparently being transported armchair and all to the concert hall itself; or it could be that we feel the concert hall has somehow come to us. This is not simply a question of semantics. The recording engineers and producers need to have their objectives clearly defined: and we too, if want our audio system to come close to 'suspending our disbelief' that we are actually at a concert and the musicians are performing 'live' for our personal delectation, must be presented with a total sound package which closely parallels the real thing. Progress towards this goal has perhaps been slower than that of reproducing the full frequency and dynamic ranges of music. Nevertheless, considerable strides have been made and more are in prospect.

Mono versus stereo

In the early days of recording and broadcasting, a single channel of communication was used. In essence this meant that our two ears were replaced by a single microphone suspended in front of the musicians. A microphone is simply a device which converts the energy present in sound waves into an alternating electrical current. It contains a thin diaphragm, the equivalent of the eardrum, which is set into sympathetic vibrations by the changing air pressures. This causes a tiny electrical generator to produce an alternating current whose changing frequencies and amplitudes mirror the pitch and loudness of the original musical tones.

When this single signal is recorded or transmitted to us by radio and reproduced through a single loudspeaker, the best aural illusion we can hope for is that of eavesdropping on the concert through a kind of porthole. There can be a degree of front-to-back perspective lent to the various voices or instruments partly by their relative loudnesses but more significantly by the graduated amounts of reverberant sound which lend distance to the sound sources more remote from the microphone. We have no sense of lateral spread across the stage, so that all the players might be imagined as sitting one behind the other on a centre line. All distances recede from one point behind our loudspeaker grille and no sound sources can be imagined as transported into our room. It might be thought that the reverberation of our own room would clothe the emerging sounds in a useful ambience and in this way recreate the feeling of being in a concert hall, with the reflected sounds coming to us from all sides. Yet, except in very large listening rooms, this added ambience or 'bloom' counts for very little in practice. The room dimensions are so small that the first reflections arrive at our ears within a very few milliseconds of the original and so little impression of ambience results.

From around the middle 1950s records, and later broadcasts, began to use stereophonic techniques and the previous single-channel sound became referred to as 'monophonic' or 'mono'. As described in Chapter 2, stereo recording relies on a pair of microphones (in the simplest case) designed to simulate the action of a pair of ears. Special care in regard to the disposition and directional properties of the microphone elements captures the same directional clues as human hearing, namely intensity and time-of-arrival differences. When the resulting two channels of electrical information are kept separate, or 'discrete' all the way from the microphone through to a pair of suitably spaced loudspeakers, a reasonable illusion of the original left-to-right spread of the musicians can be preserved.

Notice that stereo is at best an illusion. After all, though the left and right loudspeakers are being fed with separate signals meant to convey the left and right directional information, *both* our ears receive the sounds from *both* loudspeakers. The brain therefore has more unravelling to do than in the real case at a concert, when our left and right ears contribute discretely different signals to the brain.

Nevertheless, when recorded and reproduced correctly, two-channel stereo can be remarkably lifelike. When the listener sits at the recommended distance from the spaced loud-speakers, namely the same distance from each loudspeaker as they are from each other, his aural stage spreads out from the narrow porthole of mono to a 60° arc. The musicians will appear to be disposed over an area extending backwards from the speakers and bounded on either side by the speakers themselves. We might almost imagine that the wall behind the loudspeakers opens out directly into the concert hall. There remains a certain sense of isolation and of eavesdropping on the concert from some distance away. Yet this kind of stereo reproduction may be the best we can do by way of bringing the concert hall to our homes.

Surround sound

However the other approach, of transporting ourselves in imagination to the concert hall, remains a tantalising dream for audio engineers and many attempts have been made to capture the full 360° soundfield existing in the hall and somehow reproduce it in the home. If indeed it were possible to convey to the listener's ears the same changing patterns of air pressure which would be experienced by a member of the audience, the magical desired effect would be the result. It would then be as if all four walls of our room had disappeared and we were sitting in the concert hall. The orchestra would still be occupying its proper place on the platform but we would be immersed in just the same mixture of reflected sounds from front, back and sides as occurs at a concert.

For about eight years, from 1970 onwards, the recording and broadcasting industries did experiment with four-channel systems but the public reaction was at best mixed. Under the generic name 'quadraphony' these systems used arrays of four microphones or complex mixing arrangements to produce four signals to be reproduced from four loudspeakers arranged in a square around the listener. The added expense and inconvenience of a four-speaker system with the necessary quadraphonic decoder unit did much to diminish the commercial success of these techniques, but the public lack of interest was more likely due to three other causes. First, the industry failed to agree a standard for the method of encoding the four signals on to disc, and so competing systems came on to the market whose discs did not function well on each other's equipment. Second, the surround sound effect produced was at best rather vague and diffused. Third, it required the listener to remain fixed in a central position, with any approach towards one of the loudspeakers resulting in that direction immediately becoming dominant.

Deeper research into both the way in which a three-dimensional soundfield can be captured by microphones, and the psychoacoustics of human directional hearing, holds out a very real promise of a much more successful approach to surround sound in the future. This is discussed in Chapter 15.

Room acoustics

An important factor which acts against a truly realistic reproduction of any musical sounds in the home is the effect of room acoustics. We have seen that concert halls each have individual reverberation characteristics and it is the same with small rooms. Indeed the problems are made worse by the smaller dimensions. What happens is that the room behaves like a three-dimensional organ pipe: the length, breadth and height each tend to tune or resonate to one particular fundamental frequency and its family of harmonics. The fundamental frequency is that for which the dimension equals half a wavelength, so that a room measuring $8 \times 5 \times 3$m, for example, would have main resonances at 21.25, 34 and 56.67Hz, plus harmonics at 42.5, 68, 113.34, 63.75, 102, 160.01Hz, etc.

The effect of these room resonances, or eigentones as they are called, is to boost the intensity of notes at these frequencies and so give an exaggerated booming bass. This explains the peculiarly male pleasure of singing in the bath, the non-absorbing bathroom walls forming excellent resonators at bass (or baritone) frequencies. Yet, where correct reproduction of music is concerned, this singling out of individual frequencies is clearly undesirable. A barely furnished cube-shaped room would be worst because very little absorption would take place and the dimensional resonances would coincide for the length, breadth and height. Heavy curtains spaced a fair distance out from the windows and wall are helpful, as are large pieces of furniture and a sprung wooden floor. It also helps if the dimensions are unequal and in no simple arithmetic ratio, so that the eigentone harmonics do not coincide, and deep recesses or non-parallel walls will spread the frequencies usefully.

An ideal listening room would also have a fair degree of symmetry. That is to say the stereo loudspeakers could be placed symmetrically at one end, in front of a moderately absorbent wall to avoid strong reflections, and the two side walls would have similar features to each other so that reflections from the two sides would not throw the stereo image seriously off balance. These counsels of perfection can rarely be achieved in practice, as real rooms will always have doors, windows and other prominent features placed asymmetrically. However, if the principle of acoustic balance is understood, the placing of loudspeakers and one's listening position can usually be moved around for reasonable results.

Another aspect of room acoustics is background noise, which is an ever-present distraction even when low enough to be heard only subconsciously, and can mask or completely submerge quiet passages in the music. Even in the quiet countryside, ambient noise levels of about 30dB above the threshold of hearing are common, and city and suburban homes have to contend with much higher levels due to the amalgam of traffic, air conditioning and aircraft noises. As a result, a certain average volume setting will be needed if all the music is to be audible, right down to the quietest pianissimo.

We may then run into another problem, the risk of annoying neighbours when the music gets too loud. Concert halls, cinemas and recording studios are specially designed to achieve high levels of insulation against external noise, ventilator noise, etc. And the insulating shell of the building or individual studio simultaneously prevents the musical sounds from being transmitted outwards to neighbouring areas. Unfortunately domestic building structures do not provide such efficient sound insulation. The party wall in a typical semi-detached house, for example, attenuates sounds at middle frequencies by only about 55dB, and this reduces to just 40dB at low frequencies. So listening to reproduced music which peaks to more than 90dB in homes where the ambient noise level is perhaps 35dB will begin to constitute a nuisance, with the bass frequencies predominating.

This leaves a usable dynamic range of 55dB between the quietest music that we can be sure of hearing and the loudest music that our neighbours cannot hear. Modern 'audiophile' gramophone records, and the coming generation of digital discs, can contain much wider dynamics than this. We have therefore reached a stage in the evolution of music systems for the home where source material can possess a wider dynamic range than many homes can comfortably handle. It may be necessary for future audio systems to provide facilities for compressing the dynamic range for use in the home or car.

Headphone stereo

It will be readily appreciated that listening on headphones avoids some of the problems associated with loudspeakers, and of course it makes the room acoustics irrelevant. Physical balance can be exact and indeed the headphone designer can specify the acoustic loading and environment with great precision. The sound quality, while of course varying between one design and another, at least presents a stable image which is independent of the particular room or the place in the room where one is listening. Ambient noise becomes much less of a limiting factor. We are no longer obliged to make a subconscious effort to ignore background distractions, and so head-phones make it easier, and less fatiguing, to concentrate on the music. As we shall see in Chapter 11, some headphone designs completely enclose the ears to provide a very high degree of isolation and make listening a uniquely private and rewarding experience, perhaps even surpassing real life concert going.

The questions of loudness, and the nuisance value of loudspeaker audio, are completely under the headphone user's control. He can choose as loud a listening level as he personally likes—though taking care not to go to intensity levels which might become fatiguing or even damaging over long periods—without needing to worry about other people.

The actual stereo effect tends to be too divided for complete naturalness. This is because the majority of stereo programmes were intended to be listened to on loudspeakers where, of course, both ears receive the signals from both loudspeakers. In headphone listening, each ear is exclusively hearing its own channel, so that the left/right spread tends to be exaggerated with the centre image depressed. There are other psychoacoustic vagaries depending on the individual which prevent a centre-front image from appearing at all convincingly. However, some very impressive results have been obtained using the technique known as 'dummy-head' or *Künstkopf* recording (see Chapter 2).

5
How Records Are Made

Many radio broadcasts of classical music, and a rather smaller proportion of pop music broadcasts, take the form of a direct relay as the concert or recital is being performed 'live'—that is, before a live audience. This puts a certain strain on the producer and engineers since they must have their microphones already carefully arranged in the best positions before the concert begins, and the only opportunity they will have had to check the musical balance will have been at the rehearsal, if any, in the empty hall. They can therefore only guess at the amount of deadening of reverberation which the absorption due to the audience will bring about, and they will not know exactly how the dynamics of light and shade will emerge during the creative progression of the actual performance. Add to this the likelihood of audience coughs and other noises, and a 'live' relay is seen to be rather a chancy business.

In practice, listeners to a live radio or television broadcast are fairly tolerant of audience noises and other distractions. They will even accept slight flaws in the music itself—errors of intonation, late entries, or a cracked note from the French horns—which will inevitably occur somewhere in nearly every performance. After all, there is the compensating benefit of hearing a continuous interpretation of the music, spiced as it is by the ever-present possibility that something might go sadly wrong.

However, when we listen to a gramophone record we become much more intolerant of distracting noises, and critical of musical fluffs or blemishes. This applies on a first listening to a record and of course is aggravated on repeated hearing. This is why the majority of recordings are made without an audience, in a soundproofed studio or other location where extraneous noises can be controlled, and using procedures which allow the musical results to be refined by repeating passages which seem to be less than perfect at the first attempt. The final recorded performance then consist of a number of best 'takes' edited together. Clearly this raises the question of sustaining a consistent interpretive flow through a given piece of music. However, most musicians can cope with this problem, and the

6 For their recording of the Berlioz Requiem in Walthamstow Town Hall, EMI used all the available space to accommodate the London Philharmonic Orchestra and Choir, soloists and four groups of brass players (*Photo Clive Barda*)

7 During the Berlioz recording, some of the principals moved into the control room to listen to a digital tape playback. Left to right, André Previn (conductor), David Bell (editor), Suvi Raj Grubb (producer), Christopher Parker (balance engineer, standing), Malcolm Hicks (chorus master) and Peter Andry (executive producer) (*Photo Clive Barda*)

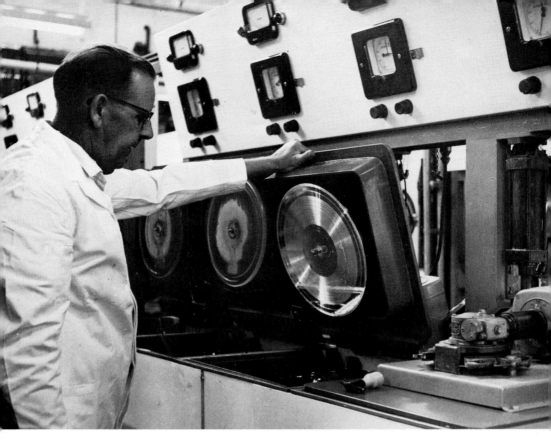

8 The metal stampers from which LP records are pressed are produced in electroplating baths (*Photo EMI*)

9 Musicassettes are duplicated at high speed on banks of 'slave' recorders from signals on the continuous-loop 1in master tape, visible through the glass panel on the left (*Photo Phonodisc*)

advantage of being able to eliminate the occasional wrong note or badly shaped phrase are considerable.

A classical recording session

The decision to make a recording of a given classical work with selected performers is usually taken long before the actual recording sessions are booked. It can be taken for granted that the conductor, players and singers are already familiar with the music to be recorded. Indeed in the case of complex works like a Mahler symphony or opera or oratorio it is becoming increasingly the practice to book the recording sessions close to the time of a public performance. Then the time and expense of rehearsals is doubly useful. At the recording session itself, all those taking part can concentrate on the business of committing a polished performance to tape.

The procedure is to run through and then record either a whole movement or section (Plate 6). The recording equipment, which consists of a mixing console and one or more tape recorders, is situated in a separate room out of earshot of the main hall or studio. This control room, specially designed for the purpose in the case of a recording studio and improvised in a dressing-room or vestry in the case of a concert hall or church, is also equipped with a pair of high quality loudspeakers. These enable the recording team to judge the sound quality as picked up by their microphones and either relayed directly through the mixing console or replayed from the tape.

The conductor and other key performers will usually come into the control room to listen to a playback of the first take (Plate 7). Discussions can then take place as to its success or otherwise—musically as well as technically—and sections may be re-recorded if necessary before moving on to the next scheduled section. A long work may be recorded in sections out of sequence, perhaps to suit individual soloists who may have other engagements—or, where a choir is involved, all choral passages may be recorded at a single evening session because most choirs are largely amateurs and available in the evenings only. The producer has the responsibility of planning the order of recording in consultation with the conductor and soloists. He must mark up the score with the editing points and a complete log of the best takes. The score and tapes are then passed to an editor who will prepare a finally edited version for approval.

Widely different microphone techniques are used. In a hall or studio with good acoustics it should generally be possible to use only a few microphones. This produces a more natural musical balance and also makes it easier to preserve the true perspective and left-to-right layout of the musicians. Two microphones represent the minimum number for stereo, European engineers mainly preferring to use directional microphones and to mount these as close together as possible. This is the so-called Blumlein technique, named after its inventor, and gives excellent spatial recordings. American engineers often prefer to use non-directional microphones spaced anything from 1.5m to 4.5m (5ft to 15ft) apart. This gives wide-sounding stereo but can suffer from a 'hole in the middle' effect, unless a third microphone is added at the centre with its output mixed into both the left and right channels.

When the hall acoustics are unsympathetic, or not well enough known in advance, the engineer will often play safe and position numerous microphones throughout the orchestra. This gives him the possibility of overcoming problems with echoes or internal balance, but of course introduces new difficulties. He must now rebuild the true orchestral sound from scratch, by fading up violins, cellos and so on—and even allocate them to believable positions in the stereo stage by 'panning'. This requires a good deal of experience, and of course should be checked with the conductor who no longer has full control of the orchestral balance as recorded. Once a satisfactory balance has been agreed, it then becomes important that the engineer leaves well alone—and resists the temptation to fade individual instruments or sections up and down as the music proceeds. Unfortunately many recordings have been spoiled by this kind of 'spotlighting'.

Pop recording

There are at least as many styles of popular or 'pop' music as classical music, and even more different ways of making pop recordings. However, it is possible to generalise about some aspects of pop recording. Whereas in classical music the live performance is regarded as most important, with recordings judged to be good or bad according to how closely they recreate the live sounds, the situation is actually reversed for pop. The recording almost always comes first and, when the fans go along to a live concert, they hope that the sounds they then hear from the stage (and loudspeaker system) will closely resemble the sound of the discs. In practice this is often difficult or impossible to achieve.

Pop recordings are built up, sometimes over a period of several weeks, through several processes of recording and re-recording (dubbing). An essential ingredient is felt to be 'separation' between each instrument and voice. Therefore acoustically very dead studios are used and large numbers of microphones placed very close to each instrument or singer. A drum kit, for example, may have six or more microphones only about an inch away from each cymbal, etc. Very complex mixing consoles are used, with facilities for changing the balance of treble or bass, adding artificial reverberation or repeat echoes, and allocating each instrument to any desired position across the stereo stage. If this does not give enough separation between the instruments, they can be played one at a time with each new instrumentalist listening to the previous recordings on headphones so that he can synchronise his playing. All these recordings are kept on separate tracks of a multi-track tape machine (twenty-four tracks is normal) so that they can be replayed in synchronism. The final decision on the mixture and electronic treatment to produce the eventual two-track stereo version is postponed until a mix-down session. Here a computer and digital memory store may be used to assist the producer and engineer in arriving at the definitive performance.

So it is little wonder that a live performance will often lack the full impact of the disc, even when complicated arrays of microphones, loudspeakers, amplifiers, synthesisers and prerecorded tapes are employed. Yet few fans will complain, and indeed the special atmosphere of a concert, with plenty of stage action and lighting effects, produces a unique experience for which the disc can then act as a souvenir. So-called 'live' albums of pop concerts do appear from time to time, but these will generally have been subjected to a certain amount of studio remixing to overcome technical difficulties which may have arisen in the concert hall.

The recording chain

It will be realised that many of the techniques available to modern record producers, such as editing and multi-track dubbing, owe their existence to the emergence of magnetic tape recording in the early 1950s. Prior to this the chain of equipment for recording consisted of one or more microphones connected by cables to a rather rudimentary control desk. The output of the desk was fed to a disc cutting machine. A blank disc, originally made of wax but later of lacquer-coated aluminium, was placed on the turntable and driven at a precisely controlled speed while the cutter head traversed the disc from the outer edge towards the centre, to cut a spiral-shaped groove on the disc surface. This head contained a sharp cutting needle or stylus which, actuated by the electric currents from the control desk, vibrated in such a manner as to imprint a copy or 'analogue' of the music signal waveform in the groove.

From about 1950, all record companies introduced a tape recording stage, with the final copying of tape to disc delayed until all refinements had been carried out to produce an approved 'master tape' (see Fig. 5.1).

In recent years, two variants on this recording chain have appeared, each claiming to give improvements in the overall sound quality.

(a) *Direct-cut disc recording* consists of a return to the earlier practice of recording straight on to the cutting lathe with no intermediary tape stage (see dotted line in Fig. 5.1). The advantages claimed are avoidance of any distortions or noise normally introduced by tape recording, and indeed a modern cutting lathe can perform better than most tape recorders in such matters as frequency response, fast response to transients and quiet background. Such 'direct-cut' discs have therefore built up quite a reputation amongst hi-fi enthusiasts or 'audiophiles' who want the very best disc quality to show off their hi-fi systems. Several artistic disadvantages should be noted, however. The performers are

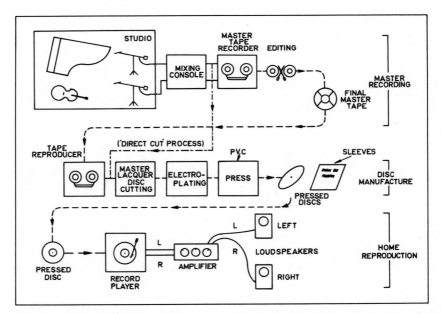

Fig. 5.1 The recording chain from studio to listener. The dotted line shows the short route taken in 'direct-cut' recording when the tape recording and editing stages are bypassed

obliged to play the music for a whole side of the disc note-perfect and without stopping. This may create an inhibiting atmosphere in some circumstances. Also the cutting engineer cannot rehearse and refine his disc transfer levels as he can when working from a master tape, and may be obliged to play safe by cutting at a relatively low average level, or restricting the amount of music per side.

(b) *Digital recording* replaces the conventional 'analogue' tape recorder with a machine which stores the musical waveform as an encoded series of short pulses. The very real advantages of this technique include the fact that such recordings are secure against the intrusion of noise, distortion or speed fluctuations in the tape mechanism. A wide dynamic range is possible, with musical climaxes and quiet passages often very impressive. The very high cost of digital recorders must be seen as a disadvantage, at least initially, and a learning process has had to be gone through to discover whether there are factors in this new technique which might lead to new and unexpected forms of signal degradation. Digital recording and its emergence as a medium in the home are discussed in detail in Chapter 15.

Disc processing

However it is produced—direct-cut or via analogue or digital tape—the master disc has first to be given a very thin coating of silver to make it electrically conducting. It is then placed in an electroplating bath for several hours until it becomes coated with a layer of nickel (Plate 8). When this nickel plate is carefully stripped from the lacquer disc it becomes a matrix or master, with ridges corresponding to the original grooves and vice versa. It could therefore be used as it stands as a mould for pressing out records in some suitable plastic material. In practice, as an insurance against damage and to allow the production of large numbers of 'pressings' (as the final records are called in the trade), two further electroplating stages are usually employed. First, a replating of the master produces a metal replica of the original disc. This is called the positive or mother and can be played as a check on quality before in turn being replated—as many times as required—to produce a whole generation of further negative metal plates known as stampers.

As their name implies, the stampers act as the moulds used in the disc presses. One stamper for each side of the record is clamped into the jaws of a press. Then, in a pressing cycle which takes less than 30 seconds, the two labels are inserted along with a lump of preheated vinyl plastic: the jaws close for a brief period and then cooling water flows through the system, the jaws open automatically and the record can be removed.

Types of record

The recording industry standard has been the LP (long play) disc ever since this format was introduced soon after the Second World War. The LP disc is nominally 12in (30cm) in diameter and runs at $33\frac{1}{3}$rpm (revolutions per minute). There are on average about 250 grooves to the inch and this gives up to around 25 minutes' playing time per side. In practice, modern cutting lathes normally employ a special technique which automatically varies the pitch (number of grooves to the inch) as the cutter tracks across the record. The tape being transferred to disc is passed over a 'preview' head before it reaches the normal replay head, and the previewed signal can be used to open out the groove spacing when loud passages are detected and close up the grooves during quiet passages. This varipitch technique allows the engineers to maximise the average level of recorded signals, thereby keeping inherent record noise to a minimum, and it can on occasion permit extra-long sides to be recorded of up to 30 minutes or even longer.

At about the same time as the 12in LP was introduced (by CBS) the RCA company launched a smaller 7in (18cm) disc running at 45rpm. Between them they soon completely eclipsed the record format which had been the sole disc medium for almost half a century. This was a coarse-grooved disc (about 100 grooves per inch), made in two sizes, 10in and 12in, running at 78rpm.

Stereophonic (stereo) gramophone records first appeared in 1958 and of course necessitated the carrying of two mutually independent channels of information in a single groove. Up until then, monophonic (mono) records had consisted of a single lateral waveform which generated the required output electric current by driving the stylus from side to side. Some experimental stereo discs were made by combining this lateral drive with a vertical waveform for the second channel. However, the combined lateral and vertical cut records were soon felt to lack the desired symmetry and a happier solution was found by turning the axes through 45°. Thus, looking at the cutter head or playback pickup cartridge from in front, the signal corresponding to the left stereo channel consists of vibrations in a plane at 45° to the record surface effectively on the left-hand wall of the groove. The right channel is similarly modulated in a plane at 90° to this, on the right-hand wall.

Disc distortions

Certain forms of distortion are inevitable in the disc record format, and will be discussed in more detail in Chapter 7. First there is something called end-of-side distortion. Since the record is turning at a fixed rotational speed, it follows that the linear speed of the groove under the stylus falls progressively as it spirals towards the centre. The recorded waveform therefore becomes more cramped. As we saw in Chapter 3, there is a direct relationship between the wavelength at any particular frequency and the speed of motion (velocity = frequency × wavelength). The wavelengths recorded on a disc are therefore continually shrinking and, since the smallest wavelengths correspond to the highest frequencies, there can be a considerable loss of high frequencies at the end of each record side due to the inability of the stylus tip to explore the tiny waveform properly.

Second there is a form of distortion due to what is called tracking error. As we have seen, the cutter head tracks straight across a radius of the disc and is always lined up at right angles to the groove. Unfortunately a pivoted pickup arm (the most usual type) sweeps in an arc across the record and so it is continually shifting its angle with respect to the groove and this leads to distortion. Third we have a 'pinch effect' which results from the different tip shapes inevitably used for cutting and playback styli. The cutting stylus must of necessity be V-shaped and, to take the simpler case of a lateral mono groove, will therefore cut a groove of constant width. A reproducing stylus, however, must be rounded and so will be obliged to rise and fall twice during each cycle of the recorded waveform—thus generating a certain amount of second harmonic distortion. The situation is worst with a spherical tipped stylus and progressively less serious with a properly dimensioned and aligned elliptical or 'fine line' stylus.

Cassette duplication

After a slow start, prerecorded cassettes or 'musicassettes' have increased in popularity to the point where they can compete on nearly equal terms with LP records. The record companies now make simultaneous releases, at least of their classical repertoire, on disc and cassette. Many people find that they need both discs and cassettes to meet their various audio requirements: discs for highest fidelity on their home system and cassettes for convenience in the car, or at parties since they are less liable to damage than discs.

The economics of cassette mass-production are very different from disc processing. Each cassette tape must be recorded individually, which is clearly more complicated than the simple pressing out of discs. The raw materials for the cassette tape and its case tend also to cost more than the disc equivalent. Techniques have therefore had to be evolved to keep costs to a minimum, and it is the successful solution of this problem which has gradually brought the price of cassettes down to the same level as discs.

Starting with the studio master tape, which may be analogue or digital, an analogue copy is made at $7\frac{1}{2}$ips (19cm/s) on to a special 'running master' of one-inch-wide tape. This has four tracks to carry the stereo channels of both sides one and two of the final cassette (with side two running backwards). The ends of this tape are joined together to form a continuous loop with a short length carrying a cue tone at 6Hz. The tape is loaded into a special machine which drives it continuously at high speed (usually thirty-two times normal—ie 240ips). The resulting signals are fed simultaneously to a dozen or more slave recorders (Plate 9). These are similarly running at thirty-two times normal cassette speed, ie $32 \times 1\frac{7}{8} = 60$ips (152cm/s) and carry large spools of cassette-type tape, enough for about twenty repeats of the music programme. When these tapes have been completely recorded they are taken off the machines and placed on tailoring and winding machines. Here the 6Hz tone is used to locate the beginning and end of each music programme. Empty cassette cases with lengths of leader tape already attached to the two hubs are loaded into the machine. One end of the music tape is spliced on to one leader. Then the tape is wound into the cassette at high speed until the end tone is detected, when the tape is cut and joined to the second leader. Labelling and packaging sequences follow.

It is interesting that the running master is played with side one running forwards. Therefore the spools of twenty cassette programmes are taken off the slave machines tail-side out. They then run into the cassette cases so that the cassettes are ready to play side one without rewinding. Also, when the programmes for sides one and two are first transferred from the (two) studio masters to the running master it is usually arranged to make side one longer than side two (when the music allows) and the opening of side two is lined up with the actual end of side one. This allows the user to play side one to the end and, on turning over the cassette, find the music of side two ready to begin immediately.

6
The Shapes of Audio

The component parts of a complete audio system are shown in outline in Fig. 6.1. They comprise the three main sources of music in the home—disc, tape and radio—an amplifier/control unit and a pair of loudspeakers. In fact only one loudspeaker is needed for mono, but the vast majority of home audio systems cater for stereo, and so a pair of matched, suitably spaced, loudspeakers is essential. A microphone and a pair of headphones are also shown in the diagram, and indeed 'live' recording and the alternative of private listening on headphones should certainly be considered for inclusion in all installations.

On the building-brick principle, it is possible to combine the units shown in Fig. 6.1 in numerous ways, and omit some of the sources if these are not wanted initially. This chapter considers the advantages and disadvantages of buying and assembling a system entirely made up of separate units, as against the various integrated models available such as music-centres and rack systems. Just a few of the possible combinations are: a mono one-piece radio with built-in speaker; a Walkman cassette player with headphones; a music-centre with separate speakers; a system of 'separates'; a stereo radio-cassette recorder with two built-in speakers.

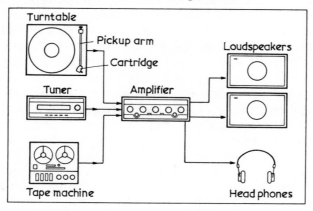

Fig. 6.1 The component parts of a typical stereo system

Audio evolution

Fashion seems to play almost as important a part in the shaping of home audio equipment as it does in other areas of human interest. As a result, the size and shape of the units and the degree of integration of units into composite cabinets gives very little guide to the sound quality to be expected. This is to be regretted only in so far as it makes the task of choosing audio equipment a little more difficult. However, so long as one has enough patience and determination to insist on a thorough demonstration prior to purchase—and that one's final choice is made primarily on the basis of pleasing sound quality—the proliferation of audio shapes should at least include something that pleases the ear without offending the eye, or fitting awkwardly into the given living-room.

Historically, audio began with Edison's one-piece cylinder phonograph in the 1870s. This was both recorder and reproducer to begin with, but later the emphasis shifted to improving the playback quality from commercial prerecorded cylinders. This led to the development of quite hefty, and sometimes quite handsome, pieces of phonograph furniture selling alongside the small portable machines. Disc-playing gramophones, from their inception in the 1900s, similarly aimed to satisfy both the cheap portable market and the more quality-conscious buyer. Cylinders and discs continued in competition right up to the middle 1920s, when the easier duplication and handling of gramophone records finally ousted the cylinder for good.

All these machines were acoustic, that is the sound energy was entirely derived from stylus (needle) movement in the groove. The sounds were amplified, so to speak, by attaching the stylus via a lever arrangement to a diaphragm of mica or similar material in the soundbox. The diaphragm could radiate only moderately loud sounds into the air, and the frequency coverage left much to be desired, particularly at the bass end. The remedy was to direct the diaphragm soundwaves into some form of horn whose ever-widening cross-sectional area gave further boosting of the loudness and whose flared opening made an efficient match to the outer air. Ingenious adaptations of this horn-loading idea led to many fanciful shapes— compared with which today's audio looks positively dull.

When radio broadcasting began in the early 1920s, there were dark mutterings that this would be the end of the gramophone. If people could receive hours of music by 'wireless', why would they continue to buy records? In the event these forecasts, like others since, proved wide of the mark, and indeed the emergence of radio sets gave the gramophone a new lease of life.

Already something of the variety of choice we now know faced the intending purchaser. He could buy a radio, with a built-in or separate loudspeaker, and either add a separate new electrical gramophone unit or fit an electrical pickup to his old acoustic gramophone and plug the pickup output wires into his radio. Very soon he was being offered 'radiogramophones', which combined radio, gramophone and loudspeaker in a single floor-standing cabinet. Around 1950, the first tape recorders began to appear, and the business of 'separates' or 'integrated music systems' began all over again.

The case for separates

In those postwar years, it was quite definitely an advantage to buy, or build for yourself, separate units. The technology of sound reproduction was advancing so quickly that only the high-fidelity enthusiast who had, and understood the workings of, a separate turntable, pickup arm, cartridge, amplifier, loudspeaker and perhaps a tape recorder could keep up with the latest developments. He would buy each component from a different manufacturer, and mix and match the units until he achieved a sound quality that suited him personally. Also the cost of replacing individual items could be quite small, and so he could experiment and upgrade his system fairly easily. Many men had come out of the armed forces with an interest and practical experience in electronics and so home construction of amplifiers, radios and loudspeakers was very popular. This could both save money and sometimes give better sound quality than the shop-bought units.

Against this, it has to be said, the hi-fi rig was often an unsightly accumulation of ill-matched components—from the aesthetic point of view. It also had a bird's nest of connecting cables and needed special knowledge to persuade it to perform correctly. Hi-fi was an antisocial hobby, and the rest of the family were usually warned not to touch the hi-fi—but to use the homely radiogram instead.

The case for integration

Then, as now, there were also good arguments in favour of buying an integrated system. Since all the component parts had been designed and interconnected by one manufacturer, it could be assumed that they were sensibly matched to each other in terms both of cost and performance. An integrated system is much easier to accommodate in the average living-room where it has to coexist with other activities. The connecting wires do not trail all over the place, and anyone can put on a record or tune in the radio without needing special skills or knowhow. If the quality of reproduction from a conventional radiogram fell somewhat below that of a properly matched and aligned rig of hi-fi separates, this was of less importance to many people than the absolute need for quick and easy operation, plus an acceptable degree of orderliness. And at least the quality standards were likely to be consistent, whereas the hi-fi addict could occasionally make expensive mistakes. He might upgrade one component out of all proportion to the rest and, on the principle that 'a chain is only as strong as its weakest link', fail to get the overall improvement he expected.

The modern music-centre

The latest embodiment of the radiogram principle is the music-centre (Plate 10). This has the controls for both the radio tuner section and the amplifier section conveniently grouped together. It also has the record-player deck and a cassette tape deck built in, with all the interconnecting leads conveniently out of harm's way (and out of sight). The only cables needed are a single mains lead to be plugged into a wall socket, an aerial lead-in and the flex leads to a pair of speakers suitably positioned for good stereo listening.

 Inevitably a music-centre tends to be quite large, but it need not be unsightly. It is a great convenience that the cassette recorder is permanently wired up and ready to record a favourite radio programme at a moment's notice. By using a suitable electronic timer, either supplied as part of the music-centre or bought as a separate add-on unit, it is possible to set up the system to switch itself on, record a given programme and switch off again unattended while one is away from home. In short, the best designed music-centres have put operational convenience high up on their list of desirable features. And this ability to choose entertainment from disc, tape or radio at the flick of a switch—without having to change over connections or operate knobs on separate units—makes a music-centre a good investment for many homes.

 Prices range widely, but as a rule you get what you pay for and there is no real reason why a music-centre should not perform every bit as well as a set of separates costing an equivalent amount. When making comparisons, remember that disc, tape and radio are all included. Because the price of a music-centre may appear quite a large sum, it has unfortunately become the practice to skimp on the quality of the loudspeakers offered as 'included accessories'. With a few exceptions, therefore, it is a good idea to avoid the apparent bargain offered by such inclusive packages and ask the dealer to help you choose separate loudspeakers of a standard likely to match up more closely the potentials of the particular music-centre.

Rack systems

In recent years a considerable market has been created for rack-mounted systems of separates (Plate 11) which claim all the convenience and domestic harmony of the one-piece music-centre, together with the high performance and individual choice associated with component hi-fi. To be honest, most of these rack or 'tower' systems fall quite a bit short of the quality standards achievable by putting together a chain of genuine high fidelity products. Also they are less tidy than a music-centre since too often each of their units has its own mains lead, requiring up to four separate connections to the house supply, and the interconnecting cables are often too long and liable to fall out or get tangled up.

However, there is a useful degree of flexibility about these systems, which partly explains their popularity. For example it would be perfectly possible to omit the cassette deck or radio tuner, perhaps to limit the original outlay or because that particular music source was not immediately required or was felt to be supplied adequately by a unit already owned. Adding the matching unit at a later date would be perfectly straightforward. Again, many manufacturers offer rack systems at several price levels. Therefore it is often possible to splash out more money on the unit or units felt to be most important, and economise by buying other units from one of that manufacturer's cheaper systems.

The racks themselves take numerous shapes, being either in vertical towers or horizontal frameworks with handy storage space for records, tapes, headphones and other accessories.

Of course the inspiration for these home rack-mounted systems came from professional studio installations where serried ranks of duplicated units, including standby units ready for quick changing in emergency, are a common feature. So the domestic designers have often sought to give their units a sometimes spurious 'professional' look by fitting vertical metal handles at each end of the front panel, copying professional controls and meters, and even constructing their units to fit precisely into the 48cm (19in) rack width which has evolved as a professional standard. The results can be impressive, but the total visual effect is often too technical and complicated to suit some tastes or merge happily into the living-room environment.

Mini systems

Electronic components have gone through several phases of progressive miniaturisation in recent years. First the tiny transistor replaced the thermionic valve and, since it required lower working voltages, it did away with the need for large and elaborate power supplies. Then integrated circuits (ICs) came along compressing the functions of scores of transistors into the area of a postage stamp, to be followed by large-scale integrated circuits (LSIs) and eventually the mind-boggling microchip.

Not surprisingly, therefore, the cabinets of audio units have progressively become more and more empty. They have retained their traditional dimensions, mainly because human fingers have preferred to operate the traditional types of knobs and switches—and also to some extent to preserve that 'professional' look—while the circuitry inside has become miniaturised.

However, by ingenious designing and the use of new miniaturised controls such as touch-sensitive switches, a new breed of 'mini' or 'micro' hi-fi systems has appeared (Plate 12). These can be built to almost any level of technical performance, and of course will appeal most to people with limited space. Indeed, mini systems always attract immediate attention in dealers' showrooms, on the basis that 'small is beautiful', though some sales resistance has been reported on the unreasonable argument that potential purchasers often feel that they are not getting as much for their money.

A typical top area size for mini systems is only 25×20cm $(10 \times 8$in) so that, while all other component units can be stacked on top of each other to occupy a minimum of space, the record-player deck stubbornly refuses to shrink. In order to satisfy the demand, real or imagined, for total space-saving, some designers have produced record decks with top areas which are literally no greater than an LP record sleeve, ie 30cm (12in) square. These have a short linear-tracking pickup arm built into the lid, with a clamp to hold the record on to the platter and the stylus tracking force applied by means of a spring. The whole deck can easily be stacked on top of a mini hi-fi system, or can even be positioned vertically against a wall.

Features versus performance

There are even record decks and music-centres built with vertical turntable operation as standard, and at least one design has a linear-tracking pickup on both sides of the record (which is clamped at the centre label area only). Either pickup can be selected by means of a switch and a 'search and play' system will play any chosen sequence of tracks from the two sides.

This illustrates a certain dichotomy in the design philosophy of audio systems. If the strictest sound quality standards are given first priority, then such features as the record deck and amplifier will necessarily be massive and almost devoid of auto-operation features and other frills. This type of equipment will generally be very expensive, since each tiny increment of improved performance at this level involves an increasingly large cost factor. True high fidelity equipment is therefore designed with the professional or keen hobbyist in mind. A degree of expertise in setting up and operating the equipment can be assumed, and cosmetic or space-saving features are less important.

In the wider domestic audio context, ease of operation, attractive appearance which will blend with room décor and furnishing, and reasonably low cost all take precedence over that last ounce of sonic fidelity. Since the market for equipment in this second category is much greater than that for specialist top-quality hi-fi, even more research and development seems to be directed towards 'convenience audio' than sound improvements. In music-centres and matching rack systems in particular, one new feature or styling gimmick seems to follow another with surprising speed. Some systems, for example, now offer complete remote control of all operations (Plate 13), with the act of cueing the record-player automatically starting the cassette deck for copying purposes (strictly against the copyright laws) and so on. Spoken words of command will even be accepted by some systems—provided the instructions are spoken by the voices previously learned by the built-in microprocessor.

The intending purchaser is indeed fortunate in having such a wide choice of audio equipment types. There is a real need to decide one's priorities in advance, however—performance versus features—and each feature should be examined to see whether it will be really useful in the given environment, or just a superfluous gimmick.

Audio shopping

Other basic decisions should be made before you go audio shopping, so as to narrow the choice and avoid expensive mistakes. You should begin by trying to put an upper price limit on the project, perhaps guided by a quick sortie to the local stores to see the range of asking prices. Then you should try to imagine that the new audio system is already installed in your living-room, and clear your ideas as to how you want it to look and what tasks it will have to perform—serious listening, or just background, etc. Are disc, tape and radio equally important or can you economise on one of these? Should the tape side be adaptable to hobby or self-education recording projects? Are existing shelves or a room divider the best place for the new audio system to sit? Should the loudspeakers be floor-standing or do convenient shelves or stands already exist?

You may not want to get too deeply involved in technical jargon, however. All you need to be able to make sense of equipment specifications will be found in Chapter 12, 'How to read specifications'. Once you have sorted out your ideas for the type of system, its price and general size and shape, you should visit your nearest reputable dealer. It makes sense to shop locally since you may be able to strike up a friendship at a local level and the dealer can reasonably expect you to come back to him for further items. He may very well assist by offering to demonstrate or set up the equipment in your own home. This kind of relationship is so much better than the almost neurotic mistrust which some nervous shoppers have of hi-fi salesmen. There may be unreliable or over-pushing dealers, but the majority are knowledgeable and trustworthy—or, quite simply, they would not survive.

Describe your requirements and ask for a demonstration of suitable equipment. It is quite a good idea to take along a record you know and like, or ask for records of your own taste in music to be played. Now is the time to start trusting your own ears. Allowing for the unhelpful acoustics of the average shop or showroom, satisfy yourself that the music sounds reasonably natural, with no sharp edges or boominess. Is there ample volume without rattling or breaking up? Do the controls feel stable and are they logical and simple to use? With the volume control at a normal setting, or slightly higher, and no record playing, is the remaining noise emerging from the loudspeakers no more than a very faint background hiss?

When you are satisfied on all these points, it should be safe to go ahead with the purchase. By sticking to well-known brand names and an established dealer you should be secure against failure of parts and the normal hazards of buying any piece of electronic or mechanical equipment. Otherwise ask about the guarantee position.

When you get the equipment home, install it with due attention to all the instructions, experiment a little with different loudspeaker positions and tone control settings, then leave well alone. You bought the equipment primarily for the music; so just sit back and enjoy it. If it is a modest budget hi-fi system, it will probably exhibit a few mid-fi symptoms. Yet by following the above suggestions you will surely have met your basic music-in-the-home requirements and obtained value for money, which is the basis of sensible shopping.

Audio budgets

As a very approximate guide to apportioning the money to be spent on an audio system, you should expect to pay roughly the same amount on the four component parts—record-player deck, cassette deck, amplifier-plus-tuner (or receiver) and a pair of loudspeakers. Thus, towards the low end of the range, a £100 turntable unit might be teamed up with a £100 cassette deck, £100 tuner-amplifier and £100 speakers. Moving up the performance and price scale, a £300 turntable deserves a £300 tuner-amplifier and a pair of loudspeakers at about the same price, etc.

As-evidence that such recommendations can be of only limited accuracy, the ranges of prices of individual units and systems at the time of writing are as follows:

pickup cartridges £8–250, pickup arms £60–200, record decks (including pickup arms) £60–500, cassette decks £80–650, radio tuners £80–700, amplifiers £80–800, loudspeakers (per pair) £80–1,000, music-centres £300–750, receivers £100–800.

These figures ignore several esoteric models at even higher prices, but already show such a wide spread of prices that wise shopping at a reputable store is indicated.

7
The Record-player

As we saw in the previous chapter, audio systems come in all shapes and sizes. Nevertheless the same basic ingredients will be present, either as separate units or integrated into composite boxes of one kind or another. Let us now examine the make-up and finer points of each of the component parts in some detail. We shall begin with the three basic programme sources—record-player deck, tape deck and radio tuner—all of which are desirable in a complete audio system, though each could be omitted in an initial outlay either to cut down in costs or space. Then we shall discuss the preamplifier/control unit into which the programme sources are connected and its associated power amplifier, and finally the loudspeaker and headphones.

The turntable (Plate 13)

The unit on which we play our gramophone records can be considered as made up of three parts, namely the *turntable*, the *cartridge* and the *arm*.

A primary requirement of the turntable is that it will rotate the disc at precisely the correct speed, that is the speed used when the original master disc was cut. Only then will the music be reproduced at the correct pitch. A fast-running turntable would raise the pitch (and incidentally speed up the musical tempo), while a slow turntable would lower the pitch. In practice, while it is obviously desirable that the speed should be exactly right, most listeners cannot detect small speed/pitch errors, and so the international standards permit a tolerance (or error) of $\pm 1\%$. As a reference, we may note that a 6% change is equivalent to raising or lowering the musical pitch by one semitone. Long-term speed changes, or 'drift', tend to go by unnoticed for the same reason.

On the other hand, human hearing is very critical of short-term speed fluctuations which are audible as pitch wobbling. The effect is described as 'wow' when the fluctuations occur at a low speed, say less than twenty times per second (20Hz) and 'flutter' at high speeds. A single *wow-and-flutter* rating is given in technical specifications. The other principal performance rating for turntables is *rumble*. That is a measure of the level of unwanted low-pitched noise generated within the electrical motor or the turntable platter's main bearing.

Types of drive

Until a few years ago, the electrical motors used to drive turntables were comparatively simple devices causing their drive spindle or capstan to spin at around 1,800–3,600 revolutions per minute. The necessary speed reduction to drive the platter at the standard disc speeds of 33⅓, 45 and 78rpm was achieved through an intermediary rubber-tyred idler wheel (Fig. 7.1a). This was driven by the capstan and, since it also pressed against the horizontal rim of the platter, caused the record to revolve at the required speed. The dimensions of the idler wheel did not affect the speed reduction, which was solely dependent on the ratio of the capstan and platter diameters. The different record speeds were selected by physically moving the idler wheel so that it lined up with the appropriate portion of the stepped-diameter capstan. In some turntable designs (notably by Goldring-Lenco) a tapered capstan was employed to give continuously variable speed over the range of, say, 30–90rpm. This allowed users with perfect pitch to correct faulty records, or make it possible to retune the recorded music to the home piano and allow 'playing along' with the record. To be honest, this ability to fine-tune record speed is seldom required, but is still found on many modern record decks.

While idler-wheel drive had the advantage of simplicity and could impart a powerful starting torque, it had a number of serious drawbacks. Rumble was an ever-present problem since any motor vibrations were transmitted directly to the platter. Also wear or dust on the idler wheel or platter rim contributed further low frequency noise. Wow-and-flutter could be kept to acceptable speed levels only if a very heavy platter was used to smooth out fluctuations by its flywheel action. This added to costs and made a well-designed bearing absolutely vital.

Two basically more refined drive techniques have now replaced the idler-wheel system for all except the cheaper record-changer market. They each have clear advantages and disadvantages, with the best examples of both types being capable of exemplary performance.

The first, called *belt-drive* (Fig. 7.1b), uses a thin rubber belt to transmit the torque from the motor capstan to a flange or sub-platter on the underside of the main platter. Immediately we can see that rumble should be very low indeed, the natural elasticity of the belt acting as a barrier between any motor irregularities and the platter. The motor itself can be quite small, and located at a distance from the pickup cartridge line of traverse to minimise hum induction. Starting torque is rather weak, so that time must be allowed for the record to reach correct speed. This will be particularly noticeable when a heavy platter is employed, as on the better designs. Some belt slip may occur, and of course the belt (like the idler-wheel) may need to be replaced after a few years' use. A slight nuisance too is the need to build in a mechanical 'finger' or other device to shift the belt to another portion of the drive capstan to change turntable speed. Indeed, this task has sometimes to be carried out by hand.

The second drive system now in vogue is *direct-drive* (Fig. 7.1c). This avoids the need for intermediary wheels or belts by employing a motor, built around the centre spindle, which actually runs at normal record speed and, instead of a relatively thin capstan, has a spinning platform on which the

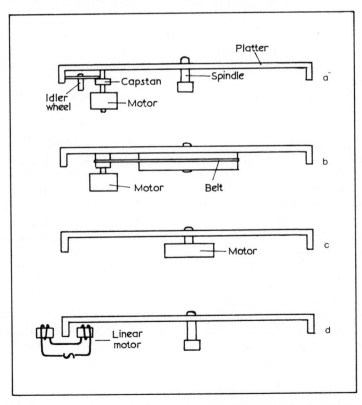

Fig. 7.1 Types of turntable drive: (a) idler-wheel; (b) belt-drive; (c) direct-drive; (d) linear-motor

record platter sits or is firmly bolted. It must be said, however, that the apparent simplicity of this arrangement—and its undoubted benefits in terms of long-term consistency of performance—is generally accompanied by quite complex electronic control circuitry. Note too that special care is needed in designing the bearing which, though it is operating at very low speed and therefore subject to low wear, will have any inherent vibrations transmitted directly to the platter. An incidental advantage of direct-drive is that phenomenal start and stop facilities can be provided, allowing accurate cueing to less than one revolution of a record. There is also the advantage that the spindle bearing is not subjected to side pressures, compared with idler-wheel and belt systems which both exert a lateral force.

Various techniques are used to maintain exact speed on direct-drive turntables. The true instantaneous speed of the platter can be monitored continuously, for example, by printing an alternately black and transparent pattern on the underside and monitoring this by means of a lamp and light-sensitive diode. Alternatively the underside of the platter may carry a ring of magnetic coating, like that used in tape recording, on which a fixed number of signal pulses have been recorded. A small magnetic replay head can then monitor the pulse rate produced as the platter rotates. The frequency of the resulting pulse stream from the optical or magnetic monitor can be compared with that of a calibrated quartz-crystal oscillator. Any error signal can then be used either to modify the voltage of a voltage-controlled DC motor, or directly control the frequency of a special oscillator driving an AC motor.

In the best designs, these servo-controlled systems can reduce speed drift to very low values, and they will correct errors due to changing load conditions. This is a problem with some idler-wheel and belt-drive turntables in which the tracking force of the pickup alone, or the use of a tracking record cleaner like a Dust-Bug, or even heavily modulated passages of music, can produce sufficient drag to slow the turntable significantly. However, an inferior servo design may introduce a new type of wow-and-flutter problem known as 'hunting' or 'cogging'. This means that speed is never quite correct but is continually drifting and being corrected.

For completeness, yet another drive system introduced by Bang & Olufsen in their Beogram 8000 may be mentioned. This is *tangential-drive* (Fig. 7.1d) and makes use of the linear motor principle found, for example, in a number of linear-tracking arm designs. Here the motor coil assembly has an air gap in the shape of an arc, having the same radius as the platter rim. The motor therefore drives the aluminium platter tangentially, with no vibration-carrying link between motor and platter. Starting torque is high and an optical sensor and microcomputer comparator control running speed with an accuracy better than 0.02%.

Speed indicators

Many turntables incorporate a speed indicator. This is helpful on decks possessing a fine speed adjustment—to confirm that the nominal speed has been correctly set, or that the unit is in fact running fast or slow. However, remembering that most ears are not sharply critical of precise musical pitch, any slight drift in speed must be regarded as of little consequence. It is therefore quite unnecessary to keep adjusting the speed because the indicator is not reading dead true. It must also be remembered that some of the more elaborate speed indicator designs are linked directly to the speed servo local-oscillator and are showing the degree of accuracy with reference to the oscillator, not the true rotational velocity of the platter.

The traditional speed indicator is the stroboscope, which may take the form of a simple printed circular card to be placed over the record spindle, or a more ambitious system with a lamp, mirror and platter ridges. The principle is to illuminate the rotating pattern with light which is glowing bright and dark at some fixed rate. Then the pattern will appear stationary when the rotational speed causes each bar or dot to be precisely replaced in position by the following one each time that the light glows brightly. AC lighting has the required property of glowing twice in each cycle of the mains frequency, ie 100 times per second for 50Hz mains, or 6,000 times per minute (and 120 times per second, or 7,200 per minute, in the USA, for example, where a 60Hz mains supply is used). To calculate the number of marks required for any given turntable speed, it is simply necessary to divide the rpm speed into 6,000 or 7,200 (see Table 7.1). It will be seen that the $33\frac{1}{3}$rpm speed is exactly correct in the UK and the USA, while 45rpm runs fast in the UK and 78rpm is inaccurate everywhere.

Table 7.1 Stroboscope markings

Nominal speed (rpm)	50Hz lighting		60Hz lighting	
	No. of bars	Actual speed (rpm)	No. of bars	Actual speed (rpm)
$33\frac{1}{3}$	180	33.333	216	33.333
45	133	45.113	160	45
78	77	77.922	92	78.26

Some of the more elaborate oscillator-controlled turntables permit true selection of turntable speed and incorporate a numerical display. Some even allow this speed to be increased or decreased in discrete steps of 0.1rpm by tapping a button.

Platters and mats

Since all turntables rely to some extent on the flywheel action of the platter to smooth out speed fluctuations, the platter must be reasonably massive or, if lightweight, shaped so that most of its mass is concentrated at the outer rim. Castings of aluminium or alloy are usual, steel being unsuitable because it would exert a pull on magnetic cartridges and add significantly to their effective tracking force. The main spindle bearing of course is crucial to rumble-free performance. In the best examples it is turned and polished to perfect roundness and with its bottom point precisely concentric. This rests on a plastic pad, or ballbearing, while the spindle body is arranged to be an exact fit in a circular bearing designed to keep the spindle truly vertical but with very low friction.

The pickup stylus cannot distinguish between forces acting on it which are due to the recorded waveform in the groove and those which might arise from spindle rocking, or indeed from odd resonances occurring within the platter itself, or elsewhere. Yet the very precision of construction of the platter makes it prone to resonate in response to any external vibration and so it needs to be damped. In many cases the mere existence of a substantial mat on top of the platter is enough to damp out its ringing tendencies, but in other designs a bitumastic or other loss-introducing coating may be applied during manufacture.

There is some debate as to the virtues of different sorts of mat, and some designers dispense with a mat completely, preferring to build hard ridges or circles on top of the platter. In theory at least there are good reasons for supporting a record over the whole of its surface. Only then will the playing stylus be bearing down on a uniform base comprising the disc and a firm backing. Also, a supported disc will be less liable to vibrate under the action of external shocks, or motor rumble, or the action of a tracking cleaning device or even the stylus itself. Unfortunately most discs are not completely flat but are either dished or warped to some extent. An inflexible mat will therefore support the disc at certain points only, perhaps with air trapped underneath in places.

The solution can either be to employ a soft mat material on to which even badly warped discs will settle evenly, or to provide firm supports at selected points only, as already described, in the hope that air pockets will not add to vibration problems. Both approaches have been found to succeed, when judged in terms of the reproduction of more stable bass and stereo imaging. And they can be helped further by the provision of a weight or clamp fixed over the centre spindle and pressing down on the label area. There are even clamps to fit over the record rim and flatten out warps almost completely; but we are now entering the world of the hi-fi fanatic, and most record users will be perfectly happy with a well-designed mat.

Some mats offered as hi-fi accessories are very thick and heavy. The extra weight is itself useful, of course, since it will increase the flywheel action of the platter and iron out speed fluctuations, as well as damping disc vibrations. However, adding a very heavy mat must put an extra strain on the drive motor and should not be attempted on low-budget record-players. Similarly, the very thick mats raise the effective height of the record, and this will alter the vertical tracking angle of the pickup. Therefore a player which allows arm height adjustment is necessary.

Another function offered by many mats is a reduction in the nuisance value of static charges on records. This problem is discussed in Chapter 14, and there is a good case for providing a permanent leakage path to earth while a record is playing. The rubber mat supplied on most record-players will act as a barrier between the static on the record and the leakage path from the metal platter to earth. Special replacement mats can therefore be purchased which contain carbon fibres or other conducting materials, and a noticeable reduction in static problems, including the annoying discharge crackles, is usually obtained.

Deck mounting

Any relative movement between a pickup stylus and the body of the cartridge will generate an output voltage. The musical signal we want to reproduce is of course generated by the stylus as it follows the microscopically small undulations of the recorded waveform in the groove. An ideal record-player deck would provide a rock steady playing platform in which no other unwanted stylus motions took place. In particular, it pays to mount the pickup arm pivot and the main spindle bearing on the same solid plate or subchassis. This will preserve the arm and disc relationship even when quite violent forces are at work trying to rock the plate.

Provision must be made for cushioning the assembly from

external shocks, footfalls, etc—and vibrations transmitted back from the loudspeakers. The latter effect is called 'acoustic feedback' and can occur through the floor and furnishings. The necessary shockproofing can be introduced either between the aforesaid platter/arm plate and a solidly mounted plinth, or between the plinth cabinet and the shelf or table on which it stands—or both. Spring mounts are the usual answer, but their precise location and design are very important. The weights of the motor, platter and arm are unevenly distributed across the motorboard area, and yet the springs must be so positioned as to keep the whole assembly truly horizontal when at rest and inhibit any tendency to rock when driven by external forces. This is achieved in the best designs by placing the points of spring suspension equidistant from the centre of gravity of the whole system and spaced on equal arcs.

The suspended system will inevitably possess a resonant frequency at which it will rock or ring—revealed, for example, by pushing the spindle and observing the rate of oscillation. However, provided this resonance is down around 2–4Hz, it will have little audible effect on performance. The suspension does require to be damped, to reduce the peak at resonance, and this is conveniently done by inserting foam or rubber pads inside the springs.

The cartridge

It is impossible to overemphasise the importance of the pickup cartridge in a record-playing system. After all, this is the component which makes contact with our precious records. And many of the factors affecting the quality of the final sounds we hear are determined in that first stage in the reproducing process. Modern disc cutting techniques have extended the range of sounds which can be inscribed on a disc to a point where it is the reproducer which introduces most of the distortion. Again, the electromagnetic parts of the better cartridges are relatively refined and it is the actual mechanical conversion of the groove undulations into stylus lever vibrations which remains the weakest link in the chain. For the sake of logic, let us follow the path of the signal as it proceeds from the disc surface to the electrical output.

The stylus

Basic differences exist between the tip shapes of cutting and playback styli. This is inevitable, considering the different tasks they have to perform, but it does lead to distortions which can be minimised but never eliminated completely. The cutting stylus is like a V-shaped chisel (Plate 14) and removes a continuous thread (called 'swarf' or 'chip') from the lacquer coating of the blank disc during cutting. The groove is therefore V-shaped in cross-section, with an included angle of 90° (Fig. 7.2a).

The playback stylus must be smooth, rather than sharp-edged, and is made with an included angle somewhat less than the groove's 90° (Plate 15). The traditional tip shape is hemispherical, so that the stylus in fact rests on the disc at single points on the two groove walls (Fig. 7.2b). The standard tip radii for spherical styli are 25μm (0.001in) for mono and 13μm (0.0005in) for stereo discs. One problem that arises immediately is that the recorded wavelengths get smaller than this at high frequencies towards the centre of a record, and so the stylus simply cannot reproduce these frequencies (the so-called 'end-of-side' distortion). In any case, the top width of the groove effectively narrows twice during each recorded cycle. This forces the stylus to ride up and down twice per cycle—so generating second harmonic distortion (the so-called 'pinch effect'). This is of little importance on mono records but significant for stereo. Another ever-present problem is 'tracing distortion' due directly to the difference in shape of the cutting and reproducing styli. The centre of a round-tipped stylus playing a smooth waveform actually traces an asymmetrical waveform—which means distortion.

An even smaller tip radius might seem to solve these problems of tracing the groove, but the stylus would then ride on the bottom of the groove where dust resides and the cutting stylus operates less cleanly. Other stylus shapes have therefore evolved having the standard tip radius in the plane lying across the groove, to preserve a proper playing height, but a narrower radius at right angles to this. This basically produces an elliptical shape in the horizontal plane (Fig. 7.2c), and indeed elliptical styli have taken over from sphericals as the norm in medium-priced cartridges. It should be noted, however, that elliptical styli are quite a bit more expensive to manufacture than sphericals and introduce a new problem in that they must be very accurately installed at right angles to the cartridge axis or distortion will result. Also the 'footprint' of an elliptical stylus as it presses against the plastic groove wall is quite narrow, so that record wear may be accelerated unless a proportionately smaller tracking force can be employed.

The improvement in tracing performance brought about by elliptical styli was taken a stage further when 'line-contact'

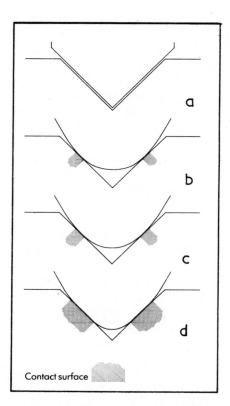

Fig. 7.2 Stylus tip shapes: (a) cutting
stylus; (b) spherical stylus; (c) elliptical
stylus; (d) line-contact stylus

Contact surface

styli appeared around 1971, though again at a cost. The
original versions, made by Shibata in Japan, were developed to
extend the frequency response up to 45kHz and beyond. This
was a requirement of the new CD-4 'discrete' quadraphonic
records which contained a supersonic (30kHz) subcarrier tone
to cope with rear-channel signals. While CD-4 records have
fallen from favour, the basic Shibata shape has continued to be
popular with audiophiles and versions are used by most
cartridge manufacturers for their top-of-the-line models, with
names such as Hyperelliptic, Pramanic and Aliptic. In effect,
these styli present an even smaller minor radius to the groove
wall, but their contour in the vertical plane has been
straightened out to increase the area of groove contact (Fig.
7.2d). This is claimed to provide excellent high frequency
response without the risk of accelerated record wear, but of
course demands special care in orientation during manufacture. In fact, the contact area is about 47 square microns—
more than twice that of an elliptical and nearly twice that of a
spherical stylus. Yet this still corresponds to a playing
pressure of about 213kg per square centimetre (1.35 tons per
square inch) for a tracking force of only 1g. Little wonder that
the groove wall is deformed (though one must hope only

temporarily) as it passes under the stylus, and little wonder that tracking force is such a critical adjustment.

Such precise shaping of stylus tips, with any hope of preserving these tiny dimensions over a reasonably long working life of, say, 1,000 hours, makes diamond—the hardest material known—the obvious choice. Lower cost diamond styli consist of just the shaped tip of diamond cemented on to a metal holder which in turn is mounted on the cantilever. Superior 'nude' styli are all-diamond, and therefore lighter and better able to track high fequencies. Using a square shank and a square hole in the end of the cantilever helps in proper alignment of elliptical and 'line-contact' styli.

Since the cantilever is part of the moving system of a cartridge, carrying the stylus at one end and an electricity-generating element at the other, it must obviously be kept as light as possible. Thin-walled tubes of aluminium or alloy are common, though metals employed in spaceship applications because of their superior stiffness-to-weight ratio are gaining in popularity—such as boron or beryllium. There is even a new generation of cantilevers made of industrial-quality precious stones including ruby and diamond. Reducing the length of the cantilever will reduce its mass, and there is at least one manufacturer who claims that it will also reduce 'dispersion' distortion due to the different frequencies having different propagation velocities along the cantilever. However, there will inevitably be reduced output voltage (sensitivity) and other practical difficulties of record clearance and dust if the cantilever is made too short. Besides being very light, the cantilever must be extremely stiff, since any flexing would reduce the proper transmission of stylus motion to the 'business' end, ie the electromagnetic generator. Yet the end remote from the stylus needs to be anchored in some type of universal hinge—or single-pivot suspension—allowing deflection in the horizontal and vertical planes. A centring collar of rubber or other elastic material will also be required, to hold the stylus in its proper relationship to the generator components. Then, when the pickup is lowered on to the record and the playing weight (tracking force) is set to the recommended value, the stylus assembly will flex by just the right amount to achieve perfect symmetry of the generator circuit.

An important aspect of the stylus geometry is the vertical tracking angle (VTA). This is the angle between the surface of the record and a line joining the stylus tip and the cantilever pivot point. Because the pivot point is at some distance behind, and above, the stylus, the latter moves in a plane which is angled forward of the vertical plane when tracing a stereo groove. Similar conditions apply when a record is being cut and, though angles used to be somewhat arbitrary, the recording industry is now standardizing on a VTA of 20°, and cartridge designers should specify 20° for their products when the cartridge has been properly set up. This is a function of both the arm height (normally correct when the main arm tube and cartridge top are parallel to the record surface) and an applied tracking force within the manufacturer's recommended range.

VTA errors are unimportant with spherical-tipped styli since the groove contact will suffer little or no change. With elliptical and line-contact styli, however, VTA errors can be the cause of distortion. Notice that another aspect of stylus geometry is sometimes mentioned in the technical literature. This is the stylus rake angle (SRA) between the stylus axis and the vertical. Clearly changing the VTA also alters the SRA, but the latter is essentially a question of the way in which the stylus is cemented into the cantilever.

The generator

Almost all the cartridges used in home audio systems work on the electromagnetic principle (Plate 16), and so it will be possible to postpone a description of other rare types until the end of this section.

Electromagnetism relies on the trick of nature whereby any relative movement between a magnet and a conductor of electricity such as a length—or better still a coil—of wire, will cause an electric current to flow in the wire. Three basic variations on the application of this principle give us the three main types of electromagnetic cartridge.

(a) *Moving-magnet* (Fig. 7.3a)   This has a fixed pair of coils, one each for the left and right stereo channels. A tiny magnet set into the inner end of the stylus cantilever rocks in response to the stylus vibrations and so induces current into the coils. The coils are mounted at right angles to each other and so disposed as to reproduce the signals arising from stylus movements in the ±45° planes with as little crosstalk between channels as possible. Moving-magnet cartridges are perhaps the most common of the magnet types and present few problems. They can be made with extremely light moving parts, give good record tracking and average signal output levels of 0.001 volt (1mV) upwards.

(b) *Moving-coil* (Fig. 7.3b)   This reverses the roles of the magnet and coil. The magnets are fixed and it is the coils which

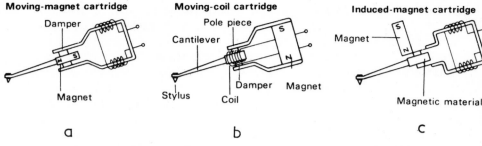

Moving-magnet cartridge

Damper

S

Magnet

a

Moving-coil cartridge

Pole piece

S

Cantilever

N

Damper   Magnet

Stylus   Coil

b

Induced-magnet cartridge

S

Magnet

N

Magnetic material

c

Fig. 7.3 Types of magnetic cartridge: (a) moving-magnet; (b) moving-coil; (c) induced magnet (moving-iron)

are attached to the inner end of the stylus cantilever. Naturally the coils have to be microscopically small and light, which tends to make this type of cartridge more expensive. On a practical point, the resulting signal output level is generally about one tenth that of other magnetic cartridges so that an extra transformer or booster preamplifier is almost always required—adding further to the cost. However, in the best examples, moving-coil cartridges are capable of wide and smooth frequency response with low distortion, and are therefore often chosen by quality-conscious audio enthusiasts.

(c) *Moving-iron* (Fig. 7.3c)   This category relies on a fixed coil and magnet assembly, with a very light iron armature at the end of the cantilever. Stylus motion causes changes in the magnetic field distribution, and therefore produces the desired output voltage. Several variations on this basic theme exist, called 'variable reluctance', 'variable magnetic shunt', etc. They can all be regarded as interchangeable with moving-magnet cartridges in practice, and produce the same order of signal level output. Their main advantages are the extreme lightness of the moving parts, and indeed of the cartridge as a whole.

For completeness, mention should be made of the other (non-magnetic) cartridge types. First there is the crystal or ceramic type which relies on the piezo-electric property possessed by certain crystalline materials. When such crystals are bent or distorted, an electric charge appears and this can be used in designing pickup cartridges, microphones, etc. Advantages are cheapness, and a high voltage output which makes such cartridges attractive for very low-cost record-players. However, the sound quality is usually limited and may change with temperature or humidity.

At the other end of the performance scale, a few quite refined cartridges have been designed using the electrostatic (condenser) principle. This arranges the two plates of a capacitor, one fixed and the other moved by the cantilever, so that the varying plate spacing generates the desired electrical output. Quality can be excellent, though a slight complication is the need to provide a high DC voltage to polarise the plates. In more recent designs this difficulty has been overcome by using 'electret' plates which have been given a permanent charge during manufacture, rather like the 'permanent' magnetisation of a magnet.

The pickup arm

Having built a pickup cartridge, with its fine stylus to trace the groove and its tiny electrical generator to convert the stylus vibrations into a usable electrical signal, we need some form of carrier. This must support the cartridge, allowing just the right downward force or playing weight to keep the stylus securely in the groove, and enable it to track smoothly inwards as the groove spirals towards the record label.

In practice, most pickup arms take the form of a pivoted beam (Plate 17). The length from stylus to pivot is generally about 230mm (9in) to give plenty of clearance across the record and platter area. The beam extension to the rear of the pivot can be much shorter, since it carries a substantial metal weight to counterbalance the combined mass of the cartridge and the main arm beam. Given that the counterbalance weight has first been set at just the correct distance from the pivot to give accurate 'seesaw' balance, the required cartridge down-force can be applied either by moving the weight slightly closer to the pivot or by using a calibrated spring.

Unfortunately, this use of an arm pivoted near one end and swinging in an arc across the record gives rise to a form of distortion which, though it can be kept quite small, is still significant. It arises from what is called 'tracking error' which is a direct result of the fact that the pickup cartridge does not follow the same path across the record as the cutter head. During cutting of the original master disc, the cutter head is carried on a suspended block which tracks in a dead straight line from the outer edge towards the exact centre of the record (see Fig. 7.4). At all times, therefore, the vibrations of the cutting stylus take place in a plane which is precisely at right angles to the groove. By contrast, a pivoted arm causes the replay stylus to travel over the record along the arc of a circle whose centre is the pivot, and whose radius is equal to the pivot-to-stylus distance. If the pivot is placed at exactly this distance from the spindle centre, so that tracking error would be zero at the centre, there is a very substantial misalignment or 'tracking error' angle across the grooved part of the record. Luckily this error, and the consequent distortion, can be greatly reduced by two tricks of geometry. First, the pivot point is moved forwards, so that the pivot-to-spindle distance is made shorter than the pivot-to-stylus arm length. This makes the error angle quite large, but much more consistent over the playing surface. Second, the cartridge itself is turned or offset through an angle which reduces the tracking error angle to zero at some chosen point on the record radius. In this way the maximum error angle can be kept to a mere 2° or so, which reduces the distortion to fairly acceptable limits. In fact, the distortion for a given angular error increases towards the centre of the record and so it is important to set the arm overhang distance for minimum distortion rather than minimum error.

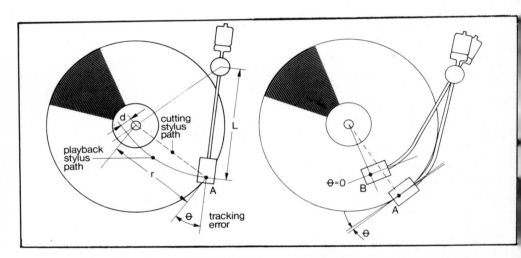

Fig. 7.4 Showing (left) the straight-line radial path followed by the cutting stylus and the arc followed by a pivoted pickup. A straight pickup arm would give a very large tracking error angle, even when an overhang *d* is introduced. Introducing an offset angle (*right*) reduces tracking error to a much smaller value

Three basic arm shapes are used to incorporate the desired offset angle. The straight-line arm with an offset headshell is perhaps the easiest to design with optimum stiffness and low mass. The J and S shaped arms allow straight insertion of a plug-in headshell but need accurate geometrical design and installation.

The whole problem of tracking error can be avoided if the pickup is carried in a straight line radially across the record, following the path of the original cutter. Until recently,

10   A typical music-centre has disc, tape and radio facilities all housed in a single cabinet, with separate loudspeakers (Sony HMK 5000)

11   Rack hi-fi systems can be bought with a matching cabinet providing storage space for LP records and cassettes (Philips F516 system)

12 This mini hi-fi system has the power amplifier on top, with a separate preamplifier/control unit, radio tuner and cassette deck (Aurex Micro 15)

13 A typical high quality record deck, showing the stroboscopic bars on the edge of the platter and the lightweight precision arm (Thorens TD160)

designing such a 'linear-tracking' arm presented apparently insuperable difficulties. A carriageway had to be built along the back of the motorboard, on which the arm could run. Friction had to be kept almost impossibly low, since the whole carriage was propelled solely by the groove action, and there was the need to ensure that the arm stayed tangential to the groove at all times. In recent years, tiny drive motors, sometimes of the linear type, have been developed capable of driving the carriage noiselessly. Also optical systems have been made capable of monitoring the tangential state of the arm to the groove and so controlling the arm-drive motor (Plate 18). Such linear-tracking arms were first used in the more expensive turntables but are now becoming available in lower priced systems.

Antiskating

In all record players, the friction between the record surface and the stylus exerts a force which is attempting to pull the pickup away from its base. An undesirable consequence of the overhang and angular offset on the conventional pivoted pickup arm is that this frictional pull is directed not in a straight line through the centre of the pivot, but obliquely. There is a resulting component pulling the pickup inwards towards the record centre. This force has a certain usefulness, since it opposes any side-friction in the main bearing of the arm, but is generally undesirable since it unbalances the playing force on the inner and outer walls of the groove and can, in extreme cases, cause the pickup to skate across the record.

Many arms therefore include some method of compensating for this unwanted sidethrust, the device being called a bias compensator or antiskating unit. The most common method is to suspend a weight on a thin nylon thread which runs over a bracket and is attached somewhere near the counterbalance weight. The procedure is to adjust the outward pull exerted by this weight so that it just compensates for the frictional sidethrust. The adjustment will always be approximate, in practice, because the inherent force depends not only on the playing weight and stylus tip shape but also on the groove radius and even the modulation level of the music. Apart from the weight-and-thread type, antiskating devices may use springs, magnets or simply a weighted lever to apply the desired outward force. It is a further advantage of linear tracking arms that no sidethrust compensation is necessary.

Pickup resonances

Any mechanical system which has mass and some form of restoring force tending to return the mass to its natural position when it has previously been displaced has a natural frequency at which it will vibrate. Examples include a weight on the end of a spring, or a pendulum where the restoring force is not a spring but the force of gravity. The natural or 'resonant' frequency depends on the mass and the restoring force (or, just as legitimately, the 'compliance' which is the opposite of restoring force, being the force required to displace the mass through a given distance).

Two basic resonances occur in pickups, one at a high frequency and the other low. The high frequency resonance is important since it sets a limit to the range of frequencies which the given cartridge can reproduce. The relevant compliance or elasticity is that of the record surface itself. This has a known average value but is a function of the vinyl used and beyond our control. The mass is the effective mass of the moving system at the stylus tip. The smaller this mass, the higher the resonant frequency and so, since output falls rapidly above the resonant frequency, the tip mass should be made as small as possible. A value of about 1mg will place the resonance at an acceptable 20kHz, but even less mass is better still. Tip mass also affects the tracking ability at high frequencies, and the desirability of good tracking is a further reason for seeking low tip mass.

The low frequency resonance met in pickups is of even more importance. This depends on the total mass of the arm, headshell and cartridge as measured at the stylus, and the compliance of the stylus/cantilever suspension. Unfortunately there is a wide variation in the values met in practice and, since the resonant frequency is quite critical, the correct matching of cartridges and arms can present problems. Essentially we want the bass resonance to occur at some subaudible frequency, that is below 20Hz, so that it will not be triggered off by musical signals and perhaps cause groove jumping. At the same time, the resonance should not be so low as to coincide with the recurrence rate of record warps which tends to peak at around 4Hz. The safe region is usually taken as 8–13Hz, and the chart in Fig. 7.5 shows how the values of cartridge compliance and total mass should be chosen to give a resonant frequency in this region. A common value for the mass in a mid-budget record-player might be 25g, of which 6g is contributed by the weight of the cartridge itself. It will be seen that a fairly low compliance cartridge should be chosen (about

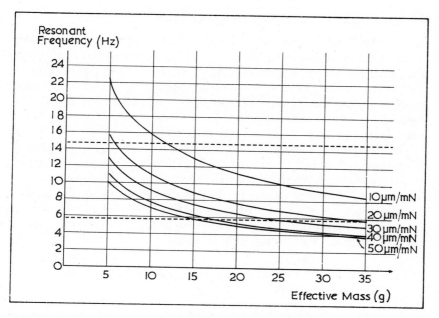

Fig. 7.5 Graphs relating effective mass and resonant frequency for given values of cartridge compliance

$10\mu m/mN$) to keep the resonance at an acceptable 10Hz. If a lightweight arm/cartridge combination can be used, however, weighing say 9g, a high compliance of $30\mu m/mN$ would give the same 10Hz resonance. Needless to say, the latter combination has advantages from the high fidelity viewpoint, since higher compliance means improved tracking ability at low frequencies, and lower effective mass means less record wear.

The ill effects of too sharp a bass resonance will be reduced if selective damping (friction) can be introduced, rather like shock absorbers in the suspension of a car. Some cartridges incorporate damping pads, and a few arms have silicon fluid reservoirs or dashpots for the purpose. However, we are once again in the highly specialised audiophile field and most ordinary record users need not worry about this hard-to-adjust refinement.

The electrical output

There has been very little standardisation throughout the audio industry of such things as distance between a cartridge stylus and the holes by which the cartridge is mounted in the headshell, etc, so care is needed at almost every stage in the mechanical installation and setting up of a record-player.

However, there are standards so far as the electrical output is concerned. Even in the elementary matter of the four output pins at the back of a stereo cartridge, there is a standard colour code: white and blue for the positive and earth pins of the left channel, red and green for the right. In the more vital matter of the way in which the electrical output is related to the recorded waveform in the groove, there is also a good degree of helpful standardisation. This can be understood if we trace the signal's progress from groove to output pins.

The magnitude of the voltage generated by a magnetic cartridge is proportional to the number of (imaginary) lines of magnetic flux crossed by the coil per second. This in turn is a function of the strength of the given magnet (the flux density, or number of lines in a given space), the effective length of the coil—both of which are fixed by the design—and the actual rate of the relative magnet/coil motion.

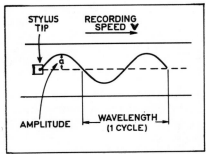

Fig. 7.6 The recorded wavelength is the distance occupied by one cycle: the stylus travels from side to side a distance 4a during each cycle

To see what this motion might be in any situation, let us look at the simplest possible groove waveform. We can consider a single-channel mono groove (provided we remember that stereo grooves actually contain a combination of two such waveforms at right angles to each other). Also, for simplicity, we can consider just one frequency (provided we remember that each musical note consists of several frequencies—the fundamental plus its series of harmonic overtones). The result is the familiar sine wave (Fig. 7.6) whose amplitude, a, is a measure of the strength (loudness) of the signal. The stylus is displaced through this distance a and back again twice in each cycle, first to one side and then to the other. So the total distance travelled per cycle is $4a$. And if the frequency (number of cycles per second) is f, the total distance travelled per second is $4af$. We define this as the average velocity v, and so write:

$$v = 4af.$$

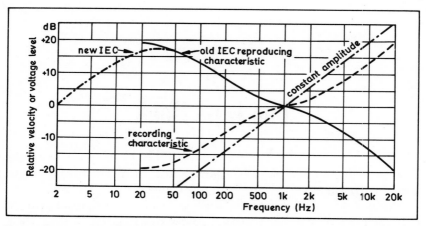

Fig. 7.7 Showing the IEC standard disc recording and reproducing characteristics, the 6dB per octave 'constant amplitude' graph and the new IEC bass roll-off

It is this velocity which decides the output voltage from a magnetic cartridge, and we see immediately that recording with a *constant velocity* (to give the same voltage at all frequencies) would mean that each halving of frequency would be accompanied by a doubling of the amplitude. This would lead to impractically large amplitudes at low frequencies, making a very large groove spacing necessary. The industry has therefore chosen to record with something more closely resembling a *constant amplitude* characteristic (see Fig. 7.7). This means that a standard amount of bass cut and treble boost, relative to the level at the centre 1,000Hz frequency, is introduced. This is referred to as the RIAA (Radio Industry Association of America) or IEC (International Electrotechnical Commission) characteristic since both bodies have incorporated it in their published standards. It follows that the playback amplifier used to reproduce discs must have the opposite characteristic, also shown in Fig. 7.7. The considerable bass boost can unfortunately present problems, since it will simultaneously raise the level of any unwanted mains hum (50Hz and harmonics) and motor rumble (anywhere around 20Hz) present in the given record-player installation. Indeed, a recent revision of the IEC document recommends a small degree of cut at extreme bass frequencies, as shown by the broken line in Fig. 7.7, to take account of this, and some newer amplifiers have this curve built-in. The high frequency boost during recording does have an incidental advantage, however. Since an equivalent attenuation of treble takes place in the playback amplifier, some of the inherent disc surface noise is reduced in level at the same time.

8
The Tape Deck

The tape deck plays a very special role in any audio system. Except for a few playback-only decks, it will not only reproduce prerecorded tapes and so act as a simple magnetic counterpart of the LP record-player, it will also *record*. This can open the door to the exciting and creative hobby of live recording, or at a more basic level enable the user to enjoy the time-shifting convenience of recording radio programmes for later listening. Plainly it will also make it possible to copy gramophone records on to tape, but all tape users should understand that such copying infringes the Copyright Act. Pending government legislation on a proper procedure for licensing such copying or imposing a levy on tapes or machines, it is imperative that copies of commercial records should be used for personal listening only. This applies whether the material is copied direct from the disc or via a radio broadcast.

How tape recording works

Magnetic recording tape consists of a clear base film with a coating of crystalline magnetic particles embedded in a suitable varnish. In the demagnetised state, as when you buy a blank tape, the tiny magnets are randomly distributed with their microscopic north and south poles pointing in all directions. If exposed to a magnetic field, however, they will align themselves with the field and will retain this magnetised state. Thus, when a tape is transported across the face of the recording head, which is an electromagnet producing a field varying in accordance with the signal current flowing in its coil, a record of the signal remains in the form of a magnetic pattern laid along the tape (Fig. 8.1).

For playback, the tape is again carried past an electromagnet, which may be the same head as used for recording now switched to the playback mode or a separate one, so that the changing field on the tape links with the head coil. This has the effect of inducing an alternating current resembling the original signal. After suitable amplification, this can be fed to loudspeakers or headphones as desired. It is clearly more expensive to provide separate record and replay heads but there are distinct benefits. In the first place it is possible to monitor the signal just a fraction of a second after it was recorded. The separate replay head is always situated 'downstream' of the record head. Therefore each portion of the tape reaches the replay head a short time after passing the record head, and can be auditioned as a continuous means of checking for sound quality and freedom from unwanted noise, etc.

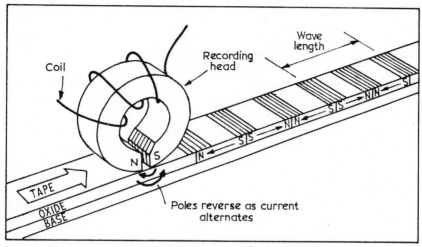

Fig. 8.1 In tape recording, the alternating current passing through the head-coil produces a reversal of magnetic poles twice per cycle

A second advantage is that the two heads can be designed and built specially for each function. In particular, this means that the head gap width can be optimised. Each head is made with a tiny gap at the front to help concentrate the magnetic field effectiveness at the point of tape/head contact. The vertical length of the gap is related to the width of the track on the tape (of which more later) whereas the gap width determines the resolution, or ability to reproduce short wavelengths. For this reason, the gap in the replay head should be as narrow as practicable or else short wavelength (high frequency) signals will be attenuated. Indeed, when the gap width equals the wavelength, the output falls to zero. The recording head, by contrast, should ideally have a wider gap which helps magnetic field penetration at low frequencies, the high frequency performance in the record mode being mainly a question of straightness of the gap edge. Typical gap widths are about 1μm for a replay-only or record/replay head and 4μm for record-only.

The record head has also to carry a special bias current. This is mixed with the music signal current at the input to the head coil—during recording only. It is at a supersonic frequency, usually in the range 50–100kHz, and so is inaudible. It is produced by a built-in oscillator and has the property of greatly reducing distortions which would otherwise occur in the non-linear recording process. There is a second use made of supersonic currents, derived either from the same (bias) oscillator or a separate one. This is for erasing any signals already on the tape just prior to recording. A special erase head is situated 'upstream' of the record head so that the numerous cycles of erase current magnetic field have the effect of returning the micro-magnets in the tape coating to a demagnetised state ready for recording. Since erasure is a non-reversible process, most tape recorders incorporate some safety mechanism to prevent the user switching to the record mode accidentally and possibly erasing a valued recording. As we shall see later, compact cassettes also have a safety lug built into their case rim.

Tape speeds

Pretty obviously, the speed at which the tape is carried past the heads has an important bearing on the sound quality. In general, a faster speed corresponds to better quality—though of course this uses up more tape per minute of music and so is more expensive. High frequencies are particularly vulnerable at low tape speeds. We can appreciate this if we realise that frequency, recorded wavelength and tape speed are all linked by the same formula as applied to soundwaves in Chapter 3:

$$\text{speed} = \text{frequency} \times \text{wavelength}.$$

Therefore, halving the tape speed halves the wavelength for a given frequency. Taking the standard cassette speed of 4.76cm/sec, we see that the wavelength at 20,000Hz is only 2.38μm, which is getting down towards the standard replay head gap width of 1μm which we mentioned earlier, and at which the head could produce no output at all. If we go instead to the 38cm/sec speed used on most professional studio recorders, however, high frequency losses become much less likely.

Another difficulty at slow tape speeds is that, exactly as with magnetic pickup cartridges, the output voltage from a tape replay head is proportional to the velocity of relative motion of the magnetic field and the coil. So sensitivity is less at slower speeds and the relative level of inherent noise is that much higher. This noise, which is due to the necessarily granular nature of the tape coating, has a characteristic hissing sound due partly to the ear's greater sensitivity at upper middle frequencies. It is such a nuisance that the cassette medium cannot be considered in a hi-fi context unless some form of noise reduction is used, such as Dolby or dbx.

Apart from granular noise, another cause of annoyance which is aggravated at slow running speeds is 'drop-outs'. These are momentary losses of signal due either to minute holes in the tape coating or lumps which cause the tape to lose contact with the head briefly. A slow tape speed will make drop-outs last longer, and increase their audibility.

Tape tracks

As well as tape speed, another factor affecting the noise level and the seriousness of drop-outs is the tape track width. When magnetic *open-reel* tape recorders first appeared in the early 1950s, they used 6.25mm- ($\frac{1}{4}$in)-wide tape and were monophonic (single channel) machines. The head gaps therefore extended over the whole tape width. Soon afterwards, it was decided that this was too wasteful of tape and half-track mono machines became popular. These had head gaps which extended only over the top half of the tape (Fig. 8.2a). Therefore, when one side of the tape had been recorded, it could be turned over and used running in the opposite direction to give double the playing time from a given tape.

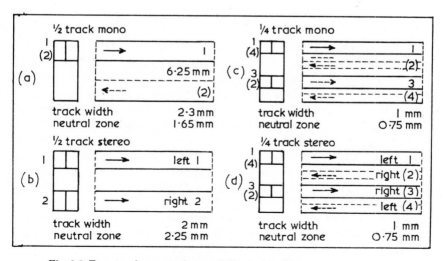

Fig. 8.2 Tape track conventions and dimensions in open-reel recorders

When stereo came along, around 1958, it became necessary to use both tracks of the half-track machines, one for the left-hand stereo channel and the other for the right (Fig. 8.2b) so playing time was once again halved. The dictates of economy in the use of tape once again took charge and quarter-track machines were introduced (Fig. 8.2c). These interleaved the stereo tracks going in the two directions, as shown in Fig. 8.2d, to ensure at least partial compatibility between half-track and quarter-track machines. Notice, for example, that a quarter-track machine will replay a half-track recorded tape quite satisfactorily even though its head gaps scan only half of the available recorded track-width. However, reverse compatibility does not apply: playing a stereo quarter-track tape on a half-track machine produces not only the desired programme on side one, say, but also the side two programme running backwards! It is also standard practice on stereo quarter-track recorders to incorporate switching to mono. Then, with either the left or right channel erase head gap out of action, it is possible to record four independent mono programmes on a given tape—two in one direction and two in the other—to get four times the nominal duration expected from the given reel of tape. As with halving the tape speed, however, halving the track width does raise the inherent noise level and the risk of trouble with drop-outs. Even today, therefore, the manufacturers of quarter-track open-reel decks often market a half-track version as well, for those enthusiasts who would rather have a superior noise and drop-out performance, even at the cost of using up tape less economically.

The Compact Cassette

It says something for the continuous research into improving the performance of tapes, heads and indeed tape transport mechanisms that, when Philips introduced their Compact Cassette format in 1963, they not only chose the slowest tape speed then current, 4.76cm/sec, and a quarter-track format but also reduced the tape width by nearly half to 3.8mm (Fig. 8.3). It is true that their first recorder—a battery-operated portable machine—did not claim hi-fi performance. However, successive improvements to every aspect of the cassette format have raised its capabilities and extended its usefulness to the point where cassette decks and recorders easily outsell all other tape formats put together (Plate 19).

One small but long-sighted feature of the original Philips conception related to the disposition of the tape tracks. They achieved more complete compatibility between mono and

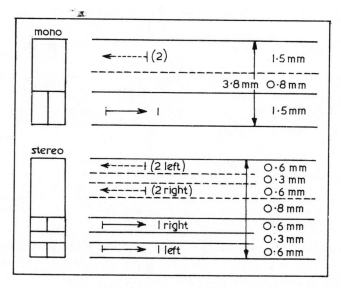

Fig. 8.3 Cassette tape track dimensions

stereo machines and tapes by arranging the two stereo tracks side by side instead of interleaved as on open-reel decks. This simple step has paid off handsomely, and even today it means that any cassette can be played on any machine. Also the record companies can issue stereo musicassettes safe in the knowledge that they are equally suitable for stereo cassette decks or mono portable and in-car players.

From the outset, Philips freely licensed other manufacturers all over the world to build cassette machines and manufacture cassette tapes. This greatly helped the format to reach the widest possible market. But they did insist on strict maintenance of such parameters as track configuration, head positioning and tape speed so that the impact of the cassette format was not weakened by offshoot developments.

Apart from its compactness, the cassette was much easier to handle than the traditional open-reel tapes. A cassette measures only about $100 \times 64 \times 12$mm ($4 \times 2\frac{1}{2} \times \frac{1}{2}$in) and yet is a fairly complicated mechanism in itself (Plate 20). The two ends of the tape are firmly anchored in free-running hubs, resembling the centres of tape spools. The tape is routed past guide pillars and pressure pads, to ensure intimate contact between the tape (which is wound coated side out) and the heads. The thicker leading edge of the cassette case has openings through which the heads press during recording and playback. During fast forward winding and rewinding, the tape is pulled along at speed by rotation of the right-hand (take-up) hub or the left-hand (supply) hub respectively. Naturally the speed increases as more tape accumulates on the pulling hub,

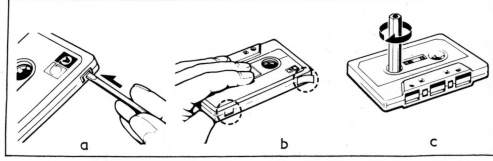

Fig. 8.4 Cassette handling: (a) removing the lug as shown will make accidental erasure of Side A impossible; (b) the anti-erasure holes can be covered with adhesive tape to allow recording again; (c) any tape slack should be taken up before loading the cassette into the machine

and so the constant-speed drive needed for recording and playback is supplied by a precision capstan which enters through a hole in the cassette casing, and presses the tape against a rubber-tyred idler wheel or 'pinch roller'. A light torque is applied to the take-up hub meanwhile, to ensure smooth spooling, and a light reverse torque or friction drag on the supply hub helps to keep the tape evenly tensioned.

Two openings at the narrower rear edge of the cassette provide a neat system for preventing accidental erasure of a recording which you may want to keep (Fig. 8.4). When you buy a blank cassette, there are plastic lugs over these holes which allow the record mode to be selected and the erase head to come into use. If you break off either of these lugs, it becomes impossible to record (or inadvertently erase) on one of the sides. The lug at the left-hand side, as you look at the cassette from the front, applies to the side whose label is uppermost. At a later date, should you then decide to erase that side, it is a simple matter to cover the hole with adhesive tape when again the record mode can be selected. Prerecorded musicassettes are supplied with the lugs already missing for safety reasons, but they too can be taped over for recording if required. As shown in Fig. 8.4c, it is good practice to take up any slack on the tape with a pencil before putting a cassette into the machine.

Tape types

A simple C-number coding of cassettes indicates the total playing time in minutes of the two sides added together (see Table 8.1). It will be noticed that the longer-playing cassettes use thinner tape and so must be considered as more fragile and perhaps liable to 'print through'. Most people regard C-90 as a sensible compromise between robustness and playing time.

Table 8.1 Cassette playing times

Type	Tape length (metres)	Tape thickness (μm)	Playing time (minutes)
C-46	70	18	2×23
C-60	90	18	2×30
C-90	135	12	2×45
C-120	180	9	2×60

Various different magnetic coatings are now used for cassettes, as summarised in Table 8.2, and it pays to understand the difference between them. In the beginning, only 'ferric' coatings were used containing tiny particles of iron oxide (gamma ferric oxide; chemical formula Fe_2O_3). Then progress was made towards finer particles—'high output'. The quality potential of cassettes then received a further boost around 1970, when chromium dioxide (CrO_2) was first introduced. The most important improvement related to high frequencies, which became clearer and less distorted during loud passages. However, these benefits could be obtained only if the level of bias was increased and if a gentler degree of high frequency pre-emphasis was applied during recording. This latter technique, known as equalisation (EQ), is a direct analogy with the RIAA/IEC frequency characteristics used in disc recording and replay (see page 91). The amount of treble boost used during recording, which must be matched by a mirror-image treble cut during playback, is described in abbreviated form by the time constant of the resistor/capacitor network

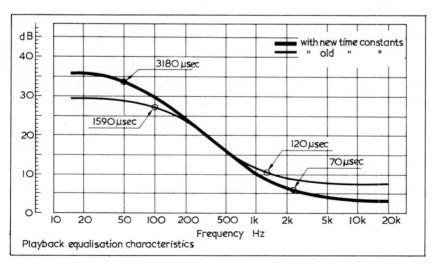

Fig. 8.5 Tape playback equalisation characteristics for ferric ('normal') tapes and the newer chrome, chrome-equivalent and metal formulations (thicker curve)

used (see Fig. 8.5). The value for ferric cassettes is 120 microseconds (μs) and that for chrome cassettes 70μs.

It therefore became necessary for cassette decks to incorporate switching to change over the bias and EQ values according to whether a ferric ('normal') or chrome cassette was being used. A change in amplifier gain was also introduced as a rule to allow for differences in sensitivity between the two types of tape. Some decks fitted separate bias and EQ switches, while others ganged the two functions on a single switch. To simplify things for the user, chrome cassettes were issued with additional holes at the rear of the case which enabled suitably equipped decks to identify the tape type and switch automatically. However, further complications were on the way.

The next development was 'ferrochrome' (FeCr) tapes which consisted of a dual-layer coating of chrome on top of ferric. These claimed the best of both worlds, the high frequency advantages of chrome and the low frequency capability of ferric, and a few decks began to appear with a third switch position. However, the indeterminate bias requirements created problems, and tape manufacturers soon found that they could modify the properties of straight ferric coatings by introducing small amounts of cobalt. These new 'chrome equivalent' or 'pseudo-chrome' cassettes achieved excellent results, used at the chrome setting.

Even better quality then became possible when 'metal' tapes came along. These use a coating of pure iron particles dispersed in a binder material and sealed against air oxidisation. Metal tapes have an extended ability to reproduce high level high-frequency signals and a significant improvement in dynamic range. However they are expensive to produce, and require even higher bias (and erase) currents than chrome. They can therefore be used to advantage only on machines having suitably designed electronics and heads. A spate of 'metal capable' decks appeared on the market as soon as metal cassettes were released, but it has to be said that some of them were technically not very good. Even now, the full advantages of metal tapes over, say, a good quality chrome equivalent type will show up only on demanding musical material and on a deck of superior design.

Table 8.2 Cassette tape types

IEC type no.	Coating	Common names	Equalisation (μs)	Bias (relative)
0	Fe_2O_3	Ferric, normal	120	100%
1	Fe_2O_3	Low-noise, high output	120	120%
2	CrO_2, etc	Chrome, chrome equivalent	70	150%
3	Fe–Cr	Ferrochrome	70	120–150%
4	Metal	Metal, alloy	70	200%

Noise reduction

An ever-present problem with magnetic tape recording is the steady background hissing noise which originates in the essentially granular nature of the coating. The problem increases as tape speed and track width are reduced, and indeed the Compact Cassette format could be said to have reduced both these parameters too far for comfort. The first person to do something positive about this was Dr Ray Dolby, an American working in Britain. He had developed a sophisticated noise reduction system for professional tapes and he adapted it in simpler form for cassettes. Dolby B circuitry effectively compresses the dynamic range of signals being recorded, over the critical 'hiss' region from about 1,000Hz upwards, and then expands the range on replay. To disguise the fact that such processing has taken place, and in particular to mask the 'breathing', which would otherwise be audible as the level of background noise is pumped up and down between loud signals, Dolby left loud signals alone and raised the quiet signals only. On replay, these signals are restored to their original level and any tape hiss is simultaneously reduced by about 10dB (See Fig. 8.6).

Dolby B was so successful that it soon became an industry standard. All better-class cassette decks incorporated Dolby circuitry (under licence) and an on/off switch in case the user wished to play non-Dolby-processed cassettes. The record companies also saw the virtues of Dolby B and went over to the process for producing prerecorded musicassettes. Other noise reduction techniques also appeared. Philips for example,

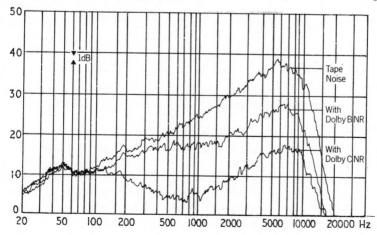

Fig. 8.6 Frequency plot of residual tape noise, showing the extent to which it is reduced by the Dolby B and C circuitry

wishing to preserve the universality of their invention, developed a DNL (dynamic noise limiter) system which operated on replay only. The principle was to introduce selective treble filtering during quiet passages only, when the music would not mask tape hiss. The system gives some cleaning up of all recordings, but tends to remove some of the treble brilliance in the music. Other manufacturers with noise reduction systems of their own include JVC (ANRS and Super ANRS), Toshiba (ADRES), Telefunken (High-Com) and dbx. The last-named, dbx, can produce spectacular noise reduction since it compresses and expands all parts of the frequency and dynamic range in the ratio of 2:1 (see Fig. 8.7). However, there is then a possibility of audible 'pumping' on certain programme material. An important advantage of dbx, from the operating point of view, is that it works equally well on any reasonable input and output gain setting.

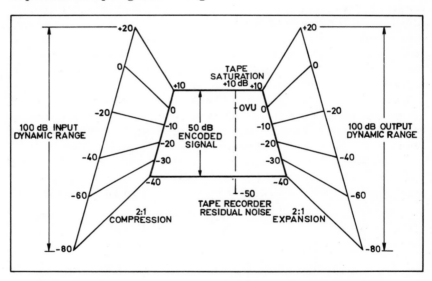

Fig. 8.7 The dbx system compresses the signal in a 2:1 ratio during recording and expands it by the same ratio on playback to restore the original dynamic range

This is not the case with Dolby B, which is level sensitive. For optimum results with Dolby, it is necessary to ensure that the mean musical signal level is the same during replay as it was during recording. If this requirement is not met, perhaps because tapes of very different sensitivity are used, there is a real chance of treble being audibly stressed or suppressed. Some more sophisticated decks therefore incorporate a built-in oscillator to allow record/replay levels to be lined up to a 'Dolby level' mark on the level meter.

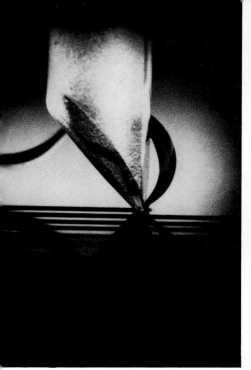

14 (*above left*) Magnified photograph of a cutting stylus during the making of a master disc, showing the thread of 'swarf' leaving the V-shaped groove (*Photo Cecil E. Watts*) and 15 (*above right*) Artist's impression of an elliptical reproducing stylus in a stereo record groove (*Photo Shure Bros*)

16 Cut-away model of an induced-magnet cartridge, showing the diamond stylus at the end of the cantilever tube, a ring magnet surrounding the iron armature and the four coils on pointed pole-pins (Ortofon VMS cartridge)

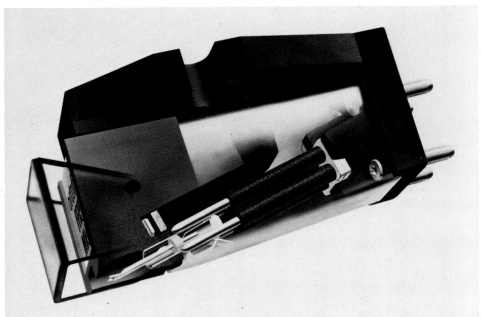

17 A typical high quality pickup arm, showing the calibrated tracking force counterbalance arrangements, silicon-damped raise/lower lever, weight-on-thread antiskating device and silicon fluid damping bath (SME Series III arm)

18 A typical record deck with linear-tracking arm instead of the traditional pivoted arm. In this design, size has been kept to a minimum by building the arm mechanism into the player lid (Technics SL-10)

19 A typical cassette deck in the more popular front-loading format which allows shelf-mounting or use in a rack system (Hitachi DE 57)

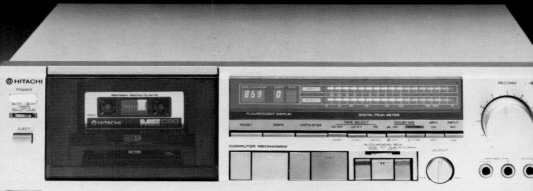

All decks with Dolby must, as a condition of the licence, have an on/off switch associated with the MPX (multiplex) filter. This is a steep treble cut filter intended to be used when recording from stereo FM radio, to suppress the 19kHz pilot tone which forms part of the 'stereo-multiplex' transmission. Inevitably, this filter affects frequencies below 19kHz to some extent. This is not particularly serious since FM radio signals are already restricted to 15kHz bandwidth (and AM radio is even more restricted), but it may make the user wish to switch the filter out when recording from other sources. If the filter is not used when recording FM radio with Dolby, the strong 19kHz tone may confuse the Dolby circuitry so that it fails to boost signals as it should.

Two more recent Dolby circuit techniques have further enhanced the performance of the cassette medium. The first is Dolby HX (headroom extension) which operates during recording only. It continuously monitors the frequency content of the signal and alters the bias and equalisation to optimise the ability of the tape to accommodate sharp high frequency transients without distortion. The second is Dolby C, which in effect behaves like two Dolby B networks in tandem to give twice the amount of noise reduction—up to 20dB instead of 10dB—and at the same time extends the effectiveness of the control down to around 350Hz instead of 1,000Hz (see lower curve in Fig. 8.6). While it is fair to say that Dolby B was considered good enough for most general purpose cassette applications, the improved performance with Dolby C raises the potential of cassettes to the most critical hi-fi level.

Other cassette deck features

The electrical signal chain through a typical cassette deck begins with the input sockets. The principal input, usually called 'line', is rated at about 0.5 volts and is intended to be connected to the amplifier 'recorder' outputs of an audio system, radio receiver, etc. The most usual plug/socket arrangement is the RCA 'phono' or 'cinch' type. This uses screened cable, to avoid mains hum, and a coaxial plug with the electrical connections made via a centre pin and outer metal collar. Of course separate connectors are needed for the left and right channels in a stereo system. The five-pin DIN plugs simplify the situation, since a single four-cored cable can combine the stereo input/record (pins one and four) and output/replay (pins three and five) connections. However, the DIN level and impedance requirements are different from those associated with the normal 'line' connectors and so it will usually be best to use DIN connectors only with European audio equipment, and choose the phono sockets (which are nearly always fitted as alternatives) for everything else. The microphone input may also use a DIN-type socket or the familiar jackplug: again the latter is to be preferred as being more robust. The microphone signal is very low, typically about 0.1mV, and so screening has to be impeccable.

On the simpler machines, the signals from all the inputs go through a single gain control knob. On more elaborate decks there are separate line and microphone controls so that mixing is possible, perhaps to superimpose announcements on musical items. An indicator of recording level is essential, and indeed failure to make proper use of the tape capabilities—by recording just up to the maximum permissible level on loud passages, and no further—is the main cause of disappointing results. If too strong a signal is allowed through, the tape overloads and the sound becomes badly distorted. On the other hand, failure to provide an adequate recording signal will mean that the volume will need to be turned up on replay and the inherent background noise will become obtrusive. The simplest level indicator is a VU (volume unit) meter and good results can be obtained with this after a bit of practice. However the needle of a VU meter is really showing average levels, and failing to indicate transient peaks. So peak reading meters, or rows of LED (light emitting diode) lamps, are fitted on the better decks with more accurate calibration of levels, including the recommended Dolby level. In situations where it is not always possible to keep an eye on the meter, as in recording interviews with a portable machine, it can be helpful to choose a recorder with automatic gain control. This limits peak levels to avoid overloading and, though a somewhat compressed sound may result, this is usually preferable to severe tape saturation.

The function controls generally consist of a row of keys, levers or touch-sensitive buttons labelled Play, Record, Rewind, Fast Forward and Stop. These are all self-explanatory except that, as a precaution against accidental erasure, the Record control is always linked with the Play button in such a way that the user must deliberately press both to enter the Record mode. Decks are said to possess 'logic' controls when the mechanism is designed to allow switching directly from Play to Rewind, etc without first going through the Stop position. Another standard facility is a Pause control. This arrests the tape motion by withdrawing the drive capstan from the pressure roller, while keeping the heads in contact with the tape. It is intended for use during replay or record where a short interruption is required followed by quick start.

It is always useful to know how much tape has been expended, or how much remains, and much ingenuity has been expended by designers on this feature. At a basic level, the user can see through the window of the cassette itself the amount of tape remaining on the supply (left-hand) hub, and there is usually an engraved scale which could be used as a very rough guide. Next in order of accuracy is the ordinary three-digit mechanical counter which is fitted on the majority of machines. Provided one makes a habit of pressing the reset-zero button at the beginning of the tape, it is possible to calibrate the counter numbers against time for each of the cassette types, C-60, etc, and thus know the elapsed time with fair accuracy. The counter readings for the start of individual recorded items can also be logged and entered on the cassette liner card as a form of index. More sophisticated decks add a memory function which permits fast winding to the zero setting when required, with automatic switching to the Replay or Record mode in some cases. Finally, there are a few machines where the arbitrary three-digit counter is replaced by a 'real time' indicator in minutes and seconds, again with flexible 'search' and play functions.

In the Replay mode, the level indicator shows the signal levels being fed from the tape to the Replay amplifier. This in its turn is generally provided with a volume control knob, or sometimes a screwdriver preset control, the signal appearing at output phono sockets or pins three and five of a DIN socket for connection to the amplifier or receiver 'tape replay' input sockets. The output is usually rated at about 1 volt and is easily matched to most equipment. There is also a headphone socket, generally of the stereo jackplug type, and this may occasionally be provided with its own volume control.

Most cassette decks are two-head machines. That is, they have an erase head and use a common head for record and replay, switched into the appropriate circuit by the action of the control keys. However, serious recordists much prefer to listen to the signal just a split second after it has been recorded. This is a much safer reassurance that all is well than simply monitoring the input. They therefore demand a three-head machine, with the replay head separated from the record one and situated 'downstream' so that it reproduces the signals almost immediately after recording. Naturally this off-tape monitoring facility adds to the cost and complication of the deck. For instance, it makes it necessary to install two sets of Dolby B, or other, noise reduction circuitry. Inevitably, some three-head machines are better than others. The best designs genuinely employ separate heads which have been built with the appropriate head gaps and other parameters to optimise both the record and replay functions. In some cases too the availability of separate heads has been incorporated into ingenious schemes for the automatic optimisation of bias, level and equalisation for any given type of tape.

Open-reel machines

The greater operational convenience of the compact cassette format has almost enabled it to drive the open-reel tape recorder out of the market—almost, but not quite. The plain fact is that, whatever heights of technical performance standards are achieved with the cassette, the best open-reel machines can always do a little better (Plate 21). It comes back to the question of the packing density of the recorded information. Open-reel tapes are wider—6.3mm instead of the cassette's 3.81mm—and they are run at faster speeds—9.5, 19 or even 38cm/s instead of the cassette's 4.75cm/s. This simultaneously enhances the open-reel tape's ability to capture and reproduce the full frequency spectrum and dynamic range of music, and makes inherent noise and drop-outs much less obtrusive.

For professional recording engineers, and the small band of amateur enthusiasts who regard the awkward shape of open-reel decks and the fiddling operation of threading the loose end of tape round the transport path a small price to pay for potentially superior quality, it is no contest. They will choose open-reel for quality, but with an eye to other advantages too. For instance, continuous recording time can be longer than the 45 minutes offered by a C-90 cassette. Also tape editing by the cut-and-splice method is very easy (it is almost impossible with cassettes) and an essential requirement for any serious sound recordist.

Two track configurations are available, half-track and quarter-track, as mentioned on page 96. The former takes up the whole tape width for stereo, whereas the latter is more economic since its two stereo tracks occupy only half of the tape width and turning over allows a second recording to be made as on cassettes. If quality is the primary consideration, however, it will pay to choose a half-track machine and use the highest available speed (19 or 38cm/s depending on the model). At this ambitious level of recording it is also best to choose a recorder which will accept the large NAB professional spools. These are 26.5cm (10½in) in diameter instead of the usual domestic 18cm (7in) spools but give much more playing time, as shown in Table 8.3, for the three basic tape thicknesses in use, standard, long and double play.

Many open-reel decks have three heads, to give off-tape monitoring, and they often provide such 'trick' effects as multiple dubbing from track to track, echo and sound-on-sound. They also cater for use with professional grade microphones.

Table 8.3 Open-reel playing times (at 19cm/s)

Spool diameter (cm)	Type	Tape length (metres)	Tape thickness (µm)	Playing time per side (minutes)
18	Standard play	360	52	30
	Long play	540	36	45
	Double play	730	26	60
26.5	Standard play	850	52	74
	Long play	1,095	36	90

The future

Two developments, travelling in exactly opposite directions, look set to change the look of domestic magnetic recording equipment in the near future. The first is the microcassette which aims to reduce the dimensions of the compact cassette format even further—with a predictable sacrifice in every one of the sound quality criteria (Plate 22).

The microcassette measures only an incredible 50×33mm and yet offers a recording time of up to 60 minutes per side at 1.2cm/s or 30 minutes at 2.4cm/s. Naturally the microcassette machines are proportionately tiny and therefore an attractive proposition for audio note-taking or interviews. The move towards the musical applications traditionally met first by open-reel and latterly by the compact cassette seem less logical, but several machines claiming hi-fi quality have already appeared, and a catalogue of prerecorded microcassettes has already built up.

The other development is digital recording, which bids fair to raise recorded quality to new heights. However, digital techniques will have such far-reaching effects on every aspect of audio that a complete chapter seems necessary—see Chapter 15.

9
The Tuner

It makes sense to discuss the radio tuner in a separate chapter. Even when it is integrated into a radio receiver, tuner-amplifier or music-centre, the tuner section is in fact built up separately and of course has a specific task to perform. This is to enable the user to select the radio transmission he wants to hear from the myriad of electromagnetic waves criss-crossing the earth at all times of the day or night. Unbelievably, any piece of wire or metal rod which we put up as an aerial (called an 'antenna' in the USA) has currents induced into it by the waves arriving from literally dozens of radio transmitters all over the world—not to mention from the electrical sparking of unsuppressed vehicles, refrigerators, etc. The latter also act as unauthorised transmitters of electromagnetic waves though the programme content consists solely of clicks and buzzes.

A good tuner clearly needs a good measure of *selectivity*—the ability to tune correctly to the desired station and suppress all others. It should also have high *sensitivity*—the ability to raise the signals from the selected station to a useful level in relation to the inherent noise floor. Other requirements will relate to user convenience, like preset button-selected stations, tuning meters and a proper coverage of the stations in the user's local area or as far afield as his interests extend.

This last question is quite important. Not only do the standards of programming and technical competence shown by broadcasting organisations vary from country to country, but they also operate on different wavebands. It therefore becomes necessary when buying a tuner to ensure that all the wavebands to which you will want to tune are built into the unit. Table 9.1 lists the wavebands used for broadcasting. I have shown both the wavelengths and the frequencies since tuning dials are sometimes marked with one and sometimes the other. Of course frequency and wavelength are again locked together in the formula which we used in previous chapters relating to sound waves, disc records and magnetic tape recording, namely:

$$\text{velocity} = \text{frequency} \times \text{wavelength}.$$

In this case the velocity is the speed of light (itself an electromagnetic wave with frequencies around 10^{15}Hz and wavelengths around 3×10^{-7}m) which is 300,000,000m per second, so a simple calculation is all that is needed to convert frequencies to wavelengths and vice versa from:

300,000,000 = frequency (in Hertz) × wavelength (in metres).

Table 9.1 Wavebands used for broadcasting

Name	Wavelengths	Frequencies	Type of wave
Long waves	above 1,000m	150–285kHz	mainly ground wave
Medium waves	200–500m	525–1,605kHz	ground wave and sky wave
Short waves	10–100m	8 bands in range 6–26MHz	sky wave
VHF—band I	7.3–4.4m	41–68MHz	direct wave
VHF—band II	3.4–3m	87.5–100MHz	direct wave
VHF—band III	1.7–1.4m	174–216MHz	direct wave
UHF—band IV	0.6–0.5m approx.	470–582MHz	direct wave
UHF—band V	0.5–0.3m approx.	606–960MHz	direct wave
Microwaves		11.7–12.7GHz	direct wave

Radio propagation

The choice of waveband by broadcasters is based on the kind of coverage they want, local-only or long distance, since the signals radiate outwards from the transmitting aerial in quite a different manner depending on the carrier frequency used. (The centre frequency of a radio station is referred to as the 'carrier' since the audio signals of speech or music are modulated on to it, to be 'carried' through the atmosphere.) Beginning at the lowest frequencies (the long waveband) the radio wave spreads outwards keeping quite close to the earth's surface, and without being appreciably absorbed or impeded by obstacles (see Fig. 9.1). The long waveband is therefore ideal for blanket coverage of a wide area.

Moving up to medium waves, similar conditions apply, but absorption of the ground wave limits the effective service area of the transmitter to a radius of about 100 miles. At the same time, part of the transmitted wave travels upwards where it will bounce off the layer of ionised air which surrounds the earth about 60 miles up to be reflected back to the earth perhaps hundreds of miles away. This can be a nuisance, since unwanted stations at or near the same carrier frequency as a desired station may interfere with one's reception. It can also lead to the problem known as 'fading' which results in areas where both the ground wave and the reflected sky wave can be received. The latter arrives a fraction of a second later than the

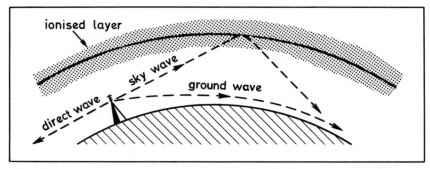

Fig. 9.1 Radio waves are propagated as a ground wave, sky wave or direct wave depending on the carrier frequency band chosen

ground wave and causes the signal strength to fluctuate. The problem is aggravated by the fact that the effective height of the ionised layer varies with the amount of sunlight passing through it. There are therefore seasonal changes and, as night falls for instance, transmissions from the continent of Europe begin to plague medium-wave listeners in Britain.

On short waves, the sky wave is deliberately used for long distance communications, sometimes even allowing for more than one hop between the earth and the ionosphere. Charts of usable frequencies and times enable broadcasters like the BBC to plan overseas broadcasting on a year-round basis. Amateurs too can transmit and receive between all parts of the globe with quite low-power equipment provided they study the sky wave propagation characteristics.

When it comes to the highest frequencies, VHF and UHF, the sky wave tends to penetrate the ionosphere instead of bouncing back down to earth. Also the ground wave is so rapidly absorbed, and scattered by obstacles such as hills and gas-holders, as to reach only a few miles effectively. We are therefore left with a direct line-of-sight wave. The transmitting aerial is usually sited on top of a hill, and receiving aerials too should be placed as high as possible and clear of all obstacles. A small amount of bending takes place, with the wave somewhat following the curvature of the earth's surface. Even so, direct-wave reception is usually regarded as limited to a maximum radius of about 60 miles, and pockets of poor reception can exist within that distance due to obstacles and 'ghost' waves arising from local reflections. Readers will recognise these problems as part of normal television reception, which uses the UHF bands (and VHF too until the 425-line standard is finally phased out).

However, it may seem odd, at first glance, that VHF band II has been chosen as the principal medium for radio broadcasting by the BBC and others. The explanation lies in the fact that a VHF carrier enables the transmitter to employ frequency modulation instead of amplitude modulation, and this introduces a number of very real advantages.

In amplitude modulation (AM), the audio signal rides on the back of the radio-frequency carrier by causing the amplitude of the carrier to vary in accordance with the audio waveform. This has two important implications. First, an absolute limit is set to the amplitude of the audio signal. This can never exceed the basic amplitude of the carrier, the so-called 100% modulation level, or the carrier would be reduced to zero on negative swings of the audio waveform and severe distortion would result. Radio engineers are therefore obliged to monitor the programme level continuously, and indeed incorporate electronic limiters to protect the transmitters from accidental overload. Second, each audio frequency fa present in the programme signal generates side-frequencies on either side of the carrier frequency fa given by $(fc \pm fa)$. The complete AM signal therefore occupies a band of frequencies whose width is twice the highest audio frequency present. Proper reception of AM broadcasts therefore requires tuner circuits capable of being tuned accurately to the carrier, as centre frequency, yet responding equally over the full transmitted bandwidth. This introduces a problem of selectivity. If programmes were up to high fidelity standards, containing audio frequencies up to say 20kHz, it would be necessary to build tuners with a band-pass of 40kHz. Then unwanted stations with carriers or sidebands falling within this range would be picked up simultaneously. In practice, due to the overcrowded nature of the medium wavebands, international allocation of station frequencies has put them only 9kHz apart. In a bid to keep interference to a minimum, adjacent carrier frequencies are mainly allocated to stations which are geographically far apart. However, particularly after dark when sky wave interference increases, a wideband tuner becomes a liability. The broadcasting companies therefore limit the transmitted bandwidth, and tuners too build in filters restricting their acceptance band to not much more than the 4.5kHz theoretical clearance between stations—hardly hi-fi.

In frequency modulation (FM) the amplitude of the carrier wave remains constant while its actual frequency is varied in accordance with the varying amplitude of the audio signal. The 100% modulation level is set at an agreed deviation of ± 75kHz, and the mechanism of producing sidebands increases the required bandwidth to a total of about 180kHz. In practice a channel spacing of 200kHz is used. The carrier frequencies for BBC Radio 2, 3 and 4 at each local transmitting station are spaced 2.2MHz apart, so that adjacent channel interference is avoided. Again, since FM is used exclusively in the VHF band II region, where only the direct wave applies, the risks of interference from geographically remote stations is very small. A further advantage of FM is known as 'capture effect'. This arises in the receiver when two stations having a small difference in carrier frequency are received; it causes the set to reproduce the stronger signal only and suppress the weaker station. It is also common practice further to reduce the inherently low background noise of FM transmissions by a procedure known as pre-emphasis. This consists of boosting the treble audio frequencies, in somewhat the same manner as we discussed earlier in connection with disc and tape recording. The received audio signal is then passed through a complementary de-emphasis circuit to restore the treble to its original level and simultaneously reduce the audibility of noise. The time constant used for FM pre-emphasis is $50\mu s$ in the UK and Europe, $75\mu s$ in the USA.

To sum up, though calling for more complex and expensive tuners, the adoption of FM waveband confers the following benefits compared with AM on the medium and other broadcast wavebands:

(a) *Frequency range is wider*   VHF/FM programmes and tuners can cover the range up to 15kHz, whereas filtering will often be introduced at 4.5kHz on AM to limit adjacent channel interference.

(b) *Dynamic range is wider*   VHF/FM programmes need little or no compression at source, whereas AM programmes are commonly compressed quite severely because of the known greater incidence of noise and interference on AM receivers.

(c) *Radio interference is less*   VHF/FM transmissions are restricted to line-of-sight distances, and the capture effect further discriminates against weaker interfering stations.

(d) *Electrical interference is less*   VHF/FM tuners incorporate an AM rejection feature which reduces the noise from unsuppressed thermostat switches, etc. These enter the aerial as wideband AM signals and often spoil AM reception.

(e) *Stereophonic broadcasting is possible*   VHF/FM transmitters have the necessary bandwidth to accommodate the independent left and right channel signals needed for stereo, using a multiplex system (described below). Proposals for AM stereo broadcasting are now going ahead in the USA and Japan, but with restricted audio bandwidth.

Stereo broadcasting

The idea of broadcasting programmes in which the listener could sense the left-to-right spatial distribution of the musicians or actors and identify the direction of individual performers is not new. Indeed, as mentioned in Chapter 2, it goes back more than 100 years, when the Paris 'Exhibition of Electricity' in 1881 featured a series of live relays from the stage of the Paris Opéra to arrays of telephone earpieces at the exhibition, a distance of about 2km away. Separate telephone lines carried the signals to left and right earpieces, so that the actual positions and movements of the performers could be detected by exhibition visitors holding one earpiece to each ear. Though telephone subscribers could listen into concert relays in various countries, including England, for some years after this, they were in single-channel mono. And of course the emergence of radio ('wireless') in the early 1920s put paid to the telephone relays. Fifty years after Ader's demonstrations, A. D. Blumlein in England patented the classic methods for two-microphone stereo recording in 1931. During the following decade, engineers of the Bell Laboratories in the USA, collaborating with the great conductor Leopold Stokowski, carried out numerous stereo experiments producing, for instance, the multi-soundtrack cartoon film *Fantasia*.

Stereo broadcasting remained an unfulfilled ambition, however, until the emergence of two-channel 'stereosonic' tape recordings in 1955, followed quickly by the tidal wave of stereophonic gramophone records from about 1957, caused all broadcasters to work on a viable transmission system. The BBC began experimental stereo transmissions as early as January 1957 using a rather clumsy arrangement. For about an hour on Saturday mornings, the left channel was broadcast on the Radio 3 wavelength and the right channel on the sound portion of BBC Television. Enthusiast listeners were invited to tune their radio and television sets to these two stations and space the sets suitably while special stereophonic demonstrations and LP records were transmitted. Clearly this was an impossibly complicated arrangement, yet it was not until July 1966 that the BBC was able to begin regular stereo broadcasts using a system which met all the following requirements:

(a) *Single-channel transmission/reception* Stereo broadcasts should be no more difficult to tune in, and not significantly more demanding of bandwidth, than mono transmissions.

(b) *Wide service area* Stereo broadcasts should not significantly reduce the area for satisfactory reception for either mono or stereo listeners.

(c) *Compatibility* Mono receivers should give equally satisfactory (mono) reproduction whether tuned to a mono or stereo broadcast.

(d) *High quality sound* Stereo broadcasts should give comparable sound quality to other stereo sources such as LP records and tapes. In practice, a frequency range of 15kHz is achieved with very little interchannel crosstalk.

After consideration of many systems, international agreement was reached on a particular form of matrix known as Zenith-GE multiplex. This first of all passes the left and right stereo signals through circuits which produce sum $(L+R)$ and difference $(L-R)$ signals. The sum signal is then modulated on to the VHF carrier in the ordinary way, so that mono receivers produce an acceptable mono $(L+R)$ signal with no modification. At the same time, the difference signal is modulated on to an inaudible supersonic subcarrier (38kHz is used in pratice) which is also applied to the main carrier (though with the subcarrier suppressed for practical reasons). By simultaneously introducing a so-called 'pilot tone' at 19kHz, it is made possible for the receiver to reconstitute the 38kHz subcarrier (by simple doubling) and so detect the $(L-R)$ signal. Having access to the demodulated sum and difference signals, the receiver is able to derive the original left and right stereo information by further algebraic adding and substracting, thus:

$$(L+R)+(L-R) = 2L$$
$$(L+R)-(L-R) = 2R.$$

While the 38kHz subcarrier frequency is of course inaudible, and the 19kHz pilot tone beyond the hearing capabilities of all but keen-eared young people, they can still be a nuisance and must be removed by filtering. They cause trouble in particular whenever a tape recording is being made from a stereo broadcast. These high frequency tones, and their harmonics, can beat with the high frequency bias/erase signals to generate difference tones well down into the audible band. Most FM stereo tuners and receivers incorporate suitable filtering but, in case they do not remove the tones effectively enough, it is common practice to build a multiplex (MPX) filter into tape machines. Since this filter would attenuate high frequencies in the programme material too, it can be switched out when not required—as when making live recordings through a microphone.

Most tuners provide some indication that the station being received is broadcasting in stereo. This 'stereo beacon' can consist of an indicator lamp or meter and is simply activated by a circuit which detects the presence of the 19kHz pilot tone and reconstituted 38kHz subcarrier. The latter tones are also used to give automatic changeover of the tuner mode of operation from mono to stereo, without the need for the user to do anything. However, situations may arise where the user would like to override this auto-switching. For example, when a weak stereo transmission is wanted, the background noise may be uncomfortably loud when listening in the stereo mode (noise is normally about 20dB higher in stereo than mono). A reduction in this noise can be achieved by switching the tuner to mono operation. Then only the (L+R) component of the signal is used and, of course, sent equally to both the left and right output sockets. Some tuners allow a manual or automatic compromise to be reached called 'quasi-stereo'. This preserves some of the stereo effect, when tuned to a weak stereo station, by allowing a certain amount of crosstalk in antiphase at high audio frequencies. This reduces the annoyance value of the noise, though at some sacrifice of stereo channel integrity.

The audio output voltage is usually amplified to about 500mV at the tuner sockets. As with cassette decks, the phono-plug socket is the most common, with DIN sockets fitted on many European models. Sometimes the tuner output level is fixed, but a good number of tuners have an output volume control. In general it will be best to turn this to a fairly high setting consistent with producing a comfortable setting of the main amplifier volume control. This will keep any induced noise or mains hum in the connecting cable to a minimum, and allow comparable volume levels to result when switching between the tuner and the record-player. When using the AM wavebands, or mono reception on FM, the left and right output sockets feed identical signals to the two stereo channels of the amplifier.

Aerials

Except for the audio signal output sockets, the only other connections to a tuner are for one or more aerials. Some confusion can arise because of the different types of aerial connecting cable used in different parts of the world, and this problem will now be discussed along with the desirable features of the aerial itself.

Since the whole process of radio reception begins with the aerial, it would seem axiomatic that every home audio system where good sound quality is considered important would provide a decent aerial. Unfortunately many do not and, while this is a less serious omission on AM, it must mean that the full benefits of VHF/FM—which does require a good aerial signal—are often being lost. The job of the aerial is to pass into the tuner as high a signal voltage at the required carrier frequency as possible. In practice, any piece of wire insulated from the earth will contain tiny currents at all the radio frequencies arriving at that point in space. So within limits it could be said that any piece of wire will act as an aerial. Many people have found that even the human body can act as an aerial: simply putting one's finger on the aerial terminal will produce some level of signal from a tuner or receiver.

Now in the case of the AM wavebands, the signal we hear is recognisably feeble from a poor aerial, and gets progressively better as we improve the aerial. This is logical, and so anyone who is interested in decent reception of long, medium or short waveband signals will quickly see the virtue of a good aerial. By contrast, it is in some ways unfortunate that VHF/FM transmissions produce quite a loud audio output from the tuner with only the most rudimentary aerial. The purchaser may therefore take a new tuner or receiver home and find he gets seemingly adequate results with the built-in aerial or piece of divided flex often supplied. In fact, better suppression of inherent noise and distortion could almost certainly have been obtained with a loft or outside aerial.

There are three important ingredients in the production of a good aerial: its dimensions, its directional properties and its siting.

Aerial dimensions

It turns out that the actual length of a wire or piece of metal rod causes it to resonate, that is respond selectively, to radio waves having certain related wavelengths. This can be turned to advantage when an aerial is cut to the correct length for a given carrier frequency or waveband. The desired signals will be enhanced and the unwanted signals, which constitute nothing more than interference and noise, will be suppressed. Two basic types of resonant aerial exist, the Hertz-type which tunes to the radio frequency for which the aerial is precisely a half-wavelength long, and the Marconi-type which is a vertically mounted variant only a quarter-wavelength long with the earth, or some other conducting plane such as a car body, supplying the remainder of the system.

A glance back at Table 9.1 will show that wavelengths in the medium waveband measure several hundred metres, so that resonant receiving aerials are just not practicable. However VHF band II, used for FM radio, has wavelengths around 3m and so a half-wave Hertz aerial—called a dipole—is both practicable and highly desirable. Any good conductor of electricity can be used for an aerial, copper and aluminium alloys both offering a better proof against the ravages of climate and oxidisation than iron. Thin wire could be stretched between supports, or stretched out straight on to a wooden board (see Fig. 9.2), but tubing will have enough rigidity to stand on its own. An incidental very important advantage is that such tubing tunes less sharply to the resonant frequency,

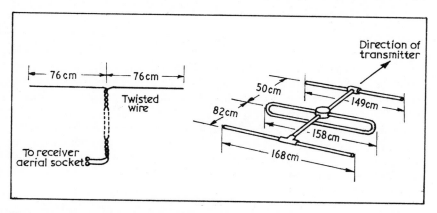

Fig. 9.2 Suggested dimensions for home-made VHF aerials: a simple dipole of twisted (insulated) wire flex (*left*) and a folded tube dipole with reflector and director rods added (*right*)

allowing adequate coverage of the whole VHF band and very good coverage of the three BBC radio stations grouped at the standard 2.2MHz spacing in each local area. The effective length of such a dipole is about 5% greater than its measured length. This gives the formula for calculating half-wave dipole lengths as:

$$\text{length (metres)} = \frac{145}{\text{frequency (MHz)}}.$$

For the centre (Radio 3) frequency from the BBC Wrotham transmitter, for example, this becomes:

$$\text{length} = \frac{145}{91.3} = 1.59\text{m}.$$

Aerial directivity

A further means of enhancing the performance of an aerial is to make it directional, and orientate it in such a manner as to boost its reception of the desired transmissions and simultaneously help it to reject unwanted stations and reflections from large obstacles. The half-wave dipole is inherently directional: it responds most efficiently to radio waves arriving broadside on and produces hardly any signal from waves arriving along its length. If a polar diagram is drawn representing the effective signal strength at each angle by the distance out from the centre, the result for a simple dipole is a figure-of-eight (Fig. 9.3a). Clearly such an aerial should be orientated so that the loop of the figure-of-eight is pointing straight towards the transmitter.

A dipole can be made more sharply directional by mounting an array of similar metal wires or rods (elements) parallel to it at calculated distances. Adding a single element at about a quarter-wavelength more remote from the transmitter has the most dramatic effect (Fig. 9.3b). The second element acts as a 'reflector' and reinforces the signal received by the dipole— almost doubling it—from the desired direction while greatly reducing signals arriving in the opposite direction. This obliges the user both to direct the dipole broadside on to the desired transmitter and ensure that the dipole is on the transmitter side of the reflector.

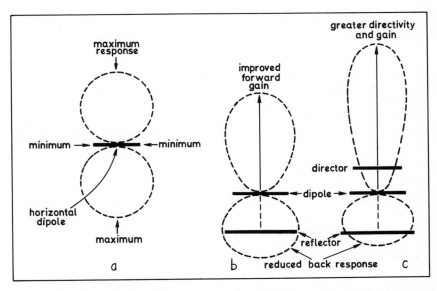

Fig. 9.3 Aerial directivity patterns for: (a) a simple dipole; (b) dipole plus reflector; (c) dipole plus reflector and one director

So far we have produced the familiar H-aerial very commonly used for reception of the older VHF band I (425-lines) television broadcasts, the two arms of the H being the dipole and reflector respectively. If now one or more additional elements are placed at approximately one-eighth wavelength intervals in front of the dipole (Fig. 9.3c), these act as 'directors' and progressively increase the front-back efficiency of the aerial system (now called a Yagi array). Figure 9.2b shows the dimensions for a do-it-yourself directional array based on a variant of the simple dipole known as the 'folded dipole' which simplifies matching to the aerial cable. The very short wavelengths used for UHF television (about 50cm) have made it practicable to design extremely directional arrays having as many as sixteen director rods. Indeed the greater incidence of unwanted 'ghost' multipath reflections from obstacles, when operating in the UHF bands, has made such highly directional aerial arrays almost mandatory. As a consequence, TV viewers on the continent of Europe for example who wish to tune into a number of transmitters in different directions may feel obliged to fit a rotating aerial array controlled from a knob or handwheel in the living-room.

VHF band II transmissions are intermediate in wavelength between VHF band I and the UHF bands, and a simple H-aerial or Yagi array with three or four directors will usually be considered adequate. Correct orientation is still needed, however, and once again a few radio-listener fanatics in Europe and the United States have found that a rotator device gives them a useful extension of programme choice.

The polar diagram shape, figure-of-eight or cardioid of varying degrees of sharpness, does not apply in a single plane only. It is really a three-dimensional solid figure. The complete pattern for a half-wave dipole, for example, is doughnut shaped, with the dipole at the centre. This suggests at first sight that a dipole or array will be equally effective whether it is mounted vertically or horizontally, or at any intermediate angle. In practice, however, the receiving aerial works best when it is mounted in the same effective plane as the transmitting aerial. This is referred to as the 'polarisation' of the transmitted signals. It so happens that television broadcasts in the UK are mainly vertically polarised, which explains why TV receiving aerials are normally vertical. VHF/FM radio transmissions, on the other hand, are mainly though not exclusively horizontally polarised and so the receiving aerial should lie in the horizontal plane.

It will be realised that the normal vertical rod aerial used on cars is at a disadvantage for VHF/FM reception. Accordingly a plan for introducing 'slant polarisation' is being implemented by the BBC in the hope of producing a compromise condition to suit both home and car listeners.

Aerial siting
Ideally the receiving aerial should be situated as high and as clear of obstacles as possible. However, there are many home situations where this counsel of perfection is simply impracticable, or else it would entail such a long lead-in cable that costs and cable losses would become prohibitive. Fortunately, where good VHF/FM reception of the BBC Radio 2, 3 and 4 programmes is the only requirement, most UK homes are within 30 or 40 miles of the local transmitting station, making an indoor aerial quite a practical proposition.

Moving up from the basic built-in aerial provided on some receivers—which is really not good enough for quality reception, particularly of stereo programmes—we come to the folded ribbon or piece of twin flex opened out over the last 80cm or so to form a letter T. Clearly the top-piece of the T is intended to act as a half-wave dipole. It should therefore be positioned horizontally and orientated so far as possible so that it is broadside on to the line to the transmitter. In some rooms there may be a picture rail and a wall at just the correct compass bearing. Then the problem of positioning this awkward 1.5m length of flex is solved. In other rooms some experimenting will be necessary to find a position which is acceptable both visually and in terms of aerial efficiency.

With such a basic room aerial, it may be found that one of the BBC networks is less well picked up than the other two. This is because the thin wire gives rather sharp tuning and its length may not be equally suitable for all three transmissions, even though they normally emanate from the same transmitter site and have carrier frequencies spaced at only 2.2MHz part. The solution is to replace the flex dipole with a tubular one, available from radio dealers. This has broad enough tuning to cover the BBC networks and will do a better job of picking up BBC and commercial local radio stations too.

For homes more than about 30 miles from the transmitter, or where hills or metal-framed buildings impede reception, the indoor dipole will need to be moved into a more advantageous position such as a loft. Then, depending on space available, it will be worth adding extra elements to produce a more directional array. At least a loft position will allow such an array to be turned to the best angle, which would be impracticable in the living-room. The principal obstacle to be avoided will be the water tank.

Finally, where even better reception conditions are desired, an outside aerial is the answer. This almost certainly means that a do-it-yourself job is no longer possible. Calling in a professional will be safer, and he will have local knowledge of wavelengths and transmitter directions. He will also know best how to combine aerials for television and VHF/FM sound radio.

Aerial connections

It would obviously be a mistake to install a good aerial and then couple it to the tuner by means of an inadequate connecting cable which severely attentuated the previous signal. The key, apart from making wiring and plug/socket connections properly, is to match the impedances of the aerial, cable and tuner input. Some confusion arises because two standard impedance configurations are in use. Either works very well, but it is a mistake to mix the two.

The characteristic impedance at the centre of a dipole aerial is about 75 ohms. In the UK the standard practice is to use coaxial cable which has an impedance of between 70 and 80 ohms (a near enough match for all practical purposes) and design the tuner input to match this. The tuner aerial socket will therefore be of a suitable coaxial type, the entire system being described as 'unbalanced' since one half of the twin-conductor line is the inner wire of the coaxial cable while the other, earthed, half consists of the surrounding metal braiding. In the USA and elsewhere a 'balanced' aerial feeder is common with two identical wires placed flat side by side or twisted in a plastic coating. This produces a characteristic impedance of 240–300 ohms, and many tuners therefore possess twin (unearthed) input sockets rated at this impedance. The indoor flex aerials supplied with many VHF/FM tuners and receivers can be used directly with this two-pin input. However the UK-type coaxial cable should be connected to the coaxial socket, where provided. In practice, most VHF/FM radio equipment built for world markets is fitted with both types of aerial socket, so no problems should arise. For situations where a 75 ohms connector must be used into a 300 ohms socket, or vice versa, a matching transformer can be inserted—called a 'balun' (balanced-to-unbalanced).

Tuner controls and features

The front panel of a tuner or receiver will usually be dominated by controls and indicators associated with the basic job of selecting and tuning accurately to the desired station. The superior sound quality obtainable on VHF/FM transmissions has caused many tuners to be designed with only this waveband. On others, the medium waveband may be added — sometimes almost as an afterthought with very little attention paid to securing decent sound quality. For use in the UK, the long waveband has become a necessity in some households because of an oddity of BBC programme allocations which puts certain Radio 4 items on longwave only. Yet longwaves are seldom used in many other countries and so tuners covering this band have to be designed almost solely for the British market. The short wavebands too are used only by the minority who spend time listening to long distance broadcasts — perhaps because they are living far from their country of origin — and so are fitted in only a few receivers.

The use of the waveband switches, rotary knob or push-buttons, is self-explanatory but a word about manual tuning is called for. Most people find tuning to an AM station very straightforward. One simply rotates the tuning knob back and forth through the desired station and the centre tuning point can be identified unambiguously by ear: the sound is not only loudest at the correct tuning position, it is also more naturally balanced tonally. (Off-tune positions emphasise the sidebands and are lacking in bass.)

Manual tuning to an FM station is a little more difficult. The signal tends to pop up and disappear more sharply with no change in tonal balance. Also there may be more distant stations broadcasting *the same programme* on adjacent frequencies, and the main clue to having selected the proper station may be merely the level of inherent background noise (least noise means best reception). For these various reasons, it has become standard practice to incorporate one or more tuning aids on VHF/FM sets (see Plate 23). Two types of tuning indicator are commonly fitted. First a signal strength meter which will obviously peak up to a maximum when a station is satisfactorily tuned. Second a tuning accuracy meter, usually with a centre zero, which shows that the given station has been tuned in precisely. From this basic provision of two meters, designing ingenuity has led to the introduction of numerous eye-catching variants. Sometimes the meters are replaced by rows of LEDs (light emitting diodes) or the tuning pointer itself may glow more brightly, or even change colour, when the station is tuned in correctly. A secondary nuisance when tuning on the VHF/FM band is the loud interstation noise. This is often silenced by means of a 'muting' switch which activates the audio channels only when stations exceeding some predetermined aerial signal strength are being tuned through. It may be necessary to switch off the muting when deliberately tuning to a weak station, and the same applies to another common feature—AFC (automatic frequency control). This is a circuit design which locks on to the given station and prevents drifting due to temperature changes or other effects.

Difficulties with manual VHF/FM tuning are avoided completely on many tuners. These may provide a row of pushbuttons pretuned to give immediate—and precise—selection of one's favourite stations. Or they may be even more exotic and add automatic 'search and tune' facilities. This causes an electronic motor to drive the tuning pointer along the dial, and stop automatically for a few seconds at each station having a predetermined signal strength. The user can then go straight to whichever station suits his fancy. Some tuners do away with a conventional tuning scale and replace it with a digital display of station frequency. This feature is often combined with 'synthesiser' tuning in which a microprocessor can control the search tuning mode and even commit to memory the frequencies of selected stations which can then be summoned at the touch of a numbered button.

10
The Amplifier

As the building-bricks diagram in Fig. 6.1 (page 61) shows, the amplifier may justifiably be described as the keystone of any audio system. It acts as a kind of telephone exchange, allowing the user to select the programme source he wants to hear—disc, tape or radio—and feeding it to the loudspeakers or headphones as required. It also has the basic job of amplifying or boosting the source signals, which start off at only around 0.001 watt, to the 10 watts or more needed to drive the loudspeakers. In some high fidelity designs this latter function is carried out in a separate so-called 'power amplifier', with the switching and other functions housed in a 'preamplifier' or 'control unit'. In most cases, however, an integrated unit is used with the functions combined in a single cabinet (Plate 24).

A quick look round the back

Most connections are made through sockets mounted out of harm's way on the rear panel (Plate 25). The source input sockets are usually of the single-channel phono-plug type and so a separate screened coaxial cable and plug will be needed for the left and right channels of each stereo source. In some, mostly European, models five-pin DIN sockets are fitted instead, and then a single combined cable is used with the two pairs of inner conductors insulated from each other and from the outer screen (see Fig. 10.1). Phono-plug sockets are also the favourite choice as output connectors to feed a tape recorder but here too a DIN socket may be fitted. This has the advantage of neatness, since the common practice is to enclose both the input (tape deck replay) and output (amplifier to tape deck recording input) conductors in a single multicore cable with five-pin DIN plugs, so one cable replaces the four needed with the phono-plug system. However, some loss of flexibility of choice occurs and it is best to use either the DIN or phono-plug system exclusively. This is made easier by the fact that, when DIN tape record/replay sockets are fitted, they are usually wired in parallel with phono sockets so that the connection appropriate to the given tape deck can be selected.

Loudspeaker connections take several forms. They may consist of screw-terminals, or spring-loaded jaws designed to grip the bared tips of the loudspeaker cable. Or there is a two-pin DIN socket often used on European equipment, and a popular two-hole socket which accepts pairs of 4mm 'banana'-type plugs. With all these types there is some indication of polarity, either by means of plus and minus signs or red and black colour coding. This is to help the user always to connect the two loudspeakers of a stereo pair in the same relative polarity or 'phase' (see Chapter 13). It is an incidental advantage of the DIN loudspeaker plug that the polarity is fixed in advance, with the smaller, round pin always 'live' and the flat pin 'earth'. Many hi-fi amplifiers have a second complete set of loudspeaker outlets, with switching on the front panel to select system A, B or A + B. This allows the user to run separate loudspeakers in another room, or perhaps in the same room if he wants to experiment with a four-speaker layout for pseudo-surround sound. The headphone socket is invariably situated on the front panel, for ease of use, and is generally of the stereo jackplug type.

It used to be standard practice to fit auxiliary mains supply sockets at the back of hi-fi amplifiers, from which the record-player, tape deck, etc could derive their mains supply without running their cables directly to the wall-socket. However recent safety regulations in the UK and certain other countries made such unscreened sockets unlawful, and so they are tending to disappear or be replaced by special screened or shuttered sockets.

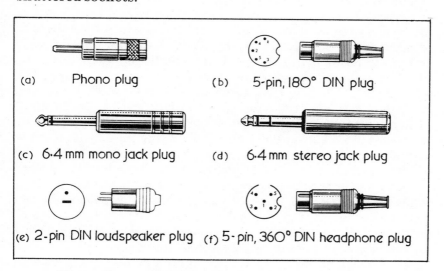

Fig. 10.1 The types of plug in most common use for audio equipment

Controls and switches

It would be impossible to describe all the combinations of controls and functions on the amplifiers on the market. However, a brief explanation of each of the basic types of control will help readers to work through their user's manual.

Source selector
Switching to the desired programme source is most often effected by means of a rotary switch or a row of suitably labelled buttons. As well as making a connection of the chosen input sockets to the main amplifier chain, this introduces appropriate impedance matching and frequency correction as necessary. Tuner and tape replay inputs have basically similar matching requirements and so it would be possible on many amplifiers to use the tape replay input for a second tuner, or vice versa. Also a separate 'auxiliary' input is often available, with similar parameters, to allow further permutations—say to include the sound channel from a television set having a suitable sound output socket.

While the sources so far described have a flat frequency response and deliver about 500mV, the inputs for gramophone record reproduction need to be a little more complex. In the first place, a magnetic pickup cartridge delivers only about 1mV and so the first stages of amplification need much more gain (about 500 times more). The input impedance is also more critical, most cartridges being designed for optimum response when loaded by a resistance of 47,000 ohms (47K). The resistance of the pickup cable is usually negligible and so it is the resistance as 'seen' at the amplifier input sockets which should ideally be 47K. If the amplifier rated input impedance is much higher or lower than 47K, the high frequencies may be slightly emphasised or attenuated respectively. As well as the electrical resistance, the capacitance of the total load on the cartridge can sometimes be quite critical. This is made up of the capacitance in the pickup cable as well as that across the amplifier input sockets. The result of adding these two together should equal the loading capacitance recommended by the cartridge manufacturer. Unfortunately there has been very little standardisation amongst the manufacturers, so that some design their cartridges for a load of around 200 picofarads (pF) and some at about 400pF or even higher. Pickup cables also vary in capacitance. A value of about 150pF was once common but, in recent years, special 'low capacitance' cables have become popular, rated at 70pF or less. As a result, amplifier designers have felt under no constraint to produce a standard input capacitance—and indeed they do not always quote a value in their specifications. So the ordinary purchaser, trying to match a record deck to an amplifier, has almost to take pot luck. It is lucky that mismatching is not often too serious. Only if the total capacitance is perhaps 50% or more at variance with the cartridge manufacturer's recommended value will an audible effect be noticed, with too high a capacitance attenuating high frequencies and too low a capacitance boosting them. Nonetheless, in a top quality system it is necessary to eliminate even such small errors. A few amplifiers therefore offer variable resistance and capacitance loading at the pickup input, and add-on accessory boxes are also available.

We have so far been considering the input sockets for standard magnetic cartridges—labelled variously 'gram', 'pickup' or 'phono'—but the increasing popularity of moving-coil cartridges (see Chapter 7) has caused some amplifier manufacturers to fit extra inputs to accommodate them. Moving-coil cartridges normally produce an output voltage of only about 0.1mV (though some 'high output' types come close to the 1mV of standard magnetic types) and are best suited to a low resistance loading of around 20–100 ohms. (They are less critical of capacitance loading.) Where special 'moving-coil' inputs are provided, therefore, they will present a low impedance and incorporate the necessary additional gain. Owners of amplifiers without such provision can buy an add-on booster unit, which may be a transformer or a 'preamplifier' designed to match the moving-coil correctly to the normal pickup inputs.

An additional requirement at both types of pickup input is equalisation for the RIAA/IEC recording characteristic used in gramophone record manufacture (see Chapter 7). As has already been mentioned, this equalisation consists of a considerable amount of bass boost, which makes it very important to avoid mains hum or other magnetic field induction at the cartridge and its connections.

A further feature which has special importance at the pickup inputs is called 'headroom'. This involves designing the input stages of the amplifier so that they give the appropriate degree of amplification of a signal at the standard rated level of, say, 1mV and 0.1mV for magnetic and moving-coil cartridges respectively but do not run into severe overload distortion when the cartridge is playing particularly loud records. Some 'audiophile' discs in particular contain peak recorded velocities many times higher than the 1cm/s used in rating the cartridge sensitivity.

Tape recording outlet

The output sockets for feeding signals to a tape recorder for recording purposes have already been mentioned. On a practical point, however, it is important to realise that this outlet is unaffected by the volume and tone controls of the main amplifier. This is illustrated in Fig. 10.2 where it is seen that the feed to the tape recorder is taken from a point immediately following the source selector switch. Thus the tape machine receives the signals from either the turntable or the tuner at a fixed level. The second switch shown is often labelled 'tape monitor' and enables the user to listen either to the original source direct or to the signal routed back from the tape recorder. On two-head machines, this latter signal is simply the source itself (unrecorded) but, on three-head machines which allow the signal just recorded to be picked up by a separate replay head, it is possible to switch to 'monitor' on the tape machine and route the off-tape signal back to the amplifier. Notice that this A/B switching to compare the direct source with the signal as recorded can then be carried out either on the tape deck or the main amplifier.

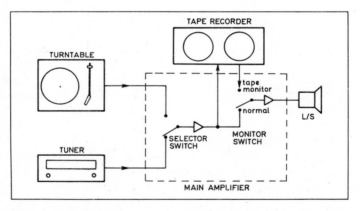

Fig. 10.2 In most hi-fi amplifiers the signal sent to a tape recorder will be that from the turntable or tuner, depending on the position of the source selector switch, and will be unaffected by the amplifier tone and volume control settings. The tape monitor input is selected by a separate switch

When the amplifier switch is moved to the 'tape monitor' position, it will of course pick up any signal connected to the 'tape' input sockets. This is therefore the accepted method of interconnecting an add-on processor of any type. A graphic equaliser, for example, could be substituted for the tape recorder in the diagram and switching to 'tape monitor' would automatically bring the equaliser into circuit. Since such processors occupy the normal tape sockets, they in turn are often fitted with tape in/out sockets so that all the necessary tape functions are retained in the set-up.

Volume control

Some means of adjusting the sound volume is a necessary feature of every audio installation. At its simplest it will be a single rotary control knob which simultaneously alters the gain in the two amplifier chains of the left and right stereo channels. Occasionally separate rotary or slider controls are provided for the two channels, so that allowance can be made for any slight differences in cartridge sensitivity or between the two loudspeakers. More usually, a volume control will be fitted in company with a *balance control*. This has a centre position where gain is equal in both channels, and can be turned in one direction to attenuate the left channel and the other to attenuate the right. A fixed 20dB attenuator or 'dim switch' is sometimes fitted alongside the volume control to cut down the sound volume when answering a telephone, etc.

Loudness control

It is a characteristic of our hearing mechanism that turning down the volume of reproduced music causes the loudness of the bass frequencies (and to a lesser extent the treble frequencies) to diminish more rapidly than that of middle frequencies. The music therefore not only gets quieter, but its character is changed so that it is lacking in body and extreme top. In an attempt to correct for this, some amplifiers have a 'loudness contour' feature which arranges that progressively lowering the volume control setting attenuates the bass and treble by smaller increments than middle frequencies. The changing response is based on the known variations in sensitivity of human hearing researched by Fletcher and Munson (see Chapter 3). In practice, however, the frequency correction can be no more than approximate and indeed the fitting of loudness controls has always been controversial, with British manufacturers tending to omit them.

Tone controls

At one time the balance of bass and treble frequencies from gramophone records, tapes and broadcasts was so variable that the provision of tone controls was a virtual necessity. More recently, however, the frequency response of source material has not only improved overall, it has become more consistent. Therefore very few occasions arise when altering the frequency balance as a corrective measure is really necessary.

Nonetheless, most amplifiers have at the very least bass and treble tone controls which can be useful in at least three ways. First, your own taste may run to plenty of bass, for example, and a judicious touch on the bass control may do the trick. Second, loudspeakers still vary in tonal balance and you may be able to rebalance the sound with a particular setting of the tone controls. Third, it is a fact of life that the acoustics and furnishing of the room can upset the tonal balance and tone controls may alleviate this problem. For example, a heavily furnished and curtained room may absorb high frequencies to such an extent as to make all reproduced music sound dull and lifeless. Simply raising the treble control may restore the natural balance.

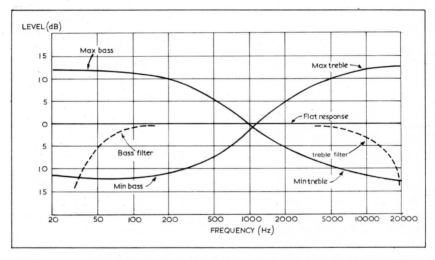

Fig. 10.3 The bass and treble tone controls give smooth boost or cut up to a maximum of about 12dB. The filters give steeper attenuation

The normal bass and treble controls give a continuously variable boost or cut on either side of the central (1kHz) frequency with a maximum excursion of about ±10dB (Fig. 10.3). This is more than enough for the situations mentioned, and indeed quite a small adjustment will usually suffice. More elaborate tone controls are sometimes provided, beginning with the addition of a third control which can raise or lower the middle frequencies. Subjectively this has the effect of making soloists sound closer or more distant, hence the name 'presence control' sometimes used. As an extension of this idea, very versatile amplifiers may incorporate eight or more controls— perhaps giving boost or cut independently over each individual octave of the spectrum (Fig. 10.4). When the controls are

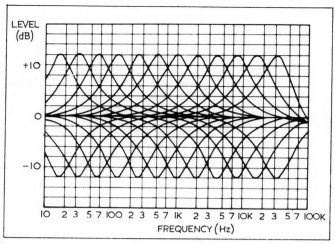

Fig. 10.4 A graphic equaliser gives independent boost or cut over a number of narrow frequency bands (twelve bands in this example)

of the sliding fader type, so that the control knob positions effectively draw a graph of the response curve, the control is called a 'graphic equaliser' (Plate 26). The sharpness or 'Q' of the boost or cut curve for each frequency band can even be altered on some versions, which are then described as 'parametric equalisers'.

Filters

In addition to the more or less smoothly operating tone controls, there is often a requirement for a sharp cut-off at the extreme bass or treble end of the spectrum. This is strictly a curative function, the bass filter being used to eliminate low frequency rumble from the disc or tape motor mechanism and the treble filter cutting out whistles or high frequency interference (see Fig. 10.4). The rate of attenuation below or above the nominal turnover frequency is quoted in decibels per octave. It should be as steep as possible: 12dB/octave is good, and 18dB/octave even better. Such steep filters are more expensive to produce, and it is to be regretted that the filters in many amplifiers have only a basic gentle slope of 6dB/octave. They then remove some of the wanted musical signals along with the unwanted rumble or interference.

How many watts?

Central to the job of an amplifier is that of producing enough electrical power, measured in watts, to drive the loudspeakers and so produce the desired levels of acoustic energy. Anything less than 5 watts per channel is likely to give only moderate sound volumes, though much depends on the efficiency with which the loudspeakers convert the electrical signals into soundwaves. Where the loudspeakers are particularly inefficient, as is the case with the majority of closed cabinet types on the market, higher amplifier powers should be chosen. It is difficult to be precise as to how many watts are ideal, though a good general rule is to err on the high side. This will allow the sharp peaks in the music, which can rise to many times the average level, to be reproduced without the amplifier running into the high-distortion overload (clipping) condition. There is admittedly a risk of supplying too high a signal to the given loudspeakers, causing the speaker drive units themselves to overload. Therefore the power handling capacity of the loudspeakers should be read in conjunction with the maximum power output rating of the amplifier to make sure that too large a discrepancy does not exist.

It is here that we run into a certain difficulty. The manufacturers of both loudspeakers and amplifiers are inconsistent in the way in which they quote power ratings. The most strictly accurate way to quote, and measure, electrical power is in terms of the voltage being applied (suitably averaged over a period of time) and the effective load resistance. Since the voltage of a musical signal varies wildly from instant to instant, the most sensible way to average it has been found to square the instantaneous voltages over one cycle of the given waveform, find the average or mean value of this, and take the square root of the answer. This gives the so-called 'root mean square' or RMS voltage. Power ratings based on this are variously referred to as 'RMS', 'continuous' or 'sinewave' (since the test signal used will normally take the form of a continuous sinewave tone at single frequency — usually 1kHz).

Unfortunately some designs of amplifier are unable to sustain a continuous tone at high power levels, and their designers have been quick to point out that musical signals consist mainly of sharp peaks of short duration — which the amplifier may handle quite happily. Various alternative power ratings have therefore been proposed, and used in amplifier specifications. These 'music' ratings inflate the rating by about 50%, so that an amplifier quoted at '60 watts (music power)' will be roughly equivalent to one at '40 watts (continuous)'. There is no real harm in this, particularly when the specification includes both ratings, but it has been known to cause confusion.

In all cases, the power rating will relate to a given level of total harmonic distortion (THD), since a higher power figure could obviously be quoted if more distortion were tolerated. It will also depend on the assumed load impedance, a 4-ohms load for example giving a higher power capability than an 8-ohms one. So, when comparing the specifications of two amplifiers, it is not only necessary to see which has the higher rating in watts-per-channel. It is necessary to check that they are both 'continuous power', for the same distortion figure (say 0.1% THD) and the same load impedance (say 8 ohms).

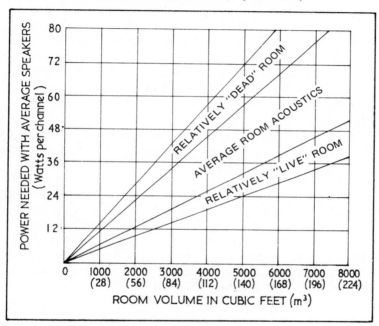

Fig. 10.5 Guide to amplifier power rating needed in rooms of different volume and three degrees of soft furnishing

To come to a final decision on how many watts you need, even the size of the listening-room has to be taken into account. The graphs in Fig. 10.5 summarise these various requirements in terms of room volume and three different degrees of acoustic absorption. For example, a 'live' room measuring $7.5 \times 4.5 \times 2.5$m ($25 \times 15 \times 8$ft), that is 84m³ (3,000cu ft) would need about a 15-watt amplifier with average efficiency loudspeakers and a relatively 'dead' room would need 36 watts.

Valves or transistors

Over the past twenty years, the old thermionic valves (or 'tubes' as they are called in America) have been almost completely replaced by semiconductor devices such as transistors and integrated circuits. The immediate advantages have been much reduced size and weight, lower voltages required, much less heat generated, greater reliability and reduced costs—in terms of the price-per-watt of amplifier power. Thus a 50-watts-per-channel transistor amplifier can be much smaller and lighter than its valve equivalent. It can also have a much smaller power supply and run cool enough to avoid all the problems of extra ventilation needed with valve designs.

Despite all these advantages, it has to be admitted that the particular forms of distortion to which transistor amplifiers are prone, when operating away from their optimum signal levels, are more disagreeable to sensitive ears than valve distortion. Early transistor amplifier designs left much to be desired in this respect and so 'transistor sound' got a bad name. Nowadays these problems can be said to have been completely solved and the best transistor amplifiers produce exemplary sound quality provided they are properly operated.

Nevertheless, a vogue for valve amplifiers has returned in some audiophile circles and a few manufacturers have built very good valve systems to satisfy this rather élitist demand (Plate 27). Transistor designers have fought back, however, with a variety of exotic circuit configurations capable of reducing all known forms of distortion to inaudible levels. The valves-versus-transistors war therefore continues, with each side having its enthusiastic adherents.

20 (*above left*) Exploded view of a typical cassette, showing the front pressure pad, loaded tape hubs and the spacer sheets which assist smooth spooling (*Photo Philips*) and 21 (*above right*) The microcassette system is being promoted as an even smaller successor to the compact cassette, with add-on tuners, etc (Pearlcorder SD3)

22 A typical open-reel tape deck capable of taking the larger 26cm tape spools (Revox PR99)

23   A sophisticated radio receiver with digital frequency display and microcomputer-controlled tuning (Revox B780)

24   The front panel of a straightforward amplifier with push-button source selection and rotary knobs for filter, bass, treble, balance and volume (Rogers A100)

25   The back panel of the amplifier in Plate 24, showing push/hold loudspeaker terminals and phono-sockets for source inputs (Rogers A100)

11
Loudspeakers and Headphones

With the loudspeaker, the process of capturing, storing and transmitting sounds in electrical form comes full circle. The loudspeaker takes in an electrical current having frequencies and level changes proportionate to the original soundwaves, and reconverts the signals so as to radiate a new set of sound waves. Given an ideal chain of events, the new waves will reproduce at the listener's ears exactly the sequences of air pressure changes which he would have experienced if he had been present at the original performance. In practice, the chain is by no means perfect, and yet the recurring miracle is that this seemingly impossible task is carried out well enough to give a very plausible re-creation of a musical performance.

At the heart of any loudspeaker is one or more transducers, that is, devices capable of converting electrical energy first into mechanical vibration and then into soundwaves (see Plate 28). The vast majority of loudspeakers use the electromagnetic principle—already found in our descriptions of microphones,

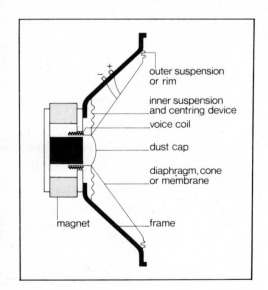

Fig. 11.1 Construction of a typical moving-coil loudspeaker drive unit

outer suspension or rim

inner suspension and centring device

voice coil

dust cap

diaphragm, cone or membrane

magnet

frame

gramophone pickups and tape heads. Figure 11.1 shows a typical moving-coil loudspeaker drive unit. The alternating signal current is passed through the 'voice coil'. Interaction between the alternating magnetic field thus created and the fixed field of the powerful permanent magnet produces a force driving the coil into to and fro vibration. Since the coil motion by itself would not set much air into vibration, the coil is cemented at the centre of a diaphragm or cone of some light but stiff material. For best results, the diaphragm motion should be piston-like, with its entire surface moving forwards and backwards in synchronism. However, it takes a finite time for the coil motion to travel outwards through the cone material so that some phase shifts take place. Also it is necessary to support the diaphragm rim in a ring or 'surround' of suitably flexible material and waves are reflected back through the cone causing further unwanted phase discrepancies.

Multi-unit loudspeakers

These difficulties can be diminished to some extent if the drive unit is asked to handle only part of the total frequency spectrum, say three or four octaves instead of the whole 20–20,000Hz audible range. This has led to the popularity of multi-unit loudspeakers in which two, three or even four drive units each handle just that part of the frequency range for which they are specially designed.

In a fairly basic two-way loudspeaker, for example, the bass unit or 'woofer' might be designed to operate best from the lowest frequencies up to, say, 3,000Hz. Thus it would be given a fairly large diaphragm to set a sizeable volume of air in motion and the coil and surround would be designed to allow the large amplitude swings needed at low frequencies. A smaller unit or 'tweeter' would take care of frequencies from 3,000Hz upwards, its principal features being extreme lightness of the moving system and an ability to respond to rapid changes in signal value.

In more elaborate designs, the middle frequencies might be given to a third driver, called a mid-range unit or 'squawker', and a fourth 'sub-woofer' unit might be added to reproduce only the very lowest frequencies. Pretty obviously these multi-way loudspeaker systems work best when each unit is carefully designed for its particular task. It also becomes desirable to divide the incoming signal into the appropriate frequency bands and send each unit its own band of frequencies only.

This is the job of the crossover network (Fig. 11.2), which makes use of the frequency discriminating properties of capacitors (condensers) and inductors (coils). A capacitor has an increasing impedance to alternating current at lower frequencies, while an inductor has the opposite effect with an impedance which increases at high frequencies. The designer can select the frequency at which he wants his crossover network to divide the incoming signal by choosing appropriate capacitor and inductor values. He can also decide in advance how rapidly he wants the circuit to attenuate the signal beyond the crossover frequency. A single capacitor/inductor arrangement produces a gentle slope of 6dB/octave. In cases where it is desirable to remove the unwanted frequencies more steeply from the drive units which are not designed to handle them he can use a more complex network and achieve 12 or 18db/octave slopes.

On occasion, a designer may be using units which are of different sensitivities. It is, however, a simple matter for him to add resistors to the crossover network to trim the sensitivity of the more efficient units and so achieve the balance he wants. In the same way, some loudspeakers have variable attenuators in the circuit to allow the user to vary the relative level of sounds from the tweeter or mid-range or both. This can sometimes be a more satisfactory method of balancing the loudspeaker reproduction in an over-damped or over-lively room, than resorting to adjustments of the amplifier tone controls.

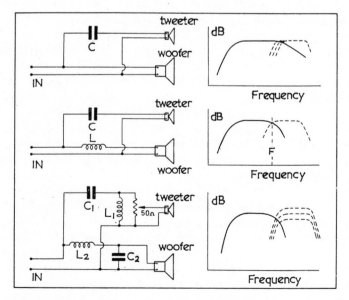

Fig. 11.2 Two-way loudspeaker crossover networks: (a) simple capacitor to keep low frequencies out of the tweeter; (b) LC network for 6dB per octave slopes; (c) more complex 12dB network with tweeter attenuator

Directivity

As well as simplifying the task of obtaining satifactory low-distortion performance over the full frequency spectrum, multi-way loudspeakers have an advantage in terms of directivity. Any vibrating diaphragm has the property of being omnidirectional (radiating equally in all directions) when its diameter is smaller than the sound wavelength. For example, a 30cm (12in) driver would be omnidirectional for all frequencies below about 120Hz. But at higher frequencies, as the wavelength becomes progressively smaller, the drive unit will become increasingly directional and beam the sounds along a more concentrated path along its forward axis. This effect is not too serious from the listener's point of view provided that the beam width does not become so narrow that the listening position for acceptable high frequency audibility becomes very restricted. The term 'listening window' has been coined to specify the minimum beam width within which an acceptable level of high frequencies will be heard. In general a listening window which gives a substantially flat response up to, say, 10kHz within a $\pm 20°$ arc in the more important horizontal plane, and $\pm 5°$ in the vertical plane is thought satisfactory.

This would be almost impossible to achieve with a single-driver loudspeaker of normal dimensions, but is quite practicable in a multi-way system since the diameters of the mid-range unit and tweeter are scaled down in such a way as to extend their radiation beam-width in proportion to the decreasing wavelength band which they are designed to handle.

Of course this use of two or more drive units must always involve compromise, and it brings several disadvantages in its train. First, the fact that different bands of frequencies are radiated from different positions on the loudspeaker front panel cannot make for ideal listening. It will certainly reduce the precision with which stereo signals can be perceived in their intended left/right spread. It helps if the designer groups the drivers as close together as possible, and if he arranges their centres in a vertical line when viewed from the front. This at least maintains directional integrity in the all-important horizontal plane, though there remain differences in direction-ality in the vertical plane, and problems of interference between the waves from the various units. Fortunately these become less serious at greater distances, and are not normally a distraction for listeners at, say, 3m or more from the loudspeakers.

Another alignment problem arises, looking at the loudspeaker from the side, in that the effective source-points of the drive units are at unequal distances from the listener's ears. We may take the voice coil to be the point of origin in each driver, and it becomes clear that simply bolting a woofer, mid-range unit and tweeter to a baffleboard will place the voice coil of the larger units much further from the listener than that of the smaller units. A time-of-arrival or 'phase' error has therefore been introduced for a typical listening position, which will upset the integrity of the relationships between the various frequencies present in any complex musical signal. Expert opinions vary as to the audibility of such phase errors, but several loudspeakers have been marketed claiming to offer 'linear phase' radiation. Their solution is to step back the smaller drivers so as to line up the voice coils either in the vertical plane or in some slightly angled plane aimed at a stated listener position.

Many of the directivity and phase troubles of multi-way loudspeakers become easier of solution if the drivers are mounted concentrically. However, most earlier attempts at building high frequency units on the centre axis of the woofer have been discontinued. The Tannoy 'dual concentric' design remains popular, however (Plate 29). This has twin radiators, with separate voice coils fed from a crossover network. The high frequency unit is at the back and radiates into an expanding horn cut through the centre of the main magnet assembly. The horn flare is continued by the bass driver cone itself and so all frequencies share a single point of origin.

Loudspeaker enclosures

If a cone-diaphragm loudspeaker unit were simply suspended in free air, it would be a very inefficient radiator of sounds. The trouble is that it actually behaves as a double radiator. While the front surface of the cone is alternately pushing forward and pulling back on the air immediately in front of it, thus sending out a train of sound waves, the back surface is doing precisely the same thing in the opposite direction. So there are two sets of waves instead of one. Notice also that the two waves are completely out of step with each other (we say they are in antiphase). A compression of the air at the front of the cone coincides with a rarefaction at the back, and vice versa. More especially at low frequencies, where as we have seen the radiation from any diaphragm tends to be more or less equal in all directions, a listener will receive both waves. Since they started out in antiphase, they tend to cancel each other out and produce only feeble sound levels.

One answer would be to mount the drive unit on a large board or baffle. This would reduce the interference between the two waves by increasing the system's directivity. Below some frequency, however, where the dimensions of the baffle approximate to the wavelength, the waves continue to be able to bend round the baffle and travel out omnidirectionally. A baffle measuring 1m across (about the largest size that most people would regard as feasible in an ordinary living-room) would work quite well down to, say, 200Hz, but cancellation effects would impair results at lower frequencies.

Building the loudspeaker into the wall between two rooms would seem to present an ideal, if not entirely practicable, solution. The front and back waves would be kept apart, except that the very lowest frequencies might be able to find their way round via doors and windows. Indeed the rooms on both sides of the wall would be well served, though strictly speaking receiving sounds in antiphase.

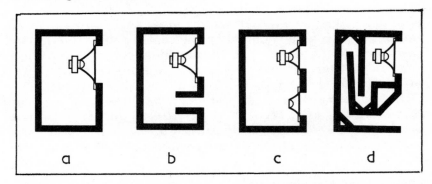

Fig. 11.3 Types of enclosure: (a) infinite baffle; (b) bass reflex; (c) reflex with passive auxiliary bass unit; (d) transmission line or labyrinth

This idea of developing an infinitely large baffle has been adapted in practical form to produce the 'closed box' type of loudspeaker enclosure (Fig. 11.3a). Here the back radiation is directed into a sealed cabinet which is lined with absorbent material. Only the front radiation is therefore put to use, while the back wave is effectively prevented from reaching the listener. Unfortunately this is not the end of the matter and indeed the designer must work quite hard to minimise the unwanted side effects. As we have said, the box is lined with absorbent material, and indeed some designers fill the whole interior with natural fibre materials or bonded acetate fibre (BAF). This tackles three problems: the need to mop up the back-wave energy, the need to reduce resonant standing waves between the parallel sides of the box, and the need to damp the

unavoidable resonance peak at a natural frequency compounded of the moving mass, the compliance of the cone
suspension and the compliance or 'spring' of the enclosed air.

The closed box is now the most popular type of loudspeaker
enclosure, despite these drawbacks, and is variously described
as 'infinite baffle' or 'acoustic suspension'. The latter description indicates that, provided the designer gets his sums
right, and includes the effect of the air in his calculations, the
complete system is capable of very satisfactory balance. In
general a moderately heavy cone has to be used, to lower the
resonance frequency which is considerably raised by the effect
of the air, and the drive unit construction has to allow for
unusually large coil excursions to produce the necessary
output at bass frequencies. The damping necessary to smooth
out resonance peaks inevitably makes this type of loudspeaker
relatively inefficient. Efficiency in this context is the ratio of
acoustical watts produced to electrical watts required from the
amplifier, and typical values for infinite baffle systems are only
about 0.5%. However, the emergence of transistor amplifiers
has made electrical watts fairly easy and inexpensive to
produce, so that inefficient closed box loudspeakers—often of
very small dimensions—and a good sized amplifier may
combine to give very satisfactory results.

To increase efficiency, some enclosures are designed to put
the back radiation to use rather than suppress it. The 'bass
reflex' enclosure, for example, (Fig. 11.3b) has a porthole (with
or without an associated tunnel or tube) whose dimensions are
carefully calculated, along with the volume of the enclosed air,
to 'tune' to the main resonance frequency of the drive unit.
When this is done properly, the mass of air in the port actually
moves back and forward in step with the cone at low
frequencies. It is as if the back radiation had been turned round
and reversed in phase, so that it now reinforces the front wave
instead of cancelling it. Greater efficiency and enhanced bass
output are the most obvious benefits, but there is also an
improvement in power handling capacity and reduced
distortion.

Bass reflex loudspeakers need to be quite large if they are to
handle really low frequencies, and various additional tricks
are often introduced. For example, the resonance peaks can be
controlled by introducing acoustic resistance (air friction) in
the port. This can consist of wool padding or even a bundle of
drinking straws!

A variation on the reflex principle is the auxiliary bass
radiator (ABR). This consists of a passive, non-driven unit
which takes the place of the open port (Fig. 11.3c). Once again

the idea is to construct a tuned double-resonant system, only now the ABR cone takes up the reinforcing vibration instead of the mass of air in the port. The designer can select values of ABR mass and compliance to ensure that the main driver is helped by the passive system at just the right frequency for smoother bass response extension. ABR loudspeakers can be smaller than the traditional bass reflex types.

A more complicated type of enclosure, which must be quite large in size, is the 'transmission line'. The idea here is that the back radiation from the main cone is made to travel down a pipe containing absorbent material so that it is sufficiently delayed to make it emerge at the end of the 'line' in phase with the front wave (Fig. 11.3d). In theory such a line should be a quarter of a wavelength long at the bass resonance frequency. This would mean a 2.8m pipe for a loudspeaker going down to 30Hz, for example. This shows why transmission line enclosures need to be large, even when the required length is achieved by folding the pipe back on itself once or twice. The bends in the pipe naturally set up unwanted resonances at higher frequencies which need careful damping and tapering of the pipe to keep under control. Not surprisingly, this type of enclosure is sometimes called a 'labyrinth'.

Where space is available, a form of enclosure design known as 'horn loading' can be used. This directs the back radiation, or sometimes that from the front, into a flared horn. The main result is an astonishing increase in efficiency up to around 50%, rather like the effect of speaking into a megaphone. The response to transients is improved and distortion very much reduced, since only small diaphragm excursions are needed. Once again, the dimensions are critical. The horn length needs to be up to perhaps 5m, with a progressive opening out of the cross-sectional area to a final opening of several metres square. Also the 'cut-off' frequency, below which very little radiation takes place, is very sharply delineated and needs to be chosen with care. Nevertheless a few excellent full-range horn-loaded loudspeakers have appeared on the market, sometimes designed for corner-mounting so that the boundaries of the room act as the final extensions of the horn.

Horn-loaded tweeters are in fact quite common. Since only short wavelengths are involved, the horn can be quite small and is mounted in front of the tweeter diaphragm to give high efficiency along with controlled directivity. And giant versions are the standard installation in cinemas and arenas, and at large pop concerts.

Other types of loudspeaker

While the moving-coil driver is by far the most common type, others do exist. The 'ribbon' loudspeaker, for example, uses the electromagnetic principle but combines the functions of coil and diaphragm in a thin strip of metal foil. This is suspended between specially shaped magnet pole-pieces and is invariably horn-loaded to increase efficiency. Even more unusual is the 'ionic' loudspeaker which has no moving parts. It consists of a quartz crystal cell in which is a small volume of air kept in an ionised state (comprising positive and negative charged particles) by the application of a voltage at supersonic frequency. When the audio signal is modulated on to the high frequency voltage, the ionised air contracts and expands, so radiating sound waves. Like the ribbon, the ionic loudspeaker is usually horn-loaded and restricted to use at high frequencies, with normal moving-coil drivers covering the rest of the spectrum.

The electrostatic loudspeaker

One unusual type of loudspeaker which is more often used for high frequencies only, but deserves special mention because it has been employed very successfully as a full-range system, is the electrostatic.

This makes use of the attraction and repulsion forces which exist between electrically charged bodies according to whether they have opposite or identical polarities. Thus if two metal plates were lined up close to each other, they could be given a high charge by the application of a DC voltage. Then, if one of the plates was fixed while the other was a thin diaphragm, it would be possible to superimpose an alternating voltage on the DC and set the diaphragm into to and fro motion. In practice, the drawbacks of this 'unbalanced' simple system are overcome by using a balanced structure (Fig. 11.4). Two fixed plates are used, suitably perforated to allow sound waves to pass through, and the thin diaphragm is suspended between them. With the DC polarising voltage applied equally to the outer plates, with respect to the central diaphragm, the 'at rest' position of the latter is dead centre. Then the alternating signal voltage is applied in a push-pull manner, with the swings in voltage first attracting the diaphragm towards one plate and then the other.

Unlike the moving-coil loudspeaker, where the driving force occurs only at the centre of the cone where the coil is situated, the diaphragm of an electrostatic loudspeaker is simulta-

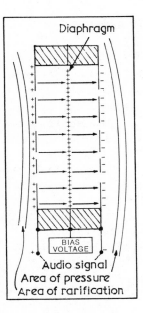

Diaphragm

BIAS
VOLTAGE

Audio signal
Area of pressure
Area of rarification

Fig. 11.4 In an electrostatic loudspeaker, the diaphragm is suspended between two fixed perforated plates and alternately attracted towards one or the other

neously driven over its whole surface area. This gives a better approximation to the ideal piston motion. Also the diaphragm can be extremely light and responsive to very sharp transients.

The best known electrostatic loudspeaker is the Quad model first produced by the Acoustical Manufacturing Company in 1957 and still going strong. It is a 'constant charge' device, the high DC voltage (6,000V) being applied via a large resistance to keep the charge unchanged during operation. A built-in transformer produces the required push-pull drive of signal to the plates and also presents a nominal 8-ohms impedance for matching to conventional audio amplifiers. In fact, the diaphragm is divided into vertical strips handling different frequency bands, high frequencies over the 15cm-wide centre area and low frequencies in 36cm strips on either side. There is no box or cabinet, only a metal-mesh protective grille with an internal plastic film to keep out dust.

The absence of a cabinet immediately avoids the problems of cabinet resonances, the downfall of so many conventional loudspeakers. It also gives this loudspeaker unique directional properties. Theoretically the system behaves like a 'doublet', that is, its radiation pattern is figure-of-eight with the strongest radiation equally on the front and back axes, and very little radiation to the sides. In practice, the precise figure-of-eight pattern is not achieved equally at all frequencies. At bass frequencies, for instance, the ability of the waves to bend round obstacles and spread outwards can lead to cancellations. Also the loudspeaker must be placed at some distance from the walls of the room, at least 1m, or reflections and standing waves will degrade the performance. There is also the usual tendency for highest frequencies to be beamed within a rather narrow 'listening window', though careful design and slight curvature of the construction are aimed at spreading the beam to some extent.

In 1981 a new Quad electrostatic loudspeaker was launched, the ESL-63, having further novel features. The single thin diaphragm is suspended between electrode plates arranged in concentric rings. By feeding the outer rings through pro-gressively longer delay circuits, the designer has been able to drive the diaphragm as if from a point source situated at some 30cm behind it. This lends a special kind of phase coherence to the sound which would be difficult to obtain with a con-ventional moving-coil system.

Electrostatic loudspeakers are not without their shortcom-ings, however. With such a high DC voltage on the plates, excessive diaphragm amplitudes could cause noisy, and possibly damaging, electrical arching. Steps have therefore to be taken to limit signal levels, particularly at low frequencies, and so this loudspeaker is not suitable for situations requiring high power operation. The special directivity pattern too, though actually beneficial in that it triggers off fewer room resonances than the conventional type, makes room positioning—and the listener's position—a matter of fairly critical adjustment for best results.

Loudspeaker connections

The signal input points on a loudspeaker resemble those used for the 'loudspeaker outlets' on an amplifier. That is, they may consist of a pair of screw terminals, spring-loaded terminals, 4mm 'banana'-plug sockets or the DIN two-pin socket (Fig. 11.5). Quite obviously for stereo it is important to connect the left and right amplifier outlets to the left and right loud-speakers respectively, otherwise the layout of orchestras, etc will be reversed right to left. It is also important to connect the two wires to each loudspeaker in the same polarity or phase. With the DIN two-pin plugs this matter is taken care of automatically, with the positive or plus wire always soldered to the round pin and the negative to the flat one. When pairs of terminals or sockets are used, however, care is necessary to get the wires the right way round. Look for a colour coding, red and black for positive and negative, or perhaps + and − signs. Then check that the twin flex used, which should also have the two wires colour coded for easy identification, is taken from the amplifier to the loudspeaker with the polarity unchanged.

A final warning relates to the need to ensure a really good metal-to-metal contact at each terminal, while avoiding any risk of a short circuit due to strands of wire from one terminal touching the other. Any increase in resistance to signal currents due to a loose or dirty contact would be wasteful and seriously degrade the performance. A short circuit would endanger the amplifier, causing the fuses to blow or worse. In the same way, higher signal levels than the loudspeaker is designed to handle could endanger the drive units. Therefore many loudspeakers now incorporate a protective fuse (see Fig. 11.5) or more complex peak detection and protection circuitry.

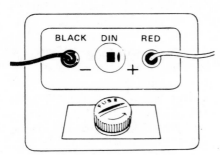

Fig. 11.5 Loudspeaker connections may use a two-pin DIN socket or colour-coded 'banana' plugs as shown. A protective fuse is sometimes fitted

The cable used, twin cable of course because a complete electrical circuit is needed with the current flowing out from the amplifier along one 'leg' and back along the other, should have negligible resistance. This means the conducting wires should be thick rather than thin (thicker conductors offer less resistance) and no longer than necessary (each metre of length adds a little more resistance). The flex described as 14/.0076in, or 5-amp lighting flex, has a resistance of about 0.04 ohms per metre and is perfectly satisfactory for runs of up to about 10m. For longer runs, thicker cable would be better (see suggestions in Table 11.1). Various exotic loudspeaker cables have appeared on the hi-fi market offering phenomenally low resistance. The best of these can sometimes add extra

Table 11.1 Loudspeaker cables

Area (sq mm)	Europe Wire type Spec.	Max length (metres)	AWG	USA Zip cord Max length (feet)
2.50	50/0.25mm	25	10	160
1.50	30/0.25mm	15	12	100
1.25	40/0.20mm	12	14	65
1.00	32/0.20mm	10	16	40
0.75	24/0.20mm	7	18	25

definition to an already top-class system, but their high price makes them not worth considering in the normal domestic situation. Also some 'special' cables have increased capacitance which can upset certain types of amplifier.

Loudspeaker impedance

All loudspeaker specifications quote a nominal input impedance. The most common value is 8 ohms, with 4 and 6 ohms occurring occasionally. In fact, the impedance of a loudspeaker is not purely resistive and so it varies quite considerably with frequency, rising to a peak of 30 ohms or more at the main bass resonant frequency. The quoted nominal value indicates the impedance measured at the first dip following this peak and is a useful yardstick when matching amplifiers and loudspeakers. Amplifiers too are generally designed with a certain loudspeaker load impedance in mind, with 8 ohms again being the most common value in use. The thing to watch here is that the speaker load should not fall too far below the amplifier rating. Thus, connecting a 4-ohms loudspeaker to an 8-ohms amplifier is less good than connecting an 8-ohms speaker to a 4-ohms amplifier but will just about work satisfactorily. Any lower load value, however, could draw too much current from the amplifier and cause distortion or overheating.

A particular case where care needs to be exercised is when extra loudspeakers are connected in parallel—perhaps to run extension speakers in another room. The rule is that the effective impedance of two similar speakers in parallel falls to about half the value of one on its own. Thus two 8-ohm speakers in parallel would 'look' like 4 ohms to the amplifier and work reasonably well, but two 4-ohm speakers would present only 2 ohms effectively and probably be unsafe.

Why headphones?

The idea of using high quality headphones as an alternative to loudspeakers in a stereo system can be said to have originated about twenty years ago. Before then, let it be admitted, the quality of sound from headphones was no better than you would expect from a product designed entirely for telephony, military communications or 'ham' radio listening. However, when the designs began to be tackled seriously as a method of monitoring the full frequency and volume range of high fidelity records, tapes and broadcasts, it was found that headphones were by no means just the poor relation of loudspeakers. Not only could headphones equal the best and most expensive loudspeakers in quality of sound reproduction, they offered real advantages over the traditional loudspeaker/room listening situation. Let us look at some of the more obvious advantages.

Advantages of headphones

(a) *Room acoustics are irrelevant* Headphones, while producing only small amounts of sound energy, are in no way dependent on the room environment. Yet they need careful design to provide a balanced response over the whole spectrum of sound frequencies. For one thing, they must be designed to produce optimum quality when loaded with the peculiar air canals which form the typical outer human ear. However, this done, the total environment can be specified by the designer and will not vary from room to room—or even from place to place within any given room.

How different is our experience in loudspeaker listening, where we are obliged to hear not only the sounds from the speakers, but also the sounds bounced from the walls and ceiling. Every speaker designer knows that his system will sound dull in one room and over-bright in another. The total sound quality is indeed a function of the room dimensions and furnishings. It will even change if the speakers are moved around. As for the stereo effect, every hi-fi listener knows that his own position with respect to the left and right loudspeakers can drastically alter the kind of stereo he hears. With headphones, the listening environment is predictable and stable.

(b) *Ambient noise is irrelevant* Measurements of the ambient noise level in even quiet suburban homes show that the music from our radios or hi-fi speakers has to compete with a continuous background at some 40dB above the threshold of hearing. This sets a very real limit to our ability to enjoy the quiet passages in music. Also, the subconscious effort we make to ignore background distractions can lead to listening fatigue.

Headphones make it a great deal easier, and therefore less fatiguing, to concentrate on the music. All designs, even the so-called 'open-air' headphones, shut out extraneous sounds to some extent. Other types are specially designed to isolate the listener very effectively from noise and interference. Personal listening at this level of isolation can be a uniquely rewarding experience, even surpassing real life concert going.

(c) *High powers are irrelevant* Because the sounds we want

to hear are radiated from points so near to our eardrums, headphones require only a fraction of the amplifier power needed for proper operation of loudspeakers. With only a modest stereo amplifier, we are free to choose any listening volume we like—including one that would prove antisocial if we sought to achieve it with loudspeakers. At last it is possible to turn up the volume on our favourite rock groups or opera choruses without reference to the rest of the household or neighbours. The decision is ours, without compromise, at any time of the day or night.

(d) *Distortion is at a new low*   As a spin-off benefit from the high efficiency bestowed by the close proximity of the headphone diaphragm to our ears, distortion can be kept to phenomenally low amounts. As a rule, we can relate the harshness that comes from waveform distortions in sound reproduction directly to high amplitudes. The low power levels we demand of the amplifier mean that a virtually distortion-free signal can be presented to the headphones.

At the same time, the amplitudes of headphone diaphragm movement are tiny by comparison with speaker cone travel. Also the smallness of the moving parts in a headphone make for extreme lightness which will enable the diaphragms more accurately to follow even the steepest wavefronts of transient sounds like the pianoforte and percussion.

(e) *Frequency coverage is high*   Designing a loudspeaker for smooth coverage of the full frequency range of human hearing is fraught with difficulties. It is a plain fact of life, as we have seen, that loudspeakers will generally focus high-frequency sounds along a specific axis, while radiating bass frequencies equally in all directions. The balance of frequencies is therefore annoyingly dependent on the listener's position in relation to the speaker axis.

In modern headphone designs, wide frequency coverage is achieved and the balance of bass, middle and treble is not subject to directivity vagaries.

Types of headphone

The largest group of headphones employs the basic moving-coil (dynamic) principle already referred to in connection with loudspeakers on page 137. This relies on a relatively heavy copper coil attached to one side of the diaphragm, which is in effect a miniature loudspeaker cone. The coil is suspended in the field of a powerful permanent magnet, the field being concentrated in an annular gap which closely accommodates the coil.

A feature of the enclosed-ears, pressure-type dynamic headphone is that the voice-coil of the diaphragm is totally enclosed by the earpiece cup. Thus the diaphragm vibrations, caused by the pulsating forces set up as the alternating signal current flows through the coil, produce pressure soundwaves which travel into the auditory canals of the listener's ears.

This form of loading on the diaphragm can be designed to give a flat bass response down to the lowest audible frequencies—provided the ear cavity is very effectively sealed. Some of the top headphones in this category possess fluid-filled cushions which promote a nearly perfect seal around the ear. The bass response is then limited only by the specifications of the supporting equipment. Clearly it is a feature of such totally enclosed and sealed headphones that sound can neither escape from the headset itself, and be disturbing to other people near the wearer, nor enter the headset from outside. This group of headphones is therefore a first choice where good isolation is a prerequisite. Ambient noise attenuation is about 40dB.

Also high in user popularity is a type of headphone which is not totally enclosed (Plate 30). This is termed the velocity type and, while still employing the dynamic principle, is effectively open to the atmosphere. The diaphragm sets two trains of waves into motion, one directed inwards towards the listener's ear and the other outwards through vents in the earpiece cup. As a result, the listener is not so completely cut off from his surroundings as with the sealed pressure-dynamic types. He can hear the telephone or front doorbell ring, for example. The cancellations between the front and rear wave-trains, which can be a limiting factor when the velocity principle is applied to loudspeakers, is unimportant here. The distances involved are so tiny that there is insufficient time for the back sound waves to interfere with the front waves. New ceramic magnets give high magnetism with small size and weight, and have led to new designs of headphone with crisp and clear performance in extremely small dimensions.

At the high end of the headphone market are a few models which employ an entirely different driver principle. These *electrostatic* types rely on the motion of a thin plate (the diaphragm) when this is built to form one plate of a condenser or capacitor, as in the electrostatic loudspeaker. The driving force depends on the presence of a DC 'standing charge' being applied between the diaphragm and the two fixed plates. Normally this DC voltage is developed within a small rectifier unit connected to the AC mains supply. Some designs derive the necessary polarising voltage by rectifying part of the AC music itself. This 'self-energising' technique, introduced by

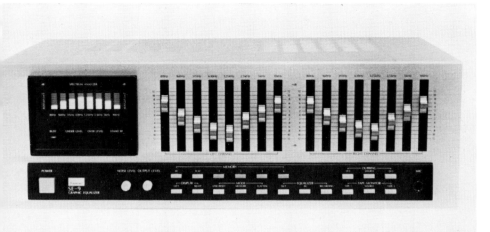

26 A stereo graphic equaliser with eight sliding faders in each channel to give independent control of each octave band (Sansui SE-9)

27 A modern valve amplifier using thermionic valves of the type originally popular twenty years earlier (STD D2000)

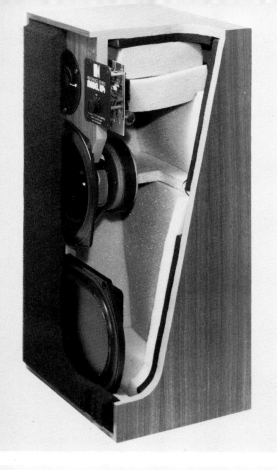

28 Cut-away model of a three-way loudspeaker showing the tweeter, squawker (mid-range) and woofer drive units and the internal acoustic padding (KEF Model 104)

29 (*below left*) A type of integrated two-way loudspeaker drive unit with the tweeter mounted at the centre of the main cone (Tannoy Dual-Concentric) and 30 (*below right*) Headphone listening allows a free choice of programme and loudness in any situation (*Photo AKG*)

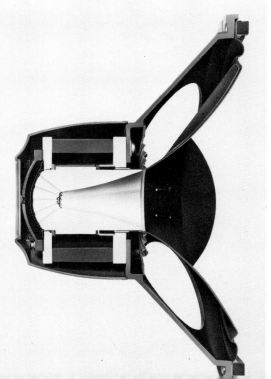

Koss, is helpful in circumstances where connection to the AC mains is difficult or undesirable. It is fair to point out, however, that a moderately high music signal level must be maintained when utilising the self-energising mode, to ensure adequate DC availability. Electrostatic headphones are characterised by a special clarity, wide frequency response and excellent transient performance.

Headphone connections

The phenomenal upsurge in the popularity of headphone listening over recent years has not gone unobserved by the manufacturers of hi-fi amplifiers, receivers and tape recorders. Accordingly it has become standard practice to fit one or more headphone jack-sockets, generally on the front of the unit. Fortunately, also, there has been a welcome degree of standardisation in the type of socket to be employed and the voltage level and matching impedance necessary for best results.

The stereo jack-plug

Most systems have standardised on the tip-ring-sleeve stereo jack-plug shown in Fig. 10.1 (page 127). The sleeve connects to the common earth (ground) point at which potential the equipment chassis and cable screen braiding will be held, so minimising hum pick-up. The left and right 'live' signal wires are connected to the jack-plug tip and ring respectively. It should be noted that amplifiers may be met occasionally with the socket left and right connections reversed. Also there are a very few amplifiers (generally models which possess a phase reversal switch for one channel) which are not designed to work with common-earth headphones. In such rare cases, it will be as well to consult a qualified hi-fi dealer.

Headphones are made in about three impedance ranges: low = 1–100 ohms, medium = 100–1,000 ohms and high = 10,000–30,000 ohms. It is worth noting the impedance of headphones when purchasing because of the question of *impedance matching*. Maximum transfer of energy (efficiency) occurs when a unit in a sound reproducing chain has the same internal impedance as that at the input of the next link in the chain. This is of great importance in the case of loudspeakers, for example, where we need to conserve energy and the popular amplifier output impedance of 4 or 8 ohms works best with 4- or 8-ohms speakers.

Impedance matching is less critical with headphones, since most amplifiers in hi-fi systems will have ample power in hand.

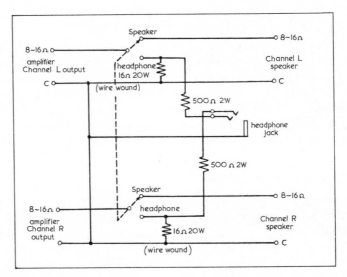

Fig. 11.6 Typical circuit for switching between stereo loudspeakers and a jack-socket for headphones

However, a serious mismatch should be avoided since, apart from a loss in efficiency, there is a chance of tonal quality being adversely affected at the same time.

Most headphones will produce ample sound volume from the standard headphone sockets on audio equipment, which usually tap off the amplifier speaker outlets through series resistors. A switch is usually fitted to silence the loudspeakers during headphone listening, or this will often consist of an automatic cut-out switch which operates as the headphone jack-plug is inserted in the socket.

In the unlikely case of an audio unit which boasts no headphone socket, a circuit as shown in Fig. 11.6 can be assembled easily enough by anyone handy with a soldering iron.

The new DIN plug

On the continent of Europe, there has been a move towards employing a new type of headphone plug and socket. This has appeared in a German DIN (Deutscher Industrie Nor- menausschuss) standard and has five pins arranged as shown in Fig. 10.1 (page 127). Pins one, two and three are connected to earth (ground) and pins four and five to the left and right signal wires respectively.

12
How to Read Specifications

In the final analysis, sound reproducing equipment must be judged by ear. Therefore, where a complete audio system is being chosen, it may be enough to follow the advice contained in Chapter 6. Fix on a price range, visit a reputable local dealer, and make your decision based on unhurried listening to your choice of music.

However, when individual units are to be chosen to supplement or upgrade an existing system, it pays to study the matching requirements. It may also be quite difficult to arrange a demonstration in which several units seemingly meeting your requirements can be coupled into a system resembling the equipment you already have. It is then that the published specifications become a sensible starting point in narrowing down your choice. When the specifications have been properly prepared, and are then correctly interpreted, they do allow the performance of the units to be reasonably predicted and compared with others.

It is a considerable nuisance that specifications are invariably expressed in technical jargon, and that a considerable amount of research would generally be needed to discover whether the performance claimed under each heading could be considered excellent, good or only fair. The following notes are intended to provide a series of quick-reference guidelines. Each audio unit is taken in turn, in the order followed in Chapters 6 to 10, and all the most common specification parameters are defined and explained. Under each heading there is a 'What to look for' guide. Studying these notes, and taking them along with you on audio shopping expeditions if necessary, should enable you to avoid gross matching errors and choose with confidence.

Turntables

1 *Nominal speeds*
Rate of platter rotation. Expressed in revolutions per minute (rpm).

What to look for   The one essential speed is 33⅓rpm. Include 45rpm if 18cm (7in) singles are to be played, or the few 30cm (12in) 45rpm audiophile discs issued. The old pre-LP speed of 78rpm is only rarely fitted on modern turntables. If you have a collection of 78s you will need to track down a special turntable (and a cartridge with the necessary larger stylus) to play them. A fourth speed, 16⅔rpm, is sometimes fitted but few records, mainly spoken word, were ever issued at this speed.

2 *Speed deviation*
Maximum error in speed. Expressed as a percentage drift from the nominal speed, caused by AC mains voltage variations in the range ±10%.
What to look for   Figures less than +1.5% to −1%.

3 *Fine speed adjustment*
Sometimes called 'pitch control'. Allows user to vary the turntable speed over a small range on either side of the nominal speed. For most purposes, selecting the nominal speed is accurate enough in these days when records very rarely appear with basic speed errors, and most ears will tolerate errors up to 2%. However, where greater accuracy is needed, perhaps by a user who is blessed with absolute pitch, or someone who wants to retune a record to his piano to 'play along' with the music, speed adjustment can be useful. Expressed as a maximum percentage speed change on either side of nominal.
What to look for   A minimum overall range of one semitone in pitch, ie ±3%.

4 *Stroboscope*
Visual speed indicator. Useful only where fine speed adjustment is available. Generally takes the form of a pattern of bars on the edge or underside of the platter. Must be viewed in AC lighting to give stroboscopic effect—pattern stationary indicates correct speed, drifting forward or back indicates speed above or below nominal. Some modern turntables show actual speed in a digital display.
What to look for   Models having a built-in neon or other light source allow daylight use.

5 *Wow-and-flutter*
Cyclic fluctuations in speed caused, for example, by irregularities in pulleys or platter. Expressed as a percentage deviation around a standard measuring frequency (3kHz or 3.15kHz). Unfortunately two standards are in use. Both use a 'weighting'

filter to emphasise those frequencies to which the ear is most sensitive, and so make the quoted value correlate more closely with the annoyance value of the pitch fluctuations. In Europe the figure is 'peak weighted' (DIN), whereas in Japan a 'weighted root-mean-square' (WRMS) figure is preferred, which is smaller than the DIN figure by a factor of about four.
What to look for   Low figures. Less than 0.2% DIN or 0.05% WRMS. Some people are very much more sensitive to wow-and-flutter than others. In case you are in this category, ask for a special demonstration of critical records—piano, organ and woodwind sustained notes are particularly revealing.

6 *Rumble*

Low frequency noise introduced by motor vibrations and motor and platter bearings. It can be emphasised by resonances in the pickup arm and the motor-board suspension. It can also be suppressed to some extent by a falling bass response in the pickup, amplifier or loudspeakers—only to reveal itself if one of these components is upgraded. Paradoxically, therefore, rumble does not often trouble the owner of a modest system with small loudspeakers, even though his inexpensive turntable may generate large amounts of rumble. In a better quality system, by contrast, a turntable with a low level of inherent rumble is mandatory, and it must be mounted carefully to keep rumble to a minimum. Expressed as a decibel level with reference to a standard recorded velocity. Again, unfortunately, two or more standards are in use. Most commonly met are the IEC 'weighted' and 'unweighted' figures related to a tone at 315Hz recorded at 3.83cm/s.
What to look for   Figures greater than 55dB (weighted) or 35dB (unweighted).

7 *Auto operation*

A fully automatic turntable will give auto-start, auto-stop, cueing and repeat cycles at the touch of a switch. Thus in normal playing of a complete record side, the switch will start the motor, move the pickup over to the record and lower it into the run-in groove; when the stylus reaches the run-out groove at the end of the record, the pickup is automatically raised and moved back to its rest and the motor is switched off. A semi-automatic deck provides only some of these functions: you may need to move the pickup over to the record by hand (this motion automatically switching on the motor) and the auto-stop may only switch off the motor, again requiring the pickup to be returned to its rest by hand. A manual turntable has no automatic functions.

What to look for   Insist on a demonstration of the automatic functions. The better models use an optical system to trigger the auto-stop cycle, rather than a mechanical detector which may place unwanted side-pressure on the pickup arm during the last minutes of the music. It is also best if an electronic mute circuit cuts off the pickup signal during lowering and raising operations, to eliminate stylus plops and other mechanical noises. Note that autochangers which could play a stack of records in sequence have gone completely out of fashion, mainly because record surfaces could be damaged by rubbing against each other.

Pickup arms

1 *Height*
Minimum clearance needed between the motorboard top/arm pedestal base junction and the turntable lid or dust-cover.
What to look for   Check that the range of height adjustment is adequate if you are likely to fit cartridges of widely varying heights or employ a particularly high turntable. Also check clearance needed below motorboard inside plinth or cabinet.

2 *Overall length*
Distance from front edge of headshell to rear of counter-balance support rod.
What to look for   Check clearance available between rear of arm and walls of cabinet or plinth.

3 *Effective length*
Distance from stylus tip to centre of pivot. This is the most important dimension so far as stylus/groove geometry is concerned. It determines the radius of the circular arc over which the stylus tracks on its journey from the outside to the inside of a record. Unfortunately there is no standardisation amongst cartridge manufacturers of the distance between the stylus and the cartridge fixing holes. So some juggling of the precise arm pivot position, or the position of the cartridge in the headshell, may be necessary to set up the specified effective length. These adjustments are critical if tracking error distortion is to be kept to minimum, and some form of gauge or protractor will normally be supplied with the arm.
What to look for   Length at least 215mm (8.5in).

4 *Stylus overhang*
Distance by which the effective length (see Note 3) exceeds the pivot-to-spindle centre distance. This, together with the offset

angle (see Note 5) determines the tracking error (Note 6).

What to look for   The specification value should give minimum tracking error. Even so, very careful alignment will be necessary, using the arm protractor or a proprietary gauge.

5 *Offset angle*

Angle between the longitudinal axis of the stylus and the line joining pivot to stylus. It is introduced to minimise tracking error, in conjunction with the stylus overhang (Note 4).

What to look for   Again, the specification value should be correct for the given design.

6 *Tracking error*

Maximum deviation of axis of cartridge from tangent to the groove. The angular error is continually changing as the pickup tracks across the record. Proper design, and alignment of the dimensions specified in Notes 3–5, will keep the error to below 2°. In practice, the alignment protractors and gauges aim to give minimum tracking error distortion, which corresponds to a slightly different stylus overhang distance than that for minimum angular error.

What to look for   A maximum of 2°.

7 *Tracking force adjustment*

Method of setting the downward force required to keep the stylus in proper contact with the groove walls as it tracks a record. Is usually accomplished by first setting the counter-balance weight behind the arm pivot to the position which just balances the arm in seesaw fashion. Then the counterbalance weight is moved towards the pivot by an amount which will produce the stylus down-force recommended by the cartridge manufacturer. Some designs of arm employ an adjustable spring, with a fixed counterweight, and most arms incorporate calibration marks to indicate the force applied.

What to look for   A range of 0–3g will cover most modern cartridges.

8 *Sidethrust compensation*

Also called 'antiskating'. Adjustable mechanism for counter-acting the inward force acting on all pivoted pickup arms due to friction between stylus and groove. Usually calibrated to correspond to selected tracking force values in grammes, and stylus tip shapes.

What to look for   Concealed spring or weight types may look neater than the classical weight on a thread, but the latter is capable of very accurate adjustment.

9 *Capacitance*
Electrical capacitance of arm and connecting cable. Expressed in picofarads. Standard values are around 150–250pF. 'Low capacity' arm/cables are about 80pF.
What to look for   Match to cartridge requirements (see Pickup Cartridges).

Pickup cartridges

1 *Type*
Most specifications state whether the cartridge is mono or stereo, and indicate the type of transducer. The vast majority of today's cartridges are 'stereo', that is they possess twin generators producing left and right channel outputs corresponding to the twin waveforms inscribed respectively at $\pm 45°$ to the record surface in a stereophonic record. However, stereo cartridges may be used with impunity on mono records—when they will send identical (left + right) signals to both channel outputs. Again the vast majority of modern cartridges have electromagnetic transducers. The types referred to as moving-magnet, moving-iron, induced magnet, etc may be regarded as interchangeable so far as matching is concerned. Only the moving-coil needs special care since it will usually be relatively insensitive and require different load conditions (see Notes 2 and 3).
What to look for   Choose stereo rather than mono, of course, but otherwise base your decisions on sound quality judged on demonstration.

2 *Sensitivity*
The rated output voltage for a stated value of recorded velocity. Usually expressed in millivolts for 1cm per second, but sometimes other reference velocities will be used such as 5cm/s, when the figure for 1cm/s can easily be calculated.
What to look for   0.7 to 2.0mV/cm/s for all 'magnetic' cartridges; 0.01 to 0.4mV for moving-coils. (Some moving-coils have the same sensitivity and load requirements as 'magnetics'. But otherwise it will be necessary to provide a booster transformer or pre-amplifier.)

3 *Recommended load impedance*
Total values of resistance and capacitance as 'seen' by the cartridge, adding together the components contributed by the arm, connecting cable and amplifier input circuit. Most magnetic cartridges are designed to work best into 47,000 ohms (47K) resistance and between 200 and 450 picofarads

capacitance. While arm manufacturers often give a capacitance value in their specifications (see Pickup arms, Note 9) amplifier manufacturers rarely do. However, an amplifier input capacitance of 50pF can usually be assumed, and then simple addition to the arm figure will give the total load value. Where a gross mismatch occurs, proprietary load boxes can be purchased, and indeed a trend towards providing switched load values as an extra feature on hi-fi amplifiers has begun.

What to look for The standard 47K resistance value, and a moderate capacitance value of, say, 200pF on magnetic cartridges. Moving-coil cartridges are much less sensitive to loading conditions, and in any case will generally need to be matched to a booster transformer or pre-amplifier (see Note 2).

4 *Frequency response*
Range of frequency coverage within stated decibel limits. Manufacturers who specify a plain 'frequency range' figure without any qualifying reference to the number of decibels (plus or minus) within which the response is maintained are being less than helpful. It is of little use having a cartridge which gives an output up to 16,000Hz, say, if the level at that frequency has fallen to 15dB below that at 1,000Hz. As well as quoting a frequency range with dB limits, some specifications include a response graph.
What to look for 40–16,000 ±2dB would be quite good; 20–20,000 ±1dB would be excellent. The DIN standard demands a minimum standard of only 63.5–8,000Hz ±2dB, 40–12,500Hz ±5dB.

5 *Channel balance*
Difference in sensitivity of the left and right channels when playing an identical signal. Expressed in decibels for a signal at 1kHz.
What to look for 2dB or less.

6 *Channel separation*
Sometimes called 'crosstalk'. Ability to reproduce left and right channel signals without serious leakage from one to the other, which would degrade the stereo 'information' and tend to produce a narrower stereo stage. Expressed in decibels as the difference in level between a standard signal on the 'wanted' channel and that measured on the 'unwanted' channel. As well as quoting a single figure at 1,000Hz, some specifications display a graph of separation over the full frequency range.

What to look for   20dB or greater at 1kHz; at least 10dB from 7kHz upwards.

7 *Stylus type and tip dimensions*
Diamond is now used almost exclusively (except for a few cheap cartridges with sapphire styli) but diamond quality can vary, with 'nude' or 'naked' diamond styli being all-diamond and generally superior to metal-shanked types with only the tip made of diamond. Tip dimensions are expressed in microns (micrometres or μm) or thousandths of an inch ('thou'). Early conical styli, on which the tip was effectively hemispherical, had tip radii of 75μm (3 thou) for 78rpm records or 25μm (1 thou) for mono LPs. For stereo this was reduced nominally to 13μm (0.5 thou), and present standards allow 15μm $\pm$ 3μm. More complicated to manufacture, but claiming advantages in terms of reduced distortion, are two families of biradial styli. The basic elliptical stylus has a major tip radius (which sits across the groove) of 18μm (7 thou) and a minor radius (better able to trace fine waveforms) of 8μm (3 thou), though values out to 9μm $\times$ 2μm are met in practice. The more recent 'line contact' styli have an increased radius in the vertical plane to give greater wall contact and reduced wear. They are usually quoted by a proprietary name such as Shibata, Pramanic, etc.
What to look for   Choose the 13μm spherical tip for a budget system. Move up in price to an elliptical or line contact stylus only if a reasonably refined pickup arm is to be used, permitting a low tracking force.

8 *Recommended tracking force*
Sometimes called 'playing weight'. Range of down-force values which will ensure safe tracking of the groove and a correct vertical tracking angle (see Note 11) during play. Tracking force is expressed in grammes or milliNewtons to indicate that we are dealing with a force rather than just a weight. Specifications are occasionally optimistic at the lower end of the recommended range and it pays to choose a value at the centre of the range or higher for safest tracking of loud passages. Stylus and record wear are obviously related to tracking force, but the increased wear due to moving up a fraction of a gramme is insignificant. On the other hand, the groove bouncing which might occur with too low a playing weight is definitely damaging.
What to look for   Values in the range 1–2.5g, with 2g an upper limit for elliptical and line contact styli.

9 *Compliance*
Ease of deflection, or 'spring', of the stylus support; the opposite of stiffness. Expressed in millionths of a centimetre, as the distance which the stylus would be displaced by a force of 1 dyne ($\times 10^{-6}$cm/dyne)—or more recently in Europe micrometres per milliNewton (μm/mN). Higher compliance means better trackability at low frequencies but demands a low tracking force and so a well designed, low-mass pickup arm.
What to look for Dynamic compliance values in the range 10–40×10^{-6}cm/dyne. Choose medium or low values except for a very low-mass arm, guided by Fig. 7.5 in Chapter 7.

10 *Stylus tip mass*
Effective mass of the stylus moving system. Affects trackability and smoothness of response at high frequencies. Expressed in milligrammes.
What to look for Values less than 2mg.

11 *Vertical tracking angle*
Angle between the vertical plane and the actual plane of motion of the stylus tip. Approximately equals the angle between the cantilever and the record surface. Should be 20° to correspond to the angle normally adopted for the cutting stylus.
What to look for 20°.

12 *Cartridge weight*
Expressed in grammes. Not a critical parameter, though the lighter cartridges require less counterbalancing to produce a given tracking force, and so permit a lighter arm system mass overall.
What to look for Values from 4 to 10g can be accepted by most arms.

Cassette decks

1 *Nominal speed*
Rate of tape travel. Expressed in centimetres per second, or inches per second.
What to look for 4.76cm/s ($1\frac{7}{8}$ips) has been the standard speed for compact cassettes since their inception. A few decks now offer half or double speed as a switched option, ie 2.4cm/s ($\frac{15}{16}$ips) or 9.53cm/s ($3\frac{3}{4}$ips).

2 *Speed deviation*
Maximum error in speed. Expressed as a percentage drift from

the nominal speed caused by AC mains voltage variations in the range $\pm 10\%$.
What to look for   Figure less than $\pm 1.5\%$.

3 *Fine speed adjustment*
Sometimes called 'pitch control'. Fitted on only a few decks, and usually operates in playback mode only, not record.
What to look for   A minimum overall range of one semitone in pitch, ie $\pm 3\%$.

4 *Wow and flutter*
Cyclic fluctuations in speed caused by irregularities in the tape transport system. Expressed as a percentage deviation around a standard measuring frequency (3.15kHz).
What to look for   Less than 0.2% unweighted, or 0.18% DIN peak weighted.

5 *Signal-to-noise ratio*
Level of inherent noise for the record/replay cycle relative to a standard reference recording level. Expressed in decibels relative to the standard recorded flux level (250 nanoWebers per metre) normally made to correspond to zero on the deck's VU level meter.
What to look for   Figures greater than 56dB (weighted) or 35dB (unweighted).

6 *Total harmonic distortion*
Degree of generation of unwanted harmonics due to non-linearity in the record/replay cycle. Expressed as a percentage relative to the zero VU level at 333Hz.
What to look for   Figures of 3% or less.

7 *Frequency response*
Range of frequency coverage within stated decibel limits for the record/replay cycle. Usually measured at a low level, at least 20dB below zero VU, to avoid high frequency tape saturation effects.
What to look for   30–14,000Hz ± 2dB would be good for ferric tapes. Expect to do better, say out to 18,000Hz, with chrome equivalent or metal tapes.

8 *Noise reduction*
Most decks incorporate special compression/expansion circuits to reduce inherent noise, mainly tape hiss.
What to look for   The Dolby B system is a must in a high quality system, if only because the vast majority of prere-

corded musicassettes are Dolby B encoded. Other proprietary noise reduction systems, including Dolby C, have individual features which can be advantageous as alternatives to Dolby B for home recording.

9 *Channel separation*

Sometimes called 'crosstalk'. Ability to record and playback desired track(s) with minimum interference from other tracks. Expressed in decibels as the difference in level between a standard signal on the 'wanted' track and that measured on the unwanted track. Two figures should be quoted for cassette decks: *stereo separation* relating to the two tracks of a stereo pair; and *mono crosstalk* relating to breakthrough of signals recorded with the tape running in one direction on to tracks in the other direction. The latter type of interference is obviously more serious than simple left/right stereo breakthrough since it will consist of an entirely different programme signal, running backwards!

What to look for   At least 25dB stereo, 60dB mono.

10 *Tape selector switch*

Enables user to select circuit conditions to suit different basic types of cassette tape. The types and their basic characteristics are listed in Table 8.2 in Chapter 8. Three parameters need to be switched, namely equalisation, bias and recording level but in practice it would be better if the user could 'fine tune' each of these to take account of the quite wide variations used, almost without reference to each other by the tape and deck manufacturers. (Such tuning is provided on a few of the more expensive cassette decks.)

What to look for   Apart from the basic 'ferric' or 'normal' tapes, it is worth choosing a machine which can be switched to suit 'chrome' tapes. These give better high frequency performance. 'Ferrochrome' has very few advantages over chrome, but a deck which can accept 'metal' tapes—though more expensive—is worth considering if you want the ultimate in dynamic range and high frequency attack.

Cassette tapes

The optimum choice of tape for a given deck is complicated by the fact that all performance features are interlocked. Thus a departure from optimum bias can degrade high, middle or low frequency response, increase distortion, restrict the maximum output level, cause compression at high frequencies, and even highlight drop-outs by failing to magnetise the tape coating deeply enough.

Racing tipsters use the expression 'horses for courses' to describe one of the more complicated guides to form they need to take into account when working out the odds on a particular horse doing well in a particular race. They know that it is not enough to assess the form of a horse in an absolute sense. They will of course note all the basic elements—the horse's parentage, its recent form, the stable, the jockey and so on. But they will pay special attention to its suitability or 'liking' for the given course in terms of the length, gradients, turns and hardness of the ground.

A very similar situation arises when we try to choose the best tapes for a given cassette recorder. There are plenty of technical properties built into the formulation of a tape which define its absolute goodness in terms of its mechanical and electromagnetic performance. However, nearly every aspect of a tape's 'form' is dependent on the intrinsic qualities and the alignment of the machine on which it is going to be 'run'. So the results that we can expect from a given tape depend on two categories of parameter:

(a) those which define its absolute form, like maximum output level for a given amount of distortion, noise level, etc;

(b) those which depend on machine features like head and amplifier design, drive mechanism and bias setting.

Basically the first category can be deduced from our knowledge of the parentage and stable of a given tape, and the 'starting price' is a fairly reliable guide to its qualities—given the right machine. The second category has to do with the compatibility of tape and machine—horses for courses—and price is no guide here. The ratings given in Table 12.1, which are based on measurements carried out by the author, are aimed solely at offering guidance in this second category.

Your best starting point is no doubt the cassette brand (if any) that was supplied along with your machine, and the list of brands which the manufacturer has recommended in his operating instructions. After all, the manufacturer has to line up his recorders on some tape brand (or according to an international standard calibrated tape, better still) so he should be anxious to guide purchasers towards tapes that will do well on his machine. This does work in a general way, but it has to be said that some deck makers print overoptimistic lists of 'recommended tapes' only some of which are compatible.

If your deck does not allow fine tuning of bias, Dolby level, etc, Table 12.1 will help you identify suitable alternative tape types. Look first at 'the devil you know', that is the tape brand

and type which came with the machine or that you have found from experience gives good results. Then run your eye down the list to discover which other tapes have similar sensitivity and bias ratings. These would then be safe bets for trying out on an experimental basis. You will have avoided gross incompatibility problems and can be reasonably certain that each tape is performing close to its theoretical best on your particular machine. Then any quality differences you detect, such as high frequency trueness, low noise, wide dynamic range or low distortion, can reasonably be ascribed to differences in the individual tapes themselves.

1 *Brand and country of origin*
Many users build up a brand loyalty over the years, and this is no bad thing since the company philosophy may be assumed to remain consistent. Note, however, that many of the largest tape manufacturers feel obliged to market a wide range of cassette types, and so one cassette type from Manufacturer X may perform quite differently from another. As a generalisation, cassette decks from the Far East have tended to creep upwards in their bias settings, while European decks have clung longer to the values laid down in the early cassette standards. Japanese tape makers quickly managed to stay with this upward trend (and presumably influenced it in the process). So, at least until recently, Japanese cassettes tended to sound better on Japanese machines than European and American cassettes. Since Far East machines now dominate the market, all tape manufacturers have been obliged to reformulate at least some of their tape types to suit a higher bias setting. Notice, for example, how the earlier BASF LH and Super LH types require a low bias whereas the later Super LH1 requires a high bias.

2 *Type*
The names that manufacturers give to their various tape types provide very few clues to their true properties. Such words as 'super' and 'extra' tell us nothing at all. However 'LH' has come to be an accepted abbreviation for 'low noise, high output' and many type names do at least indicate the sort of coating used.

3 *Coating*
This links directly with the categories as listed in Table 8.2.

4 *Equalisation*
This column again merely confirms that the selector switch on

Table 12.1 The choice of cassettes

1 Brand name (Country of origin)	2 Type	3 Coating	4 EQ (µs)	5 Relative sensitivity	6 Bias Nominal	 Test result
AGFA	LNS	Ferric	120	V. low	Normal	V. low
(West Germany)	Ferrocolour	Ferric	120	V. low	Normal	Low
	Superferro	Ferric	120	Average	Normal	Low
	Carat	Fe Cr	70	High	Fe Cr	V. low
	Superchrom	Fe Cr	70	Average	Fe Cr	Average
	Stereo Chrom	Chrome	70	Average	Chrome	Low
AMPEX	Plus	Ferric	120	Average	Normal	V. low
(USA)	20/20 +	Ferric	120	Average	Normal	V. low
	Grand Master I	Ferric	120	Average	Normal	Low
	Grand Master II	Chrome equiv.	70	Average	Chrome	Low
AUDIO MAGNETICS	Plus	Ferric	120	Average	Normal	V. low
(Switzerland)	Extra	Ferric	120	V. low	Normal	V. low
	Super	Ferric	120	Low	Normal	Low
	XHE I	Ferric	120	Average	Normal	Average
	XHE II	Chrome equiv.	70	Average	Chrome	Average
BASF	LH	Ferric	120	V. low	Normal	V. low
(West Germany)	Ferro Super LH	Ferric	120	Low	Normal	V. low
	Ferro Super LHI	Ferric	120	Low	Normal	High
	Ferro Super LHI (new)	Ferric	120	Average	Normal	High
	Chromdioxid	Chrome	70	V. low	Chrome	Low
	Ferrochrom	Fe Cr	70	High	Fe Cr	V. low
	Chromdioxid Super	Chrome	70	Low	Chrome	High
	Metal IV	Metal	70	Average	Metal	High
DENON	DX 1	Ferric	120	Average	Normal	Average
(Japan)	DX 3	Ferric (2-layer)	120	Average	Normal	Low
	DX 5	Ferric (2-layer)	70	Average	Fe Cr	High
	DX 7	Chrome equiv.	70	Average	Chrome	Low
	DX M	Metal	70	Average	Metal	High
FUJI	FL	Ferric	120	Low	Normal	Average
(Japan)	FX-I	Ferric	120	Low	Normal	Average
	FX-II	Chrome equiv.	70	Average	Chrome	Average
	Metal	Metal	70	Average	Metal	Average
HITACHI	Low Noise	Ferric	120	V. low	Normal	Average
(Japan)	UD	Ferric	120	Average	Normal	Average
	UD/ER	Ferric	120	Average	Normal	Low
	UD/EX	Chrome equiv.	70	Average	Chrome	Average
	ME	Metal	70	Average	Metal	Low
MAXELL	UD-XL I	Ferric	120	Average	Normal	Average
(Japan)	UD-XL II	Chrome equiv.	70	Average	Chrome	Average
	MX	Metal	70	Average	Metal	Average
MEMOREX	Normal Bias	Ferric	120	Average	Normal	Average
(USA)	MRX 3	Ferric	120	Average	Normal	Average
	High Bias	Chrome equiv.	70	Low	Chrome	V. low
	Chromium Dioxide II	Chrome	70	Low	Chrome	High
NAKAMICHI (Japan)	Metal	Metal	70	Average	Metal	High
OSAWA	LN	Ferric	120	Low	Normal	Low
(Japan)	LH	Ferric (2-layer)	120	Average	Normal	Low
	FC	Fe Cr	70	Low	Fe Cr	V. low
	CR	Chrome equiv.	70	Average	Chrome	Average
	MX	Metal	70	Average	Metal	High
PHILIPS	Ferro	Ferric	120	Low	Normal	V. low
(Holland)	Super-Ferro	Ferric	120	Average	Normal	V. low
	Super-Ferro I	Ferric	120	Average	Normal	V. low
	Ferro-Chromium	Fe Cr	70	Average	Fe Cr	V. low
	Chromium	Chrome	70	Average	Chrome	V. low
	Metal	Metal	70	Average	Metal	Low
SCOTCH (3M)	Ferric	Ferric	120	Low	Normal	V. low
(USA)	Superferric	Ferric	120	Low	Normal	High
	Chrome	Chrome	70	Average	Chrome	V. low
	Master I	Ferric	120	Average	Normal	Average
	Master II	Chrome equiv.	70	Average	Chrome	Average
	Master III	Fe Cr	70	Average	Fe Cr	V. low
	Metafine	Metal	70	Average	Metal	V. low
SONY	AHF	Ferric	120	Average	Normal	Average
(Japan)	BHF	Ferric	120	Low	Normal	V. low
	CHF	Ferric	120	V. low	Normal	V. low
	Fe Cr	Fe Cr	70	Average	Fe Cr	V. high
	CD-α	Chrome equiv.	70	Average	Chrome	Low
	Metallic	Metal	70	Average	Metal	Average
TDK	D	Ferric	120	Average	Normal	Low
(Japan)	AD	Ferric	120	Low	Normal	High
	OD	Ferric	120	Average	Normal	Average
	SA	Chrome equiv.	70	Average	Chrome	Average
	SA-X	Chrome equiv.	70	High	Chrome	High
	MA	Metal	70	Average	Metal	Average
	MA-R (zinc diecast housing)	Metal	70	Average	Metal	Average

the cassette deck should be set to the tape category as shown in Table 8.2.

5 *Relative sensitivity*

It is useful to know how tapes compare in relative sensitivity, that is, their playback levels from a recording made with a standard record level input. High sensitivity is an advantage, in a general way, assuming that inherent tape noise is low. More important, however, is the need to keep to tapes of a consistent sensitivity to preserve proper tracking of the Dolby noise reduction circuitry—ie exact correspondence between the average record and off-tape levels. Each machine is factory-aligned to give best results from the Dolby circuits only when the encode and decode chains are referenced to the same standard level. However, the tape sensitivity is included in this loop and so only the recommended tape, or one with similar sensitivity, should be used.

To arrive at the ratings in the table, a mid-frequency (400Hz) tone was recorded at Dolby reference level on each of the tapes, and the levels then carefully measured when this tone was replayed. Precise dB levels have not been listed, since these might be expected to vary slightly from sample to sample of a given tape type. Instead, ratings of 'average', 'high', 'low', etc have been quoted. All tapes shown with the same rating may be taken to be within about ±1dB of each other. The most obvious audible effect of using a tape of widely different sensitivity from that for which the deck has been set up is disappointing treble, caused by a step occurring in the Dolby decoding at about 2kHz.

6 *Bias*

The nominal bias is listed in accordance with the basic tape type requirements of Table 8.2. However, as was mentioned before deck and tape manufacturers often wander quite a bit from the nominal values, and the final column shows the ratings arising from my own tests. The procedure was to find the bias setting which gave the same record/replay level for tones at 400Hz and 15kHz (an accepted rule-of-thumb method for setting bias) for each individual tape type. I was then able to rate the bias requirements of each tape in relation to an established 'average' value. It should be noted that these ratings can serve as no more than an approximate guide since changing the bias level causes several parameters to alter quite drastically. If bias current is gradually increased from zero, the harmonic distortion and maximum output levels at low and high frequencies all vary considerably. Since these parameters each peak at a different 'optimum' bias level, the final choice is always a compromise. One deck manufacturer might slightly over-bias to reduce mid-range distortion, and restore any consequent high frequency loss by giving extra boost to the treble in the record amplifier. Another might under-bias to give deliberate and 'impressive' treble emphasis.

Add to all this the tolerance spread of these critical adjustments from machine to machine, and the inevitable drift with time and head wear, and we see that cassette-to-deck matching will always be a rather inexact science.

Tuners

1 *Tuning range*
The wavebands in which the tuner operates—having frequency and wavelength limits as are listed in Table 9.1 in Chapter 9.

What to look for   Insist on the VHF/FM waveband (stereo) for any high quality system. Add medium waves for longer distance reception; long waves if you regularly listen to BBC Radio 4; and short waves if you do worldwide listening.

2 *Sensitivity*
Minimum input signal needed to produce a stated signal-to-noise ratio or degree of 'quieting'. The IHF (Institute of High Fidelity) rating expresses this in microvolts (μV) for 30dB quieting but is now regarded as out of date: British Standards use 40dB for FM and 20dB for AM. Sometimes the specification will include a diagram of the sort shown in Fig. 12.1. The

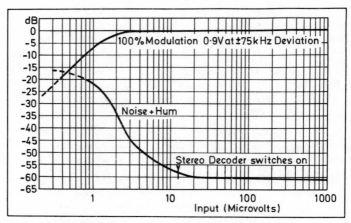

Fig. 12.1 Typical tuner sensitivity graph showing how the output increases with increasing aerial input voltage, reaching a maximum for a little over 1μV input. The noise reduction or 'quieting' curve is also shown, and the stereo switching level

horizontal scale indicates the aerial input voltage, and separate graphs show the signal level and noise level to be expected at various input voltages. It will be seen in the example that full signal level is achieved for an aerial voltage of only about 3μV and that the specification might well read 2μV (for 30dB quieting). In practice, however, about 12μV will be needed to reduce noise to the -60dB level at which the tuner's auto-stereo switching circuit has been aligned (see Note 12).

What to look for   IHF 4μV or less; BS 8μV or less (mono), 100μV or less (stereo).

3 *Adjacent channel selectivity*
Rejection of station at next standard frequency (± 200kHz). Expressed in decibels of attenuation of unwanted station.
What to look for   At least 25dB.

4 *Alternate channel selectivity*
Rejection of station two channels away (± 400kHz). Actually more important than adjacent channel selectivity (Note 3) because the latter stations are usually kept well apart geographically, so look for higher rejection values.
What to look for   At least 35dB.

5 *Capture ratio*
Ability to suppress a signal which is only a little weaker than the wanted station, even when both stations have identical or very close frequencies. Expressed in decibels of signal difference.
What to look for   3dB or less.

6 *Total harmonic distortion*
Degree of generation of unwanted harmonics due to non-linearity in the system for 100% modulation levels. Expressed as a percentage.
What to look for   1% or less.

7 *Frequency response*
Range of audio frequency coverage within stated decibel limits.
What to look for   30–15,000Hz$\pm$3dB on VHF/FM; a mere 30–4,000Hz$\pm$3dB on AM.

8 *Pilot tone suppression*
Attenuation of 19kHz pilot tone and 38kHz subcarrier, to avoid interference during tape recording. Expressed in decibels.
What to look for   19kHz 30dB or greater; 38kHz 40dB or better.

9 *Pre-emphasis characteristic*
Time constant of frequency correction needed in tuner to straighten out treble boost applied at the transmitter. Expressed in microseconds (μs). UK and European broadcasters use 50μs, but the USA uses 75μs—so imported tuners should be checked.
What to look for   50μs for UK use.

10 *Signal-to-noise ratio*
Level of inherent noise relative to a stated signal level (deviation on FM). Expressed in decibels with reference to 22.5kHz deviation.
What to look for   Better than 54dB weighted, 46dB unweighted.

11 *Channel separation*
Sometimes called 'crosstalk'. Expressed in decibels as the difference in level between a standard signal on the 'wanted' channel and that measured on the 'unwanted' channel.
What to look for   25dB or better.

12 *Mono/stereo switching*
Most VHF/FM stereo tuners automatically switch to the stereo mode when a stereo transmission (possessing the identifying pilot tone) is tuned in. However, the threshold level at which this switching takes place should be preset at the factory to a value which corresponds to the sensitivity of the given design so as to produce acceptable noise limiting on stereo (see Note 2). There is usually a 'stereo beacon' lamp or LED display which is illuminated when the auto-switching is in the stereo mode.
What to look for   A well-designed indicator and, where reception of weak station is required, a mono override switch to change to the mono mode when noise is at unacceptable levels in stereo. Alternatively, some tuners permit 'quasi-stereo' listening when reduced noise is obtained at the expense of some stereo separation.

Amplifiers

1 *Frequency response*
Range of frequency coverage within stated decibel limits.
What to look for   At least 40–16,000Hz $\pm$ 1.5dB on 'flat' inputs; 40–16,000Hz $\pm$ 2dB for pickup cartridge inputs.

2 *Channel balance*
Difference in sensitivity of the left and right channels, with the

balance control (if any) at its centre position. Expressed in decibels, for the range 250–6,300Hz.
What to look for   Less than 4dB.

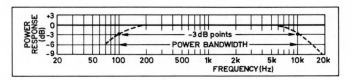

Fig. 12.2 Amplifier power bandwidth extends between the frequencies at which the output, for the rated distortion, falls by 3dB

3 *Power bandwidth*
Range of frequency coverage within which the amplifier delivers at least half its rated power (Note 6) without exceeding the rated distortion (Note 4). Expressed in terms of the upper and lower frequency limits where power output falls to half (−3dB). In Fig. 12.2, for example, the power bandwidth is 100–10,000Hz.
What to look for   At least 40–16,000Hz.

4 *Total harmonic distortion*
Degree of generation of unwanted harmonics due to non-linearities in the amplification process. Expressed as a percentage relative to the rated output power (Note 6). Many transistor amplifiers have greater distortion percentages at lower power levels, and so it is helpful if THD is quoted at more than one level.
What to look for   Less than 0.5% at full power.

5 *Intermodulation distortion*
Degree of generation of spurious sum and difference frequencies when more than one frequency is present in the input signal. Expressed as a percentage relative to the rate of output power (Note 6).
What to look for   Less than 1%.

6 *Rated output power*
Maximum electrical output for the rated distortion (Note 4). Expressed in watts per channel. The best method of measuring and expressing amplifier power for correlation between different types and conditions is to use continuous sinewave signals and quote the power equivalent to the measured RMS (root mean square) voltage across a standard load resistance (usually 8 ohms, or sometimes 4 ohms). Some manufacturers

prefer to quote 'peak' or 'music' power ratings which are respectively about two or one-and-a-half times the RMS/continuous figure.

What to look for   At least 10 watts per channel (continuous) for a high fidelity system. (See Fig. 10.7 in Chapter 10 for recommended power ratings in large and small rooms.)

7 *Input sensitivity*
Voltage required at the various input sockets to produce the rated output power (Note 6) with the volume control at maximum. Expressed in millivolts (mV) for 1,000Hz.

What to look for   Around 100–200mV for 'flat' inputs, 2–5mV for magnetic cartridges, around 0.1mV for moving-coil cartridges.

8 *Input overload 'headroom'*
Maximum voltage at the input prior to the onset of severe distortion (clipping). Expressed in volts or millivolts (mV) for 1,000Hz.

What to look for   At least 2V for 'flat' inputs, 30mV for magnetic cartridges.

9 *Signal-to-noise ratio*
Level of inherent noise. Expressed in decibels relative to the rated output power (Note 6), usually 'unweighted' and 'weighted' (ie with appropriate filtering to correlate better with human hearing characteristics).

What to look for   At least 58dB unweighted, 63dB weighted on magnetic cartridge inputs; expect about 10dB better on 'flat' inputs.

10 *Channel separation*
Sometimes called 'crosstalk'. Ability to amplify one channel with minimum interference from the other. Expressed in decibels as the difference in level between the rated maximum level on the 'wanted' channel and on the 'unwanted' channel.

What to look for   At least 40dB.

11 *Damping factor*
Is essentially the ratio of the normal load impedance (eg 8 ohms) to the much smaller output impedance of the amplifier. Though of only limited usefulness, it indicates the extent to which the amplifier output circuitry acts as a low impedance bypass across the loudspeaker coils, so damping out unwanted resonance effects.

What to look for   At least 20.

Loudspeakers

1 *Frequency response*

Range of frequency coverage within stated decibel limits, generally measured on the principal axis at 1 metre distance in an acoustically dead (anechoic) test room.

What to look for   80–15,000Hz ±3dB or better.

2 *Dispersion*

Extent to which high frequency response falls below the axial response at angles in the horizontal and vertical plane. No standard method of expressing dispersion has yet been agreed, but decibel limits at stated frequencies and angles are commonly quoted.

What to look for   Response at 15kHz maintained to within 4dB of the axial response over ±30° in the horizontal plane and ±15° in the vertical plane.

3 *Nominal impedance*

The ratio of applied voltage to resulting current flow, ie the effective resistance, at a particular test frequency. The latter is usually 400Hz (or the frequency where impedance falls to its first low point above the bass resonance frequency). In practice, designers choose agreed standard values of 4, 8 or 16 ohms with occasional compromise values such as 6 ohms.

What to look for   8 ohms is the most widely used and easiest from the point of view of amplifier matching. While 4-ohms loudspeakers are quite common in Europe, they should be used only with amplifiers offering 4-ohms capability, and never connected in parallel (as impedance is then halved, and might draw too much current from the amplifier).

4 *Impedance modulus*

Graph of impedance against frequency.

What to look for   Lowest value should not fall below 80% of the nominal impedance.

5 *Sensitivity*

(a) Voltage or power required to produce a sound pressure level of 96dBA on pink noise at 1 metre, or (b) sound pressure level produced by a similar test signal at 1 watt.

What to look for   (a) Loudspeakers requiring more than 14 volts or 24 watts are of low sensitivity; (b) below 90dBA is low sensitivity; above 94dBA is high.

6 *Efficiency*

Measure of the acoustic power delivered by the loudspeaker for a given value of electrical input power. Expressed as a percentage.

What to look for   About 0.5% is typical for a 'closed box' loudspeaker. Horn-loaded loudspeakers can achieve 5% or higher. Clearly éfficiency and sensitivity are closely linked, and the best choice is affected by room size, amplifier power rating and personal taste in regard to maximum listening level.

7 *Power handling capacity*
Guide to highest amplifier power which can safely be used. Not usually a strict measurement, but a figure related to use on normal programme material.

What to look for   At least 20 watts; higher in accordance with the rating of the amplifier used.

8 *Total harmonic distortion*
Degree of generation of unwanted harmonics due to non-linearities in the electromechanical action. Expressed as a percentage relative to the 96dBA sound pressure level.

What to look for   Less than 3% in the range 250–5,000Hz.

13
Installing and Checking Audio Equipment

Sadly, much of the audio equipment in people's homes fails to perform to the peak of its capability because quite simple precautions have not been taken. Any audio unit deserves to be properly set up and correctly linked to the rest of the system. When money has been spent on superior quality items, it becomes even more sensible to install everything with due care and attention to detail—otherwise the potential benefits of the improved fidelity and realism may not be enjoyed. Even when an audio system has been lined up for optimum results, there is a need to carry out routine checks from time to time followed by such readjustments or replacing of items as may become necessary.

This chapter gives general advice on the most important aspects of audio installation and, since very much the same operations need to be gone through for routine care and maintenance, these matters are discussed at the same time. Each element in the audio chain is tackled separately, taking the same sequence as is used in the 'audio anatomy' (Chapters 7–11), and the specifications (Chapter 12). Owners of music-centres or rack systems may have avoided some of the perils of faulty interconnections and mismatching, but they should work through each individual link in the chain just the same.

It may seem like stating the obvious to suggest that the maker's instructions should be read carefully before attempting to assemble and use anything as mechanically and electronically complex as an audio system. Yet some perversity in all of us makes us fight our way stubbornly into the end of packages clearly marked 'open other end', and optimistically plug newly unpacked appliances into the mains without so much as a glance at the instructions. Be warned. Different mains voltages exist in different countries, for example, and so in this age of international marketing multi-way switching may be fitted to audio units to suit supply voltages over a range 110–240V. Failure to attend to this apparently small detail could be disastrous. Other traps for the unwary exist all along the line. Therefore the best advice is to follow the instructions to the letter, step by step. Allow plenty of time for the initial setting-up procedures, and stop at any instruction which seems ambiguous until you have cleared up the uncertainty.

The record-player

Turntable units always arrive particularly well wrapped and so this is perhaps a good place to suggest that all packaging materials of audio units should be carefully kept, at least for the first few weeks, in case the unit needs to be returned or transported for some reason. The motor and main bearing are almost always intended to float on spring suspensions during use and so require to be clamped firmly when the deck is being carried about. The first task is therefore to loosen or remove the transit screws as per the maker's instructions. The platter, particularly when it is a very heavy item, is usually packed separately. It therefore needs to be carefully set down on the spindle/bearing and checked for free running. There is a trick to this operation on some automatic turntables in that the platter needs to be turned clockwise by hand for a couple of revolutions to make sure that the auto-stop cycle has completed its peregrinations.

Since the main spindle generally passes through a tubular orifice to rest on a point or ballbearing, it is obviously important that the deck itself should be placed on a perfectly horizontal surface, and that such spring or other adjustments as are provided are also set to ensure that the platter too is exactly level. This point needs to be checked finally when the arm and cartridge are in the playing position, since their contribution to the total suspended system may slightly alter the balance. A few decks have a built-in spirit level for this purpose, but any level-checking device can be used. It may be regarded as a counsel of perfection, to set the platter perfectly level from the sonic reproduction point of view, yet uneven wear on the spindle bearing could result in audible rumble after a time.

As well as being level, the deck support should be as solid as possible. Footsteps and other extraneous vibrations might otherwise be transmitted as shock waves to the deck and eventually to the stylus, to be reproduced as small explosions from the loudspeakers. In the worst cases, with a rickety table or wobbly rack system trolley on a sprung floor, the deck might vibrate violently enough to make the stylus jump out of the groove. Apart from these isolated and easily identifiable sources of unwanted vibration, it should not be forgotten that the loudspeakers themselves act as vibrating sources. In reproducing the musical signals sent to them, they can in turn transmit vibrations back through their bases to the floor and furniture—or even through the air—with the possibility of driving the stylus into new unstable motion. This effect, referred to as 'acoustic feedback', is often a cause of subtle discomfort in an audio system even when it is well below the level at which obvious instability or 'howl-round' occurs. A solid, heavy table or other deck support is helpful, but the design of the deck itself may often be at fault. When acoustic feedback is suspected, the loudspeakers should be raised or moved further away to see whether the trouble is alleviated, while loud music containing plenty of bass is reproduced. If the trouble persists, layers of carpet underfelt or other sound-inhibiting materials can be applied under the deck or the loudspeakers, or both.

The location of the deck should also afford a reasonable amount of ventilation, though heat from the motor is not often a problem. It is also necessary to look to such ergonomic details as allowing enough space behind the deck for the lid or dust-cover to be tilted back to a convenient angle. For right-hand users, it is also logical to position the deck to the right of the amplifier/control unit so that the pickup can be lowered and the turntable switched on with the right hand while the volume control is operated with the left.

On decks supplied with the arm and cartridge already fitted, the preliminaries are almost over. On others, the deck may be sold with only the turntable unit, to be equipped with an arm bought separately. This will involve mounting the arm on a precut board or else a blank board to be drilled and cut out according to drawings and template supplied. These operations are straightforward enough but too variable from one design to another to be outlined here.

Once the arm is satisfactorily fitted, we are ready to install the cartridge. This should be unpacked carefully and, where possible, the stylus assembly should be removed and put to one side while the cartridge body is assembled into the headshell or arm platform as appropriate (Plate 31). If the stylus assembly is not a slide-off type, the stylus guard should be left in position to shield the delicate stylus tip from accidental damage.

The first task is to fit the four signal wires. These are always made of extremely fine wire to keep weight to a minimum and they terminate in tiny push-on metal plugs. Unfortunately there is no standardisation of the thickness of the cartridge pins (1.25mm diameter is the most common, but 1mm is also used) and so it may be necessary to open out or close up the wire-plugs. This is a fiddling, not to say hazardous, under-taking and fine-nosed pliers or tweezers should be used with only the lightest pressure that will do the job (Plate 32). Colour coding of these wires is standard, and usually indicated on the cartridge pins also. White and red are used for the 'live' left and right channels respectively, blue and green for the left and right ground or earth return wires/pins. Good clean metal-to-metal contact is essential when the plugs are pushed on to the pins, and this should be checked every few months to make sure that dirt or oxidisation has not intruded.

Fitting the cartridge on to the headshell is then a matter of choosing screws and nuts from the accessory pack supplied, though some cartridge or headshell bodies are already threaded to make nuts unnecessary. In any case, the shortest screws which will fit through the two 12.7mm spaced fixing holes should be chosen to minimise weight at this all-important 'business end' of the arm.

It now becomes necessary to set the distance from the main arm pivot to the stylus tip, for the correct overhang distance which the designer has calculated will give minimum tracking error distortion (except on simpler budget decks where all these parameters will have been set at the factory for the given cartridge). In most arms there are slotted mounting holes to allow for varying the overhang distance by moving the cartridge fore and aft in the headshell (making sure not to skew it in the process). In others, such as the SME, the arm pivot pillar is moved bodily in its mounting plane to achieve the same objective. The correct setting is usually checked by lowering the stylus tip on to a protractor or gauge and adjusting the longitudinal position until the cartridge body is

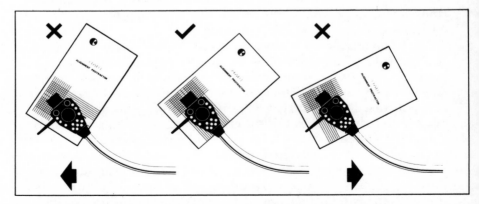

Fig 13.1 Using a protractor to check stylus overhang, the minimum tracking error distortion will occur when the cartridge is parallel with the grid lines as shown in the centre diagram (*Drawing from SME Ltd*)

seen to lie exactly parallel to the lines on a grid (when tracking error will be zero)—see Fig. 13.1. More exotic protractors can be purchased permitting even greater accuracy and avoidance of distortion at critical radii across the record.

The cartridge should now be checked for true vertical alignment when viewed from the front. The best method is to place a small mirror or other reflecting surface on the platter and lower the cartridge on to this (Fig. 13.2). It then becomes a relatively easy matter to check that the cartridge lines up vertically with its mirror image. If it does not, most arms allow the headshell to be turned in its socket to correct the error. Otherwise it may be necessary to pack a thin paper fillet between one edge of the cartridge and the headshell.

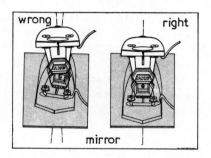

Fig. 13.2 A mirror can be used to check vertical alignment

Arm height should now be carefully set (on arms which allow height adjustment) to ensure the correct vertical tracking angle between the stylus cantilever and the disc surface (nominally 20°). A record should be placed on the turntable and the cartridge lowered on to it about halfway towards the label. Then, viewing the cartridge and arm from the side, the height at the arm pivot should be adjusted until the arm and the top of the cartridge are seen to be horizontal, ie parallel to the disc surface. As with overhang adjustment, this simple method of checking vertical tracking angle is of only limited accuracy, and dyed-in-the-wool audiophiles would expect to make final adjustments while judging by ear the angle which gives least distortion on chosen test records.

The maker's instructions for setting the recommended tracking force value will usually be quite explicit and simple to carry out. Most arms are first placed in a seesaw balanced condition by moving a counterbalance weight to an appropriate position behind the pivot. Then the required tracking force can be applied by moving the counterweight to indicated settings closer to the pivot, or supplementary weights or spring tension can be added. The calibration of these built-in tracking force devices can usually be taken on trust. Where greater precision is required, however, a wide choice of balances and gauges is available on the accessory market (Plate 33). Linked to the tracking force setting is that for sidethrust compensation or 'antiskating'. Here too the maker's instructions are usually clear enough, though yielding results of only limited accuracy. The only reliable method of checking for optimum compensation is, starting from the nominal setting, to make small adjustments in either direction and listen for the position which gives minimum distortion in both the left and right channels while a 'difficult' passage is played (perhaps with the tracking force temporarily reduced below optimum for better identification of the mistracking threshold).

An ordinary hand magnifying-glass will prove useful during some of the alignment checks, and of course is valuable for inspecting the stylus. Accumulations of dust and glue-like deposits can be readily identified. Then, after gentle cleaning with back-to-front strokes of a fine-haired brush (following the path of the record surface past the stylus) either with or without the deposition of a drop of stylus cleaning fluid or isopropylene alcohol as a solvent (Plate 34), a further examination through the magnifier should quickly confirm that the original bright appearance has been restored.

As is generally known, a simple magnifying-glass is not good enough for determining the extent of wear on a stylus. This task needs much greater magnification, special lighting and considerable experience. A better policy is to take the stylus to a suitably equipped dealer, or return it to the manufacturer or distributor, after say 1,000 LP sides. They should be able to say whether the stylus is due for replacement or can be used for a further 500 sides perhaps before being examined again. The life expectancy of diamond styli can never be predicted with any accuracy. It depends on the quality of the original stylus, the tracking force and the state of cleanliness of the records.

At the same time as routine checks are made on all adjustments and alignments of one's audio system, a careful listening test should be carried out to see whether any distortion or increased surface noise which might be attributable to a worn stylus can be identified. If well-known records in one's collection still appear to sound as clean and bright in the upper register as previously, the stylus may be assumed to be in good order.

With all these installation and alignment operations completed, it only remains to connect the record-player unit to the amplifier. Generally the connecting cable will be 'captive', that is, already wired and anchored at the arm outlet end, with colour coded phono-plugs for the left and right channels.

Similar coding at the amplifier input sockets should make any left/right confusion easy to avoid. There will usually be a separate earth wire, with instructions that this should be safely fixed to the earth terminal on the amplifier. In practice, more than one direct connection to earth in an audio system can form what is called an 'earth loop' producing quite loud mains hum.

The best plan is to connect the main component (amplifier or receiver) to the mains socket via a three-core lead and plug, and use only two-wire mains connections for all ancillary units such as the record-player, cassette deck and tuner. These will normally have a safe chassis-to-chassis connection to the (safely earthed) main component via the braided screen on their coaxial connecting leads. However, the record-player is a classic case where individual makers may adopt non-standard earthing techniques and you should be prepared to experiment. Listen carefully for mains hum with the earth wire on and off the amplifier terminal, and choose the arrangement which produces least hum. Similarly, some imported equipment has uncoded twin-wire mains leads which can lead to hum when the same polarity is not maintained for all components. The cure is to reverse the plug polarity for one or other of the components until the hum disappears. If in doubt, consult your dealer.

Another possible source of hum is direct induction from stray magnetic fields into the cartridge itself. This can be avoided by making sure that the cartridge is kept well away from the mains transformer in the amplifier, etc. Where deck/arm installation was a do-it-yourself job, it may be necessary to redress the pickup and mains leads inside the plinth to keep them well apart or make them cross at right angles.

The tape deck

Whether you are installing a cassette or open-reel deck, the same procedures apply and are much simpler than those just described for the record-player. Naturally a reasonably level and stable shelf or other supporting surface should be provided and adequate ventilation. Direct sunlight and stray magnetic fields should be avoided. Since 95% of readers will have cassette decks, we shall primarily discuss the cassette format, though open-reel decks differ in a few details.

Electrical connections are straightforward enough. The signal connectors usually comprise two pairs of double-ended phono-plug cables, two for the left and right channel inputs to the recorder (to be connected to the 'record' outlets on the amplifier) and two for the left and right channel playback outlets on the recorder (to be connected to the 'tape play' inlets on the amplifier). Attention to colour coding will again avoid any possibility of faulty left/right connections. In some European equipment, DIN plugs and sockets will be used instead of (and sometimes as well as) phono-plugs. Again, following the maker's instructions should avoid any problems. Where there is a playback volume control on the tape deck, this will clearly operate in tandem with the main amplifier volume control. To keep unwanted noise and mains hum to a minimum, though this is much less of a problem with tape decks than record-players, it is best to set the deck control as near to maximum as possible, consistent with producing a convenient setting on the amplifier control.

Once the mains supply connection has been safely made, for which the same basic rules apply as for the record deck discussed earlier, you are ready to familiarise yourself with the deck's operational features and performance capabilities. Begin with the mechanical aspects. Check that your technique for loading and removing a cassette is smooth and foolproof. It is good practice to examine the cassette before loading and, if a loop of slack tape can be seen, take up the slack by turning one of the hub centres with a pencil or finger.

While it may be assumed that the heads of a new deck will be in pristine condition, it really is surprising how soon deposits of oxide dust, shed by even the best tapes, can build up. From the very outset, therefore, plans should be made for regular head cleaning. The simplest method is to use one of the cleaning cassettes. These contain a ribbon of gently abrasive material instead of tape, enough to run for about 60 seconds at normal speed. The procedure is to 'play' the cassette once, then rewind and play again, finally rewinding once more. This will remove loose dust and hopefully restore the face of the heads, guide pillars and capstan to their original mirror-like finish. Where sticky deposits have been allowed to accumulate, however, this cleaning action may be only partly successful— though at least one brand of cleaning cassette is intended to be used 'wet' and a phial of cleaning fluid is provided with which to damp the ribbon before use.

Therefore, in addition to running a cleaning cassette through the machine after every ten cassette playings approximately, it pays to clean the heads and other points of tape contact directly at, say, fortnightly intervals or just prior to any important recording session (Plate 35). Cleaning kits are available, with cleverly angled brushes or pads and bottles

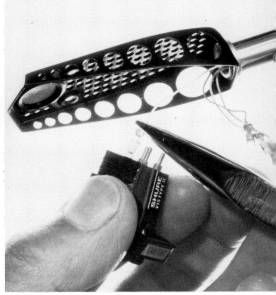

31 (*above left*) Most cartridges have user-replaceable stylus assemblies, which should be removed·for safety during cartridge installation (*Photo AKG*) and 32 (*above right*) Fine-nosed pliers or tweezers are ideal for fitting pickup tags on to the cartridge pins (*Photo SME*)

33 A separate pressure gauge can be used to check the pickup tracking force (Technics SH-50P1)

34 When using a fine brush to clean the stylus, the stroking motion must be from back to front (*Photo Bib*)

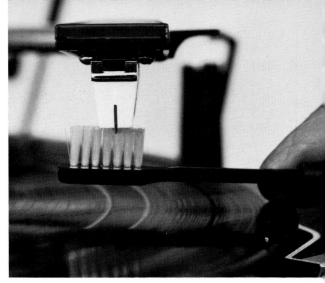

35 Tape-head cleaning kits can be obtained with specially shaped cleaning tools, fluid and an inspection mirror (*Photo Bib*)

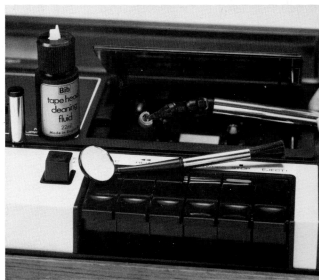

36 Magnified photograph comparing a pickup stylus tip (right) with a sewing needle (*Photo F. A. Loescher*)

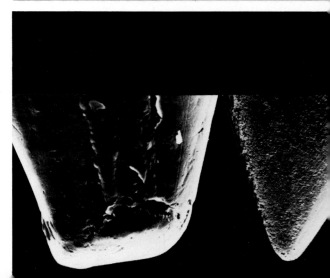

of reasonably innocuous solvent fluids. The latter usually contain small amounts of alcohol intended to soften the hard deposits but without attacking the metal plating or plastic components with which they might come into contact. Otherwise the cotton-tipped sticks used for cleaning babies' ears are highly suitable, damped with tape head or pickup stylus cleaning fluid. A gentle stroking action should be used to avoid any possibility of scouring the heads. A brown stain of oxide will soon show on the pad, but close scrutiny of the heads will be necessary to see when the cleaning job has been completed. Naturally, time should be allowed for any fluid left behind to evaporate before loading the next cassette.

Routine maintenance of open-reel tape decks will also usually include a stage of head demagnetisation. This is a precautionary measure intended to eliminate any residual magnetisation left in the heads, which are themselves electromagnets, by on/off switching surges or the effects of a magnetised screwdriver or other metal object brought too close to the heads. The demagnetiser or 'degausser' consists of a heavy coil/magnet assembly in an insulating case from which projects a pole-piece suitably shaped to concentrate the magnetic field at the tip. The unit is plugged into the mains and switched on so that a strong field alternating at fifty cycles per second is set up. The tip of the pole-piece is then brought close to each head and guidepost in turn, and then slowly moved away to a distance of about 1m before switching off. The way the unit works is that the initial strong field completely obliterates any standing magnetic charge on the heads, etc and replaces it with an alternating charged state swinging first in one polarity and then the other. Then, when the tool is slowly withdrawn, the swings of magnetic charge diminish in amplitude and reach zero before the current is switched off.

In practice, cassette decks are very unlikely to develop unwanted magnetisation. The heads are mounted out of harm's way, and there are usually circuit arrangements to prevent spurious switching surges. Therefore a degausser is probably an unnecessary luxury, except in service workshops.

Other mechanical features to be checked on initial installation include the tape position indicator function, which may have a real-time LED display in minutes and seconds but more usually consists of a three-digit counter. The business of resetting the indicator to zero should be made into an unvarying routine when each new cassette is loaded into the machine. It then becomes possible to familiarise oneself with the indicator readings associated with different elapsed times, and make reasonably accurate forecasts of how much recording time still remains on any given tape at any stage. Where a collection of tapes is being assembled, it can be very helpful to log the indicator readings for the start of each individual item—always assuming that the reset-to-zero button was pressed as the tape (rewound to the start) was inserted. All standard deck functions such as play, record, pause, etc should be practised until they can be performed almost blindfold, and any automatic trickery such as 'search and play' or auto-fade similarly rehearsed.

Unlike play-only media, a deck which actually records and reproduces programme material is perfectly made for routine performance checks. At any time one is in a position to compare the sound quality of the incoming signal with that recorded as a continuing reassurance—or otherwise—that all is well with the machine and that one's own recording technique is successful. The three-head decks are best for this, of course, since they allow instant switching between the incoming and off-tape signals. However, it is not difficult to improvise an effective comparative monitoring method for the ordinary two-head (erase plus combined record/replay) machine. Choose a radio broadcast or gramophone record which will be as taxing a test as possible, that is, containing plenty of high frequencies (since these are usually the first thing to suffer if heads become clogged or an unsuitable tape type has been chosen), long sustained notes (to show up mechanical wow-and-flutter), loud peaks (to establish what maximum meter readings can be used without distortion) and silent passages (to see whether tape and other noises are at acceptably low levels).

The trick is to make a trial recording for several minutes, then rewind to the start and replay the tape while switching on the amplifier between 'tape play' and the source in question. If you are using a radio broadcast, of course, the programme material will have moved on, but you should be able to make value judgements on the recorded quality so long as similar music is being performed. With a gramophone record, after a little practice, it becomes possible to restart the disc and tape in almost perfect synchronism and obtain exact A/B switching. This is a most revealing test of a machine's performance and its continued state of running after a period of use. Naturally there is some loss of fidelity and some ingress of noise in every recording operation, and we should not expect a perfect replica from a budget-price machine. However, this A/B comparison technique will at least serve to identify significant deterioration in performance with time—perhaps alerting the owner to the need for a proper overhaul. And it is a handy means of checking the suitability of a new brand of tape for use with the given machine, or of establishing better techniques of recording—such as the basic need to set the recording level for optimum use of the particular tape type.

Where live recording with a microphone is being undertaken, the most revealing tests of all are possible, comparing the off-tape sound with the real thing. You can even record someone reading a few sentences, then ask him to read the passage again, standing near the loudspeakers and make an A/B comparison between his real and recorded voices on the spot.

Needless to say, these subjective tests of recorded quality are an excellent way of assessing the suitability of a given tape type for use with the particular machine, following the guidelines given in Table 12.1 in Chapter 12.

The tuner

Installing a tuner is as much to do with proper choice and siting of the aerial as anything else. Mains supply and signal connections to the amplifier follow the simple lines already discussed for the tape deck. Again, when the tuner has its own audio volume control, this should be set as high as possible consistent with producing a comfortable setting on the amplifier volume control.

By all means conduct initial tests with a simple indoor flex dipole of the sort discussed in Chapter 9, but be prepared to invest in a superior loft or outdoor aerial array unless you are in a favourable area for VHF/FM reception—say within 35 miles of the local transmitter(s) and away from metal obstructions or deep valleys. A separate earth connection to the amplifier earth terminal or to a true ground (a stake driven into the earth, or a cold water pipe) will almost certainly be unnecessary. However, a quick listening test should confirm this fact if spurious hum and interference are absent. (Electrical interference from thermostats or light switches, and radio breakthrough are at least as likely to be a nuisance when listening to records as radio, and so are dealt with separately on page 204.)

As the sensitivity diagram in Fig. 12.1 shows, full signal level on FM is achieved on quite small aerial input voltages, but it is necessary to listen particularly to the background noise level to ascertain that the received signal is of sufficient strength for satisfactory reproduction. The VHF/FM waveband should be explored manually until each of the main BBC and local radio stations has been identified. It will then be possible to set the individual tuning of preset station push-buttons (when these are available). The best procedure is to switch out the AFC and muting before carefully tuning each preset station for best reception—maximum signal level combined with minimum noise—and switching them on again afterwards.

On a manual-only tuner it is a good idea to draw a chart of the tuning scale, mark the points on the scale where your favourite stations appear and keep it near the set. The precise frequencies for the BBC main programmes in your local area will normally be at 2.2MHz spacings but this can easily be checked and marked on the chart.

In the process of familiarising yourself with the tuning capabilities of the tuner, it will be possible to form a judgement as to the adequacy of the aerial. If better results seem desirable, upgrading of the aerial for both FM and AM should be tackled on the lines suggested in Chapter 9. The aerial connection should be secure, with good metal-to-metal contact, and be of a type which preserves the impedance matching needs of the feeder cable and aerial type. It is not uncommon for tuners situated very close to a transmitter to suffer overloading, and consequent distortion. While judicious rotation of the aerial may rectify matters, it is probably more satisfactory to fit an attenuator in the aerial lead. Local dealers will know about the problem and be able to offer plug-in attenuators of suitable step-down ratio.

Little need be said about AM reception, which is normally adequate in most areas, subject to the interference and fading problems after dark. Where the given tuner or receiver is fitted with a ferrite rod aerial, this should of course be tried though its effectiveness may be limited. Such rod aerials behave like a dipole, as discussed in Chapter 9, and have a broadly figure-of-eight directivity pattern. They should therefore be moved out from the chassis on the hinged bracket usually provided and tried at different angles until the best reception is obtained. If the rod is fixed at one angle, of course, it may be necessary to turn the whole unit around, which could be a nuisance. The same thing happens with portable radios having built-in rod or frame aerials, but then at least the working angle need not upset the appearance of a tidy living-room. If for any reason the rod aerial is unsatisfactory, a simple external aerial can be fitted. This can be a single wire with a suitably inconspicuous insulating covering run up the wall and along a picture-rail perhaps. Length is not critical and the reception will not depend greatly on direction. Since AM broadcasts are mainly of strictly non-hi-fi quality, they will normally be relied upon for information rather than optimum musical enjoyment.

Nevertheless, like every part of an audio system, an AM tuner deserves to be installed to best advantage, and a routine should be established which confirms that everything is up to the original standards.

The amplifier

Installing an audio amplifier, for all that it is the key unit in the system, should present very few problems. It generates more heat than any other unit, of course, and so must be located with due attention to the need for adequate air circulation. It should also be positioned for easy access to the controls, and so that reasonably short cables can be used to connect each of the source units. Note, however, that too close proximity of amplifier, tuner, etc can lead to unwanted interactions, notwithstanding the trend to stacked systems. Try to keep some spacing and, if stacking is unavoidable, put the amplifier on top rather than at the bottom of the stack. A three-wire mains cable is best, securely plugged into the wall-socket. As discussed earlier, this earth connection should be the only one in the system, to avoid earth loops and intrusive mains hum. Some imported units are fitted with a two-wire mains lead only. Though electrically less safe than the three-wire arrangement, such an amplifier should first be tried with the two wires properly connected to the live and neutral pins of the mains plug. Listening tests on records and radio should soon establish whether spurious noise is being introduced by the absence of an earth connection, or such discomfiting symptoms as a 'live' feel to the controls or odd crackles on touching the pickup arm, etc. If any of these signs appear, it will be necessary to connect a separate length of substantial wire from the earth terminal on the amplifier to a true earth, or most conveniently the earth pin on the mains plug. If in any doubt, call in an expert.

From the outset, it is good practice to switch off the amplifier at all times when the connecting leads to sources or loudspeakers are being inserted or even touched. The heavy surge of current which might occur when a pickup lead is being inserted or withdrawn, for example, could do untold damage to the loudspeakers. By the same token accidental short-circuiting of a loudspeaker cable could draw such heavy current from the amplifier as to blow the amplifier fuse, or worse. When all leads are inserted and dressed fairly neatly— for easy identification if for no other reason—then check that the volume control is turned right down and switch on. Placing your ear close to each loudspeaker in turn, check on the level and quality of residual noise in this zero-input condition. For a high quality system you should expect to find total silence or at most a gentle breathing sound. This is thermal noise generated in the stages following the volume control and of course may be audible at up to 1m in a budget system. If the noise seems unduly high or there are crackles, etc switch off immediately and check the mains plug and other connectors. The main fuse, for example, may be loose and should be removed and put back securely. If everything seems in order, and yet the noise is found to persist, the amplifier may indeed be faulty and require attention.

When all is well, advance the volume control slowly and check that any increase in inherent noise, contributed by the preamplifier stages, is reasonably innocuous. Repeat this process for each source in turn, with no music playing—ie the tuner switched off and the pickup on its rest. It should be possible to raise the volume setting to full without hum and noise, though probably quite audible, becoming objectionable or running into instability due to acoustic feedback. Any suspicious circumstance should lead you to turn down the volume immediately, investigate the source connections and cautiously advance the volume control again. When this procedure has ironed out any basic problems, you should be able to set the volume control to about half, or the setting which a quick listen suggests as normal, and investigate the effects of switching between sources and going through all the normal operations. The record-player is the most critical source since the cartridge is itself an electromagnet and liable to pick up hum. It also produces the tiniest signal voltage output, which is then subjected to considerable bass boost in the RIAA equalisation circuit prior to amplification. So pay particular attention to the mains hum level, with a 'working' volume control setting, as you move the arm across the platter area. This is a very severe test of turntable earthing and cartridge connections but, when you have managed to get inherent noise down to acceptable levels on the record-player input, the tuner and tape deck installation checks should be plain sailing. As a final step, you should equalise the average levels produced on the various sources, so that you can switch from record-player to tuner and tape without needing to readjust the volume control. Some amplifiers have screwdriver presets to adjust the level from individual sources, or the tuner and tape deck may have their own output controls.

It then remains to experiment with the switches and controls to familiarise yourself with their functions and establish 'norms'. You will then be alerted to possible faults or ageing problems when carrying out routine periodic checks. Do not regard the centre 'normal' positions of tone and balance controls as sacrosanct. Most of the time they do work out as the best positions in a well-designed system. But decide for yourself. Your taste may run to a particularly bright or bass-heavy sound: well and good. Or it may be that the particular pickup cartridge has a peaky treble response or is slightly more sensitive in one channel than the other, or your room may be boomy or asymmetrical. These are all things which can be sorted out by trial and error, and the controls set accordingly.

The loudspeakers

The simple mechanics of connecting up and installing a pair of loudspeakers for stereo have already been covered in Chapter 11. Briefly the things to ensure are that speaker cables of adequate thickness are used, that secure connections are made at each end of the cable with good metal-to-metal contact and no risk of a short circuit, and that proper attention has been given to preserving the polarity or phase of the two wires to each loudspeaker.

With both loudspeakers working happily, you are ready to investigate the frequency coverage and directional properties of the units and assess the relative merits of different positions within the room. Adopt a scientific attitude and be prepared to cheat a little, by which I mean choosing programme material that highlights the particular aspect being investigated and using one speaker at a time when necessary. This approach will save time and make your decisions much more positive and repeatable. The objective is to get the best performance from the given pair of loudspeakers. If, after completing the experiments, you decide that the best is just not good enough, at least you will be in a better position to judge and optimise the next pair you buy!

First investigate the treble performance. Cheat, as I have suggested, by choosing a record or radio broadcast with plenty of high frequencies, and even turn down the bass control if this helps you to concentrate. Now get very close to one of the loudspeakers—say about 30cm (12in)—and swing the balance control fully over to silence the other speaker if you like. Keeping at the same distance, move your head across the front of the loudspeaker, and up and down. You should find a marked difference in tonal quality as you do so, with the high frequencies most in evidence when one ear is dead in line with the axis of the high frequency unit (tweeter). You will also be able to identify the mid-range unit (if any) and get an idea of how the radiation from the units blends in the all-important frequency region where their outputs cross over and indeed overlap. As well as music, you can use 'white noise' for this test, which is readily obtainable by tuning between stations on the VHF/FM waveband (with the muting switched off). A well-designed loudspeaker will reproduce this as a smooth hissing sound, like falling rain, with no single band of frequencies predominating.

At this unnaturally close listening distance, it is an obvious drawback that, except for the few 'concentric' drive systems on the market, the division of the audio frequency spectrum between a tweeter, woofer, etc means that the music comes to us from different positions. However, you should now move progressively further away from the loudspeaker and check that a reasonable blend is established by the time that you reach what will be the normal listening distance. You will notice that extreme treble is still audible only if you are able to keep your ears fairly close to the axial line of the tweeter. There will be an inevitable falling off in treble at oblique angles, ie outside of the 'listening window' of the given speaker design (see Chapter 11). This is no great problem, so long as the need for careful positioning is understood. Suitable angling of the loudspeakers and choice of their location, and in particular their height, should enable any treble loss to be kept to an acceptable minimum.

You can reassure yourself on this point by carrying out some listening tests to good, clean, stereophonic programme material. Restore the bass and balance controls to normal, and adopt the textbook stereo layout. That is, you should arrange the loudspeakers at some convenient distance apart, 2 or 3m, and well away from walls or obstructions. Then sit facing them from a central position roughly the same distance from each speaker as they are from each other. (You and the speakers will then form the corners of an equilateral triangle, and the angular spread will be 60°.) With a suitable recording of orchestral music, perhaps chosen from the recommended list at the end of this book, it should be possible to identify the locations, across the stereo stage bounded by the loudspeakers, of the various string sections and individual wind players, etc. If not, be prepared to angle the loudspeakers inwards (Fig. 13.3) and try other adjustments until the instrumental layout is natural and consistent.

This high degree of stereo imaging can usually be obtained, with less confusion to the ear, when the drive units are mounted in a vertical line on the speaker front panel. Of course when three or more drivers are used, this calls for rather a tall

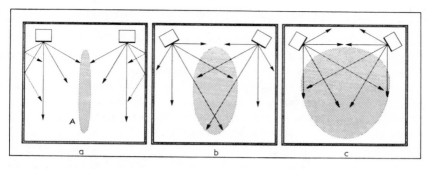

Fig. 13.3 Loudspeakers for stereo: (a) pointing straight forward may give a restricted listening area A; (b) a small angle will give acceptable stereo over a wider area; (c) a large angle may increase the effective listening area further

cabinet and so designers often settle for rather arbitrary arrangements. When the tweeter is closer to one vertical edge than the other, there is a tendency for the high frequency radiation axis to be tilted horizontally towards the nearer side. This has led some manufacturers to market their loudspeakers in 'matched pairs', with the tweeter in the left hand speaker to the right of centre and vice versa. When this bias is followed, a helpful inwards angling of the treble radiation will take place even when the speakers are placed so that they face straight ahead.

This test with an idealised speaker layout away from the walls will have kept the effects of room boundaries to a minimum. Yet the need for domestic harmony will almost certainly make such a layout impracticable. Tests should therefore be undertaken to identify any problems of sound balance which a domestically more acceptable layout will introduce. Again it may speed up the experiments if one loudspeaker is used at a time and, since the greatest problems may now be expected to arise in relation to bass frequencies, the treble tone control may be turned down.

At the root of the matter is the fact that each room boundary—walls, floor and ceiling—will act as a reflector and bounce sounds back into the room. If we consider just one boundary in isolation, say the back wall, and place the loudspeaker as close to it as possible, the reflected wave will follow very quickly after the forward wave and mainly have the property of reinforcing it. However, if we now move the loudspeaker a small distance away from the wall, the 'virtual image' source will move to the same distance behind the wall, just as our reflection in a mirror is seen to recede as we move away, and there will be certain frequencies for which reinforcement takes place, and others where the waves tend to cancel. The uneven bass response which this produces can spoil an otherwise good loudspeaker, and of course the problem is further compounded if we remember that the side wall and the floor have to be taken into account too. A few loudspeaker designers actually build their systems for a specific placement—some column loudspeakers, for example, have the woofer right down at the bottom of the cabinet to make the floor reflection as nearly in phase as possible. The majority, however, seem designed to suit a 'free-field' mounting and so need setting out from the walls and floor if the best results are to be obtained.

You can carry out listening tests while trying different room positions. It should soon be obvious that moving the loud-speaker closer to the back wall gives a spurious boost to the extreme bass. Generally any distance less than about 1m produces an audible effect, but you should be able to reach a compromise position which is both domestically acceptable and reasonably smooth in response. Moving the loudspeaker into the corner of the room will cause a more noticeable bass lift, and you may well decide that a minimum distance of 60–100cm from the side wall should be used. As for height above the floor, almost all loudspeaker types, except the specially designed floor-standing or column designs, benefit from being raised at least 30cm. This will avoid the reflected image problem, as well as odd resonances on a spring floor or mopping up of treble frequencies by a thick carpet. It will also allow you to set the tweeter axis at about the height of your ears as you sit in your favourite armchair.

Complete system checks

Once the various units of an audio system have been correctly installed and aligned, and a pleasing arrangement of loud-speakers and listening area have been arrived at, only a few basic checks remain to be carried out—channel identification, channel balance and channel polarity (phase). These are elementary, but necessary, at the end of the complete assembly operation, and they should be run through periodically whenever any unit has been moved or changed—and as a check that all is still well with the system. There are special test records on the market to speed up these tests—though of course they confirm only the performance of the record-player mode and may fail to reveal fault conditions in the radio tuner and tape deck.

Channel identification
By this is meant the proper connection of the left-hand signals

from each source through to the left-hand loudspeaker and the right to the right, which may seem too basic to need checking. Yet many home installations get this simple detail wrong. It is of no consequence when listening to mono material, of course, and may be felt to be of little importance in stereo broadcasts of plays unless one of the characters actually makes a reference to 'left' or 'right'. Nonetheless, it can spoil the realism of almost any stereophonic presentation of music, even if we do not consciously register the fact that left and right have been reversed. Orchestral layouts do vary in some respects, but it is pretty well a universal rule that the first violins will be arranged on the left, and this will be the easiest thing to listen for during a channel identification test. In the same way the first violin in a string quartet will be positioned to the left.

If a channel reversal is suspected, simple logic will usually locate the cause of the error. Swinging the balance control to left and right should shift the whole sound stage to left and right if the amplifier/loudspeaker cables have been properly connected. If it does not, then the fault has already been located and simple physical inspection should confirm that the left speaker cable has wrongly been connected to the right-hand amplifier output socket and vice versa. These should therefore be swapped over and the correctness of the sound picture finally checked.

If the balance control gives the correct left/right swing, then the unwanted channel reversal has taken place earlier in the chain. If the fault was identified on playing a gramophone record, then the left and right pickup leads should be inspected and swapped over. Clearly this will produce the desired correction of the channel reversal, but it is worth examining the plug colour coding or other left/right identification marking because one other place exists where the error could have occurred. This is in the headshell itself, where the tiny push-on wire sockets may have been connected wrongly. It will avoid future puzzles if left/right connections are corrected at all interfaces, rather than tolerating an error at one point in the chain by deliberately reversing the connections elsewhere (two wrongs actually do make a right, in this instance, but could lead to confusion in future).

There remains the possibility that left/right reversal has occurred on the other sources—tuner and tape—and a similar logical test should sort things out.

Channel balance
This is best checked by listening to a mono programme, or with the amplifier switched to mono if this is possible, from a

position exactly equidistant from the two loudspeakers. A small offset on the balance control may be necessary to move the sound image precisely midway between the loudspeakers, to compensate for differences in sensitivity in the two pickup cartridge channels (quite common) or in the loudspeakers. The test should be repeated for tuner and tape and any differences noted for future reference. Where an asymmetrical room layout has been necessary, you may decide to shift the balance deliberately to give a centre image from the preferred listening position. Switching back to stereo should confirm that a satisfyingly balanced stereo stage has been established.

Channel polarity (phase)
This will be correct when the twin wires connected to both loudspeakers are in the same relationship to the positive and negative output terminals on the amplifier. Then, if a positive voltage swing at the amplifier output produces a forward motion of the left-hand loudspeaker diaphragm, it will produce the same direction of motion in the right-hand loudspeaker. Careful attention to the colour coding or other identification on the terminals and cables should automatically give the same polarity on both loudspeakers, but it as well to check. As with the channel balance test, it is easier to use a mono programme and listen from some central position between the loudspeakers. If the polarity is correct, you will be able to identify the location of the sounds very clearly as if they were coming from a point exactly midway between the loud-speakers. When the polarity has accidentally been reversed to one of the loudspeakers, the two trains of sound waves tend to cancel each other and you will hear a sound which is lacking in bass and difficult to place in space.

If you are in any doubt about this test, you can temporarily move the loudspeakers close to each other, and then the cancellation effect in the 'out-of-phase' condition is very marked indeed. The cure is to reverse the two wires to *one* of the loudspeakers, when the reinforcement of sound, healthy bass and clear central image will leave you in no doubt that the connections are now correct.

Notice that if you were now to reverse the polarity of the connections to *both* loudspeakers, they would still sound correct (ie in phase). All that has happened is that a positive voltage swing from the amplifier now produces the opposite direction of diaphragm motion in both loudspeakers. In most contexts this reversal of absolute phase is of no real significance. However, some audiophiles are now seeking to persuade the recording and audio industries of the need for preserving this absolute phase all the way through from the microphones to the loudspeakers. Their argument, which does have some validity, is that many musical sounds are asymmetrical—the initial transient from a bass drum, for example, may have unequal half-cycles—and that they should be reproduced in correct absolute phase if maximum fidelity is to be obtained. The quest for absolute phase seems doomed to failure, since there are so many links in the chain from studio to living-room, and there is no generally agreed standard. For instance, about half the audio amplifiers on the market introduce a phase reversal while the other half do not. However, you can satisfy yourself whether your ears can detect any change in fidelity by listening first with the speakers wired in one polarity, and then with *both* reversed. The chances are that you will hear no difference at all—because so many recordings are made with a multitude of microphones and so absolute phase has no meaning. And even if you do decide that one particular record sounds better with one speaker phasing than the other, there is no guarantee that the next record you try will do the same.

Audio troubleshooting

The system checks just described form a natural conclusion to the installation of a newly acquired audio installation, or the addition of a new component to an existing system. You are then ready to sit back and enjoy the music, happy in the knowledge that the equipment is performing at its best.

However, these same simple tests can be an invaluable guide to do-it-yourself troubleshooting should any part of the equipment begin to develop a fault or show signs of ageing. It is particularly convenient that most audio systems are two-channel stereo, so that every link in the audio chain is duplicated, so to speak. This makes it possible, by the use of just a little common sense, to carry out simple substitution tests and localise the faulty component quickly. It would be quite a coincidence if any of the ills to which audio systems are susceptible were to strike down both channels simultaneously.

Say, for example, that the left channel develops a fault— severe crackles, loss of volume or absolute silence. You should begin by switching off at the mains and removing the mains plug from the wall-socket. Then, since 90% of all faults relate to connectors, carry out a close inspection of all connecting cables and plugs, looking in particular for some inconsistency in the connectors carrying the left channel signal. Very often this simple procedure will lead to the discovery of the offending circumstance and a speedy cure. If not, you should work back from the loudspeakers, changing over the left and right connections.

First, swap over the two loudspeakers, and reconnect the equipment to the mains. If, on listening, the fault has moved from the left to the right, then that loudspeaker is the culprit. It should be subjected to close examination and, if necessary, given to an expert for repair. If swapping over the two loudspeakers makes no difference, and the fault remains on the left channel, the search must be directed further back in the chain. Restore the two loudspeakers to their original channels (since both have been cleared of suspicion). Then swap over the left and right plugs at the input to the amplifier (not practicable with a five-pin DIN plug) and listen again. If the fault remains on the left channel, then the trouble lies in the amplifier at a point between its input sockets and the loudspeaker terminals. If the fault changes over to the right, then it is incoming to the amplifier and the source unit must be checked, and so on. Not surprisingly, your search will often lead you to the tiny pickup cartridge connectors in the headshell—where great care is needed. Of course, when a fault in either channel is found to apply when switching between two or more sources, this points to the amplifier and loudspeakers since these are common to the chain used for all sources.

Such common-sense procedures for narrowing down the search for a faulty component will often identify a connector or other culprit which can be put right by non-expert hands. However, genuine component faults will need expert attention and no attempt should be made to go beyond one's own boundaries of ability. Modern circuitry is much more complex than in the old days and well-meaning poking around with a screwdriver or soldering iron could do untold damage. At least your investigations will have localised the faulty unit and you can hand the repair job over to your local dealer, or the manufacturer's agent, with a helpful and fairly precise description of the symptoms.

Electrical and radio interference

Clicks, crackles and other manifestations of electrical interference can often spoil the performance of an otherwise excellent audio installation. It can be particularly exasperating when the interference seems random and difficult to diagnose—and cure. Unfortunately, such interference is on the increase as our homes rely increasingly on automatic switching of such appliances as refrigerators, central heating, cookers, hair dryers and even elevators in blocks of flats. The problem has been made worse on some equipment as new amplifier designs have a frequency response extending beyond the 20kHz upper limit of audibility and up into the RF (Radio Frequency) regions.

When any electrical switch opens or closes, it is likely to send out a wide splash of radio frequency energy. This will partly radiate outwards as an electromagnetic (radio) wave and partly pass into the mains house wiring. As a radiated impulse, the interference is all-pervading and very difficult to eliminate completely. Clearly it can enter the audio system via the aerial and then make its way through the RF stages of the tuner, be rectified or detected and appear at the loudspeakers as an audible click or crackle. This particular form of interference at least has the virtue of affecting only one's radio listening and can probably be tackled by improving or resiting the aerial. Unfortunately it may also enter through an inadequately screened chassis or faulty input stage wiring— and then affect all sources, especially the sensitive record-player input. This would need expert attention.

Luckily, such ether-borne interference is comparatively rare and is more often associated with electrical motors and unsuppressed motor vehicles than simple switches or thermo-stats. It should therefore be much less in evidence during an evening's listening to records.

The most common interference problem occurs when the spurious switch impulses are mains-borne, that is they make their way from the switch or appliance into the audio system through the house wiring. The nuisance may then appear on all or any of the sources but has the advantage of being easier to track down and cure than the radiated kind.

The first thing to do is identify the principal culprits. Each of the light switches and appliances should be operated in turn, while someone else listens for audible clicks from the loudspeakers and notes down the offending items. In the same way, the refrigerator and other appliances should be pro-grammed individually to trigger off their time switches or thermostats and again the troublesome units should be logged.

Next it becomes necessary to check whether the interference is in fact coming in through the mains wiring, or perhaps via the signal connecting cables. This can be done by temporarily unplugging the record-player deck, tuner and cassette deck from the main amplifier. Then the volume control should be turned up to its usual operating setting, or a shade higher, while the switches or appliances previously identified as trouble-makers are operated. If the trouble is roughly as bad as before, then the connecting cables and their attached sources are not seriously contributing to the problem. We can be reasonably sure that the interference is mains-borne and that the cure is to interpose some device which will block the unwanted high-frequency impulses while allowing the 50Hz mains current to flow normally.

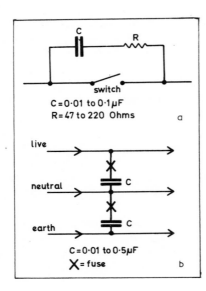

Fig. 13.4 Electrical interference: (a) use of a CR network to eliminate clicks from electrical switches; (b) use of capacitors and fuses in a mains-borne interference suppressor

The simple circuits shown in Fig. 13.4 are usually all that is needed. The first consists of a capacitor and resistor wired across the offending switch contacts. The second can be wired into either the three-wire mains connections of each device producing interference, or the three-wire mains connections at the input to the audio system. The fuses are suggested as protection against possible failure of the capacitors. The circuits are simple enough, but any tinkering with the mains wiring is not a job for the complete beginner. Therefore an expert should be called in as necessary. Alternatively a number of proprietary light-switch suppressors, equivalent to Fig. 13.4a, and mains suppressor boxes incorporating isolating transformers can be purchased as ready-made solutions.

If the earlier test with signal connectors removed produces a substantial drop in the level of the interference, then one of these cables is picking up the signals. They should be replaced one at a time until the faulty cable or unit is identified. Then a close inspection should locate the break in cable screening (the most likely cause), and this can be patched over with kitchen

37 (*top*) With practice, it becomes possible to handle records without touching the grooved surface (*Photo Cecil E. Watts*); 38 (*above*) Tracking cleaners are designed to pick up dust from records during playing (Watts Dust Bug); 39 (*below*) Some cartridges can be fitted with their own brush to collect surface dust (Pickering XLZ/7500S)

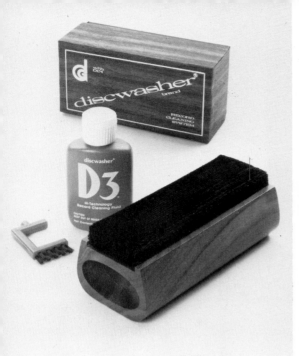 

40 (*above left*) This record cleaner uses a pad damped with special fluid (Discwasher D3) and 41 (*above right*) This pistol-shaped accessory has a crystal which produces a stream of ions to neutralise static on records (*Photo Zerostat*)

42 A Compact Digital Disc and its player unit, with a conventional LP record to show the relative size (*Photo Philips*)

foil, for example, until the cable itself can be repaired or replaced. In a few cases the trouble is not a screening fault but can be cured by purchasing a ferrite ring and winding the cable round this. The series inductance so formed acts as a block to the interfering signals. It has even been known for the loudspeaker cables themselves to pick up interference (easily confirmed by listening on headphones, or turning down the amplifier volume), and ferrite rings will again prove effective.

The two essential features of interference suppression are a methodical approach to identifying the weak points in the system, and extreme caution when making any connection to the potentially dangerous mains wiring.

The steps so far described for dealing with electrical interference will often succeed too for radio interference, which can originate in any local radio or television station, or perhaps a nearby ambulance, taxi or amateur radio installation. However, if such interference persists even after all reasonable attempts have been made to cure it, the radio and television interference investigations branch of the Post Office (Telecom) can be consulted.

14
Caring for Records and Tapes

The vinyl LP record is a phenomenal storage medium for audio signals, easily accommodating the full frequency range of human hearing up to 20kHz and beyond. At the same time, it must be admitted that it can be infuriatingly susceptible to damage and attack from dust, sticky deposits and static electrical charges.

A moment's consideration of the dimensions involved will soon show why the LP record is so inherently fragile. The finest human hair is only about 0.1mm (0.004in) thick, and yet this is already twice the minimum top width allowed for the LP groove (0.05mm). The maximum radius laid down for the V-shaped bottom of the groove is a mere 0.004mm. The tip radius of a standard spherical stylus for stereo records, as we have seen, is only 0.013mm—about one eighth the thickness of a human hair, while elliptical and line-contact styli have minor radii of about half this (see Plate 36). If we make measurements along the groove instead of across it, we find that the recorded wavelength for a 10kHz tone is about 0.05mm near the outer edge of a record, falling to about 0.016mm near the centre.

So we should not be surprised if tiny scratches, barely visible to the naked eye, contribute noise to the reproduction of records. Similarly the slightest film or greasy deposits from finger-marks will tend to fill in the microscopically small waveform and rob the music of much of its sparkle.

The most obvious enemy of LP record reproduction is dust. As viewed by the stylus, dust particles take on the dimensions of large boulders and yet they are continually being deposited on the record surface all the time that the record is out of its protective sleeve. The problem is made worse, of course, since most atmospheres also contain cooking vapours, car exhaust fumes, aerosol residues and saliva-bearing tobacco smoke. These can fuse the dust particles together and even attack the vinyl compound chemically or biologically.

The first line of defence must be good housekeeping. Records should only be exposed to the atmosphere for as long as it takes to put them on the turntable and listen to them. Then they should be carefully put back in their sleeves and returned to the storage position (of which more later). So far as possible, the record-player and its immediate surroundings should be kept clear of dust and such hazards as aerosols and tobacco smoke. A wipe around the deck area with a lightly damped cloth should keep it clean, with special attention given to the platter mat. Otherwise this may be putting dust and dirt on the underside of a record while the top side is being played.

Handling LP records with maximum safety is a trick easily learned (see Plate 37). To remove a record from its sleeve, first hold the sleeve horizontally with your left hand, and the open edge pointing to your right. Then push the sleeve edge gently against your midriff so that the open edge bows apart allowing you to insert your right hand easily. You can now take hold of the inner sleeve gently and pull it and the record out. A similar careful procedure will enable you to slide the record out of the inner sleeve, only this time you must be careful to ensure that no part of your hand contacts the grooved playing surface. You must cup the four fingers of your right hand and insert them below, but clear of, the record until the base of your upright thumb just contacts the record edge. Then you can place the tips of your fingers on the label area and draw the record, still horizontal, out of the sleeve. Having put down the sleeve, you can now bring your left hand, flat and vertically, against the opposite edge of the record and place it on the turntable. A reversal of this whole procedure should be possible, after a little practice, with the grooves untouched by human hand throughout.

Record cleaning

Even with such clinical handling, deposits of dust and pieces of lint, etc are often clearly visible on the record surface. Brand new records frequently arrive with white debris—presumably from the paper of the sleeves; and black debris—presumably from poor housekeeping at the pressing and edge trimming stages in manufacture. Also the spiralling effect on the air as a record rotates will draw air, and dust, down on to the surface.

Therefore, for these various reasons, we are obliged to adopt some record cleaning routine. Unfortunately it is all too easy to make matters worse rather than better. Where simple removal of surface dust and debris is all that is required, a minimum of cleaning should be undertaken. With the record safely placed on the turntable, or on its inner sleeve, a light wipe with a clean cloth or well-laundered handkerchief should suffice. Use a minimum of pressure and try to make a circular motion following the line of the grooves. There are numerous cloths, pads and carbon-fibre brushes on the accessory market which you may find more convenient in use. For this basic cleaning operation, a bone dry cleaner should be chosen as moisture in any quantity leads to further complications. It is a nuisance that such cleaners may shed the dust and leave a line of debris behind when they are lifted off. Also they must be wiped clean after each application or they will simply transfer dust from one disc to the next.

In many domestic situations no further steps are necessary. However, many people like a reassurance that dust—visible and invisible—is being collected during playing. And a glance at the amount of dust and sticky deposits which can accumulate on a stylus tip after playing just one LP side lends strength to their argument. The answer is one of the proprietary tracking cleaners. These resemble a lightweight pickup arm with the headshell and cartridge replaced by some form of brush. The pioneer design was the Dust Bug invented as long ago as 1955 by Cecil E. Watts (Plate 38). This has a vertical brush of specially tipped nylon bristles which loosen dust at the bottom of the groove, and a velvet roller on which the dust is collected. Other designs use fine hair or carbon-fibre brushes and have more elaborate arrangements for setting the tracking force to ensure smooth spiralling inwards as the record is played. A few manufacturers, notably Pickering, Stanton and Shure, have produced cartridges which carry a small brush to give this cleaning action (Plate 39).

At the highest levels of record reproduction, all such tracking cleaners can be criticised as being the cause of a special form of acoustic feedback known as 'needle chatter'. As the pad or bristles of the cleaner track the groove modulations, there is an action and reaction set up which can transmit the music signals through the material of the record to the pickup stylus. These may be slightly ahead (pre-echo) or behind (post-echo) the part of the music being played by the stylus, and form an annoying, though faint, background.

Wet cleaning

If the above techniques of good housekeeping and careful record handling are followed with new records, simple dry cleaning should be all that is required. For renovating older records, or coping with the extra problems of city areas or the very dry air of centrally heated dwellings, however, wet cleaning may become necessary. Accessory kits are marketed in a wide variety of types and degrees of complexity.

The simplest models consist of a plush pad behind which is a reservoir. The latter is filled periodically with a cleaning fluid which is normally made up of distilled water and a small amount of alcohol-based solvent. Others require fluid to be applied directly to the pad (Plate 40), or even sprayed on to the record, followed by a buffing or wiping action. Then again there are hand-roller cleaners which are not so much wet as tacky. These resemble cleaners sometimes used in the clothing trade to remove fluff and lint from difficult cloths. They are rolled over the record surface with a light squeeze action, and do a remarkable job of lifting off every trace of dust.

An extension of this last idea involves spraying or sponging a special liquid over the record surface. The liquid dries to form a thin film which has to be carefully peeled off—removing the dust at the same time. There are also elaborate cleaners which automatically rotate a record between a pair of vertical brushes (wet or dry), or even track it at about ten times normal speed, first with a wetting sponge and then a vacuum cleaning head. Such machinery is naturally rather expensive and better suited to use in lending libraries and broadcasting organisations than the home.

Wet cleaning is possible also in the form of a tracking cleaner, notably the Lencoclean. The tracking arm consists of a plastic tube, sloping down to the end pad which continually lays a track of fluid on the record surface as the record is played. The pickup stylus actually tracks the groove through this wet layer. Tests have shown that the sound quality is in no way impaired by this wetting, and indeed background noise can be reduced quite dramatically. Such wet cleaning has become quite popular in Europe despite its complications (for instance, the blob of water at the record centre has to be wiped dry before the record can be put back in its sleeve) but anyone tempted to adopt the technique should be warned that, once begun, it has to be continued. The fluid used, which is mainly distilled or purified water with an agent to speed up evaporation, dries on the record surface leaving the dust *in situ*. Therefore any disc once played wet is found to be noisy if played dry, and has to be rewetted at each subsequent playing—or else subjected to a thorough cleaning and restoring procedure.

Static electricity

Besides being a soft material, and therefore easily scratched or damaged, the vinyl plastic used for LP records is one of the most easily charged substances in existence. The simple action of sliding a record out of its sleeve produces enough friction to set up quite strong charges of static electricity within the material. The record will then remain in its charged state—making it attract dust, cling to the sleeve and even exert a pull on the pickup cartridge—until the charged particles have been neutralised or leaked to earth. Wiping a record with a cloth, or any of the dry pads or tracking cleaners just described, will set up even stronger charges—so that sparks may fly (and be clearly visible in a darkened room) when the stylus is lowered into the groove or the record is lifted off the platter.

The sparks of course are accompanied by loud plops through the loudspeakers, and audible crackling may continue as the record is played. Also the disc will not only attract dust particles but will make them very difficult to remove by normal methods. The pull on the cartridge will make the tracking force variable and unpredictable, almost certainly leading to distortion. It may be mentioned in passing that the acrylic dust-covers or lids on many record-players are similarly liable to acquire strong static charges when rubbed with a well-meaning duster. They will then be prone to collect an unsightly layer of dust and, even more important, may exert a lifting force on the pickup, reducing its tracking force enough to cause serious mistracking.

A leakage path to earth will avoid some of these bothersome effects. For example, since the metal platter is almost always connected to earth, if the usual insulating rubber mat is replaced by one capable of conducting electricity, merely placing the record on this mat will reduce the electrostatic field considerably. Notice that the charge is not actually removed: it moves to the underside of the disc in close proximity to the equal and opposite charge it sets up in the conducting mat surface (disc charges are always negative). The net field is therefore much reduced but the charge will largely remain in the record and makes itself evident again when the record is lifted off. Helpful antistatic (conducting) mats are now available on the accessory market, usually containing carbon fibres, and should give the amelioration described on most decks. Several turntables are now appearing with a conducting mat as standard. Sparking between the disc and the stylus cantilever can still occur and Shure, for example, have built a conducting path through the dynamic stabiliser brush on some of their cartridges expressly to avoid this problem. Note also that some cleaning brushes have carbon fibre hairs and are intended to be used with a wire connecting them to earth—which does indeed reduce record charges considerably. It also makes the basic job of sweeping up dust much more successful.

All problems with charged records are much more in evidence in dry weather or in the dry air of centrally heated homes. This gives a clue to a general method of reducing static—the introduction of humid conditions. We now see why it is that wet cleaning has strong advocates and produces such silent backgrounds. As a move towards this ideal, it is possible to place a dish of water near the turntable with a piece of flannel half submerged to produce a local area of high humidity. Alternatively a home humidifier could be considered, and will add to the general comfort by reducing the over-dryness of the air.

Another approach to removing static is ionisation of the air. This can be achieved using one of the pistol-shaped accessories which, usually, generate a cloud of positive ions when the trigger is pulled, and negative ions when the trigger is released (Plate 42). This can be very effective with heavily charged records, though some residual charge will almost always remain since it is not possible to gauge the exact dosage of ions required. Finally, and most effective of all, there are some 'permanent' antistatic fluids which are buffed on to the record and neutralise the charge, if not permanently then certainly for a period of months.

It might be asked whether the record manufacturers could not incorporate a conducting or neutralising agent when preparing the vinyl for pressing. The short answer is that such a process is possible (and I have been able to run tests on satisfactory samples) but the added cost and complication has prevented the technique from being widely adopted.

Record storage

The ideal record storage system would provide a measure of physical protection and also avoid the worst effects of dust, warping and climatic problems. For example, steamy tropical conditions might seem to have the advantage of aiding static leakage due to the high humidity, but they have often been found to cause something much worse—growths of mould and mildew.

A closed cupboard will keep out dust, but a reasonable circulation of air should also be possible. Where small numbers of records are involved, it is tempting to suggest that they be stored horizontally in piles of no more than twenty at a time. This would ensure an even downward pressure and make warping unlikely—except for some of the gatefold sleeves which can buckle the edge of the record. However, such a horizontal plan takes up rather a lot of space, unless rows of shallow shelves are constructed, and it is not particularly easy to take out individual records and slide them back again in a prescribed order.

Vertical storage is therefore more generally practical. However, it does introduce the need to ensure that the records are kept truly upright, and preferably under slight sideways pressure to keep them from becoming warped or dished. Some record storage shelves have been marketed with spring-loaded partitions to provide this side pressure. Otherwise it is best to fit frequent vertical dividers so that only up to, say, thirty records occupy each division, and devise some form of filler to help support the discs in any division which is not full. If a do-it-yourself record store is planned, this must be strong and if necessary fixed to a wall so that there is absolutely no chance of it collapsing or tipping forward.

Even when stored correctly, records can become warped or dished. Slight warping should have very little effect on playing and can be ignored. More severe undulating warps can produce pitch fluctuations and distortion. The stylus tip effectively follows a scrubbing motion while the cantilever flexes at each undulation. There is also the danger of the cartridge body 'bottoming' on the record surface or even being thrown out of the groove.

Clearly some record-players react more violently to warps than others, and this is perhaps a convenient place to point out that almost all the problems which we associate with LP records can be aggravated, if not actually caused, by the equipment. Static noise and arcing, for example, can be caused by a badly designed or ineffectively earthed turntable. It can also be made more audibly annoying by 'clipping' (overloading) in the amplifier. A single scratch across the grooves is in contact with the stylus for such a small fraction of a second that it would normally be inaudible, but it may cause certain amplifiers to overload—and the overhang or ringing which this produces will be audible.

In the same way, a well-designed pickup arm and cartridge combination may be so well damped that it rides easily over record warps, keeping a steady contact with the groove. Less well matched systems may be sent into spurious resonant vibrations by record warps, giving clearly audible instability and perhaps groove-jumping. Several add-on damping devices have appeared which can be fixed to the cartridge/headshell or at the arm pillar. These will certainly reduce the ill effects of most warps but are relatively expensive and need careful alignment. Very often the best remedy for playing warped records is a slight increase in tracking force.

Fortunately it is possible to restore warped records to an acceptable state of flatness. The aim is to apply an even pressure over the whole record surface, while at the same time keeping the record at an above-average temperature for 24 hours or longer. One method would be to use two sheets of thick plate glass and place the record between them, preferably enclosed in a protective wrapping such as its own inner sleeve. Then this 'sandwich' should be laid flat on a firm surface while pressure is applied, perhaps by a pile of large books, and left for a day or two in an airing cupboard or near to a radiator. Occasional inspection should show when the worst warps are yielding to the treatment.

Tape care

Magnetic tapes avoid many of the hazards to which LP records are prone during handling and storage. Cassette tapes in particular are enclosed and have the ends permanently anchored to the hubs, so are less exposed to physical damage than open-reel tapes. Nevertheless, reasonable care should be used if tapes of all kinds are to retain their physical and magnetic properties, and the recorded programmes are to be protected from physical or magnetic degradation with time.

Dust should be avoided, of course, since the dimensions of the recorded waveforms and the tape head gaps are again comparable with the size of stray dust particles. Therefore tapes should be returned to their boxes immediately after use, and stored away from sources of dust or dirt. Annoyingly, however, tapes are themselves a source of spurious particles since the magnetic coating itself is liable to shed with time. Therefore a regular cleaning routine must be directed towards the tape heads, capstan and guides, as described in Chapter 13. Leaving a single speck of dust adhering to the face of a replay head, for example, so that the tape is lifted away from the headgap by much less than the thickness of a human hair, can cause the high frequency response to be reduced by several decibels.

Finger-marks are less of a risk than with gramophone records, but it is worth taking care to avoid coming into contact with the tape at all times. With open-reel tapes this does call for a drill of handling spools by the edges, whereas cassette tape is exposed only at the front edge. Where a loop of loose tape is seen to emerge from a cassette, the slack should be taken up by rotating one of the hubs with a finger or pencil. If an open-reel tape were suspected of being really dirty, it would be possible to hold a cloth in the tape path to clean the tape surface during playing, and there have even been a few decks with a cleaning pad built in.

Oddly enough, the danger which most people associate with magnetic tape—induced noise or partial erasure of recordings due to stray magnetic fields—is rarely met in practice. Normal AC power lines and cables, carrying both a 'live' and 'neutral' wire, produce only a very feeble external field. The main risk areas are loudspeakers and the mains transformers in amplifiers, etc. Yet even here keeping tapes at a distance of 30cm (12in) or more will reduce the chances of accidental magnetisation to very small proportions.

Temperature and humidity both have a bearing on the physical well-being of tapes in store. The ideal ranges aimed at in professional tape studios and archives are 21°C (70°F) ±3° temperature and 40–60% relative humidity, but the precise values are less important than the avoidance of sharp or cyclic changes which can introduce undesirable changes in the stress patterns within the tape pack. Too dry an atmosphere can introduce problems with static electricity. Expansion and contraction can stretch the tape unevenly, or cause buckling. Here again the tape machine can be a contributory cause of the trouble. The tape should wind evenly in all operating modes, with the layers kept at a constant height and the tension neither too tight nor too slack. When a cassette tape creeps up or down in height, one side can be pressed against the inside of the casing and cause jamming. If this happens only occasionally, a smart tap on a firm surface will usually release the hubs but any continued tendency to poor winding should be investigated and serviced by an expert. Needless to say a smooth operating technique is just as important as having a good machine.

A common situation where tapes are exposed to excessive temperatures is when they are left in a car—in either very cold or hot weather. Sunlight can lead to very high temperatures inside a vehicle, with serious consequences to the tapes.

High temperatures have an incidental effect in that they accelerate the process known as 'print-through'. This is the cross-magnetisation which can take place between the recorded magnetic patterns on adjacent tape layers on the spool. The effect is to produce faint echoes before and after the original sound, separated on a time scale corresponding to one revolution of the spool. They are analogous to the pre-echoes and post-echoes sometimes audible on gramophone records when the cutting engineer has allowed the recording amplitude to exceed a safe maximum so that the reproducing stylus can 'read' the waveform in the adjacent groove through the thin groove wall. Tape print-through is a considerable nuisance, yet it is always liable to occur to some extent from the instant that a recording has been made. The print-through level increases with time, though at a reducing rate, and in conditions of high temperature or even weak magnetic fields. It can be catastrophic on valuable archived tapes, and indeed was at least as persuasive a reason for the adoption of Dolby A noise reduction in studios as the removal of tape hiss.

It has been found that the simple act of rewinding a tape reduces the level of print-through. Studio engineers therefore make it a rule to store their tapes 'tail out', so that they must be rewound just prior to being replayed, and print-through is then less troublesome. This idea does not work for domestic tapes unfortunately since, unlike studio tapes, they contain programmes recorded in both directions.

Two other signs that all is not well with a tape recording installation are drop-outs and insufficient erasure. Drop-outs are momentary losses of signal normally caused by uneven oxide coating. Tiny pinpoint holes may occur in the coating, or raised lumps may have the same effect by briefly interfering with the intimate tape/head contact. When the problem occurs only on certain tapes, it is likely to be an inferior batch and another type or brand should be used. If drop-outs are frequent, or increasing, the machine should be thoroughly cleaned and inspected for symptoms like insufficient back tension.

When erasure is found to be only partially effective, so that old recordings can still be heard faintly in the background when a new recording has been made, it may also call for simple 'good housekeeping' or more drastic action. The first thing to do is clean the erase head and try erasing again. If this does not cure the trouble, it may be that the machine needs an overhaul, to increase erase current, or the tape brand is at fault. Many newer tape brands have a higher value of coercivity, which makes them more difficult to erase—metal-coated tapes are particularly problematic in this aspect and should only be used on machines having the necessary high erase current and specially designed heads.

One possibility where erasure is a recurring problem is to purchase a bulk eraser. This is an electromagnet with a spindle or platform on which open-reel tape spools or cassettes can be placed and subjected to a strong magnetic field at AC mains frequency. The field is gradually reduced, either by turning down a control or physically removing the spool or cassette, so that the tape is left in its original demagnetised state.

15
Future Developments

The future of every aspect of sound recording and reproduction is so dependent on digital techniques that this chapter must of necessity begin by studying the digital process from first principles.

Put simply, digitalisation consists of replacing the audio signal waveform with a stream of pulses encoded to represent numbers. These numbers each correspond to the amplitude of the signal waveform sampled instant-by-instant during the recording process. For playback, the pulse stream is again scanned and the numbers transformed back to instantaneous signal amplitude values, so reconstituting the original waveform. The considerable circuit complexity which this technique requires at the recording and reproducing end of any audio chain, would have been quite impossible say fifteen years ago. It has become a practicable reality only because of the accelerating development of integrated circuits and micro-processors to meet the demands of industrial computers and space exploration. The most complex circuit configurations can now be assembled using only a few basic types of circuit element, many thousands of which can be encapsulated into 'chips' measuring only a few millimetres.

Sound recording has not been the only activity to benefit as a spin-off from these computer-age technological advances. Other, more homely, manifestations resulting from the huge investments of money and brainpower include the ubiquitous pocket electronic calculator, digital watches and micro-computer controlled washing machines.

Binary numbers

At the heart of all these developments is the use of a binary (two unit) scale of numbers instead of the decimal scale to which we are accustomed. This allows any number to be represented by a block or 'word' employing only two symbols or states—1 and 0. Table 15.1 shows how the binary scale works, in the particular case of a word-length of four binary digits ('bits'). More places or bits are needed for larger numbers but only the two states of 0 or 1 which can be easily related to on/off positions of an electronic switch, or the north and south poles of a magnet, etc.

Table 15.1 Decimal and Binary scales compared

Decimal	Powers of 2	Binary	Decimal	Powers of 2	Binary
0		0000	8	2^3	1000
1		0001	9		1001
2	2^1	0010	10		1010
3		0011	11		1011
4	2^2	0100	12		1100
5		0101	13		1101
6		0110	14		1110
7		0111	15	(2^4-1)	1111

Table 15.2 Range of values provided by different word lengths

Number of bits (n)	Range of values (2^n)	Signal-to-noise ratio (dB)
1	2	6
2	4	12
3	8	18
4	16	24
5	32	30
6	64	36
7	128	42
8	256	48
9	512	54
10	1,024	60
11	2,048	66
12	4,096	72
13	8,192	78
14	16,384	84
15	32,768	90
16	65,536	96

It will be seen that our four-bit word can have sixteen different values (of which one is 0) and in general a word-length of n bits provides 2^n values as shown on Table 15.2. This has a special significance in sound recording, as we shall see, since each bit in the word-length chosen gives a 6dB ($\times 2$) improvement in signal-to-noise ratio (also shown in the table). Clearly the degree of accuracy which can be achieved in purely numerical applications like calculators, as well as the highest number that can be expressed, is also directly related to word-length—which is a question of the complexity (and cost) of the given instrument. In speech synthesis, to take another example, each binary word might be made to represent a different speech sound—and again the degree of accuracy (intelligibility) could be enhanced by going to the expense of more bits per 'word'. The storage capacity of a digital 'memory' is quoted in bits: simple devices might have a capacity of only a few thousand bits (kilobits), while computer disc or tape memories can store many millions of bits (megabits).

Digital sound recording is extremely demanding of storage capacity, and speed of encoding. A high-quality system might need to handle several megabits per second. The Compact Disc, for example, has a maximum storage capacity of more than 8,000 megabits.

Analogue-to-digital conversion

In digital sound recording, the signal to be recorded starts off as an electrical imitation or 'analogue' of the original sound waveform (see Fig. 15.1). To convert this to digital form, the amplitude of the waveform is sampled at regular intervals of time and each sample is encoded and stored as a binary number corresponding to its value on a fixed amplitude scale. In the four-bit example shown, only sixteen different binary code numbers are possible (as we have seen from Table 15.2).

The digitally encoded signal is made up of pulses for the symbol 1 and blank spaces for 0, the system being referred to as pulse code modulation (PCM). The process of allocating each sample a binary code number is called quantising and clearly involves some approximation since the analogue waveform will usually be at some intermediary amplitude when sampled. This approximation leads to quantisation noise but this can be

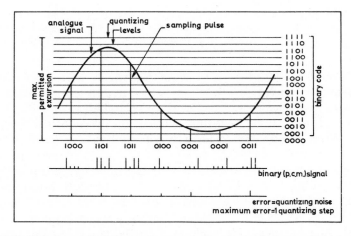

Fig. 15.1 In digital recording, the analogue waveform is sampled at fixed time intervals and each sampled level is expressed or 'quantised' in binary code. The process naturally involves some approximation which leads to quantising noise

reduced to very acceptable proportions by using more bits. This is confirmed by the last column of Table 15.2 which lists the signal-to-noise ratio obtainable for PCM systems using up to sixteen bits.

Provided the sampling frequency is more than twice the highest sound frequency to be recorded, it has been found that the waveform can be recorded and reproduced to high standards of accuracy. If an audio bandwidth of 15kHz is considered adequate, for example, a sampling frequency of 32kHz might be chosen. Where fidelity up to 20kHz is required, the sampling frequency might be 44kHz or 50kHz. To record or transmit PCM digital signals, the system requires a bandwidth at least equal to the sampling frequency multiplied by the word-length in bits. Thus a sixteen-bit system with a sampling frequency of 50kHz would need a bandwidth of 800,000Hz per channel—well beyond the capabilities of ordinary sound recording equipment.

Digital evolution

One of the first important applications of digital audio techniques was the BBC's construction of a PCM network for distributing radio programmes to its various transmitting stations in the late 1960s. Though this was only a thirteen-bit system with a 32kHz sampling frequency (audio bandwidth is in any case restricted to 15kHz on VHF/FM radio) it produced a dramatic improvement in broadcast quality. The important advantages of digital sound which appeared in this application included the following:

(a) *Reduced noise* Whereas noise is a continual nuisance in analogue distribution networks, becoming worse with each mile of landline or radio link travelled, it can effectively be ignored in the digital system. The digital-to-analogue converter at the receiving end of the line has only to recognise the presence or absence of pulses, not gauge their relative amplitudes, to be able to reconstitute the sound signal almost perfectly. The BBC's thirteen-bit system gives a signal-to-noise ratio of 78dB regardless of network distance (see Table 15.2)—much better than analogue.

(b) *Reduced distortion* Normal analogue networks introduce considerable non-linear and phase distortion, whereas the digital process restores the original waveform practically undistorted.

(c) *Wide frequency response* The full 15kHz range is preserved in the digital system, whereas high-frequency losses were almost inevitable in analogue lines.

Around 1972, the Nippon Columbia Company of Japan (Denon) began PCM sound recording, using professional videotape recorders to provide the necessary bandwidth. The conventional analogue LP records which they produced from these digital master recordings showed a degree of clarity compared with discs manufactured from analogue tape masters. In addition to the three advantages of the digital process mentioned above, the new master tapes possessed the following:

(a) *No wow-and-flutter* Because the replay system relied on an accurate quartz clock to synchronise the sampling rate on replay with that recorded, the usual short-term pitch fluctuations normally associated with tape (and disc) systems were eliminated.

(b) *No tape modulation noise* Analogue tape introduces several types of noise such as granular hiss, modulation noise and print-through. These are all avoided in digital recording.

(c) *Improved channel separation* As the left and right stereo signals are encoded separately, very little interchannel crosstalk takes place.

With such a formidable array of advantages, it is not surprising that most of the major record companies and independent studios soon followed the Nippon Columbia lead and installed digital machines for master recording. The designs varied, some using videotape equipment and others data storage units. This made it difficult to exchange recordings between studios, since each digital master could only be played back on the same type of machine on which it had been recorded. However, the in-house benefits were considerable. Masters did not deteriorate in store and copies could be virtually identical to the original.

By 1980, many of the LP records coming on to the market bore the word 'Digital', and the companies stressed the advantages of the new recording technique in their advertisements and sleeve-notes. It was, however, perfectly obvious— and often reiterated by the critics—that the different digital mastering machines gave inconsistent sound quality: that indeed these early digital recorders had limitations as well as advantages. These limitations included:

(a) *Increased distortion at low levels* While distortion in analogue recording increases at high signal levels, the opposite occurs in digital. Resolution deteriorates at low quantising levels leading to quite severe distortion. Techniques exist for disguising this effect, so that it is barely audible under most conditions. Nevertheless, degrees of acoustic dryness and tonal hardness were noticed in many early digital recordings, suggesting that the reverberant 'tail' of musical sounds, and the harmonics of certain instruments, notably strings, were not being reproduced cleanly.

(b) *Bandwidth restrictions* All professional digital recording systems used a sampling frequency in excess of 40kHz, thus permitting an audio bandwidth of 20kHz. This might seem to meet all hi-fi requirements but it is a feature of PCM encoding that a very sharp filter must be included to cut off all frequencies above the chosen upper limit. Such filters, with slopes of up to 100dB per octave, run the risk of 'ringing', that is, producing audible side-effects, unless designed very carefully. By contrast, analogue recordings tend to roll-off more gently at high frequencies.

Other practical limitations of the early digital equipment affected the way in which it was used. Editing was more difficult, for example, so that musicians were encouraged to make longer 'takes' with fewer stoppages. Ironically, this gave rise to some favourable comment from critics, who felt that editing had previously become too prevalent in the recording studios. Again, digital masters were mainly two-track only, so that balance engineers often felt obliged to go back to a simpler microphone technique and mix-down straight to two-track stereo. This was in contrast to the multi-microphone multi-track procedures evolved over recent years, yet, as with the simpler editing, it frequently produced a more natural, cleaner sound balance which drew critical acclaim for many of the new 'digital' LP records, even though it was an indirect, rather than a direct, consequence of the adoption of a digital mastering process.

Digital discs

While the so-called 'digital' LP records could, in the best examples, be identified as possessing at least some of the benefits inherent in the original studio master recordings, they were nevertheless cut and pressed in analogue form and by the old traditional methods. They were therefore subject to all the same limitations and just as easily damaged or invaded by dust and static as conventional LPs.

It was obvious that, if all the benefits of digital recording were to be enjoyed in the home, the sounds must be retained in digital form right up to the moment of playback. Research into truly digital disc systems was intensified and soon about half a dozen competing types were being demonstrated at engineering conventions and trade shows. This diversity of incompatible domestic systems, with each disc unplayable except on its own machine type, was much more serious in commercial terms than the similar lack of standardisation amongst professional studio equipment. The general public would like to be able to buy records in the shops without having to select a particular format suited to their own player unit. A great deal of confusion already exists in the videotape market, for example, where three quite different incompatible tape cassette formats are in general use—VHS, Beta and V2000.

At the time of writing (early 1982) three distinct digital audio disc formats are in an advanced state of development and all three seem likely to be launched commercially in the coming months. Brief descriptions of all three systems follow, though it is to be hoped that the manufacturers concerned may yet reach agreement on just one system and avoid the confusion which must inevitably accompany a 'war of the formats'.

The Compact Disc

Pride of place must be given to the laser-scanned Compact Disc developed by Philips in Holland, with subsequent collaboration from Sony in Japan (Plate 42). This is the most technically advanced of the systems so far on offer and has a number of important practical, as well as high-quality, features.

As with the earlier Philips invention, the Compact Cassette, the small size of the Compact Disc is already an attractive feature. The disc is only 120mm (4.7in) in diameter and consists of clear PVC 1.1mm thick. The digital sound signals are pressed into the PVC, on one side only, in the form of tiny pits or indentations measuring a mere 0.6μm across. The binary code is represented by pits for the 1 symbols and blank spaces for 0. The track spirals outwards from the disc centre and the microscopically small track spacing of 1.66μm gives up to 60 minutes of stereo music per disc. During manufacture, the stamped out PVC surface is given a thin coating of reflective aluminium and this in turn is overlaid with a transparent 0.15μm coating. A fixed linear track speed of about 125cm/s is employed and so the rotational speed decreases as the record plays, being about 500rpm at the centre and 215rpm at the outer edge.

As shown diagrammatically in Fig. 15.2, the optical playback system consists of a laser light-source, a series of lenses and mirrors and a light-sensitive detector. The laser beam is

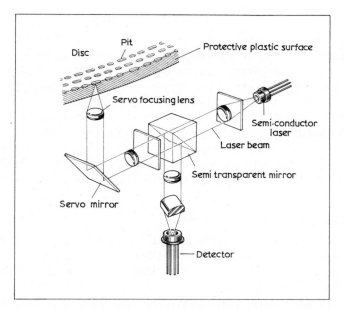

Fig. 15.2 Playback system for the Compact Disc, showing the semi-conductor laser light-source, the system of lenses and mirrors, and the detector which receives the pulses reflected from the disc surface

reflected and focussed so as to scan the helical track of pits and blank spaces from underneath the disc. As pits and blank spaces are scanned, the laser beam is either scattered or strongly reflected back downwards to be picked up by the photo-electric detector and converted into pulses of electric current. Thus the original digital signals have been reproduced and can be changed back into analogue form by a digital-to-analogue converter built into the player. The stereo electrical output of a Compact Disc player is therefore similar to that from a conventional record-player, tuner or cassette deck and can be connected to any hi-fi amplifier or domestic system.

Though the mass-production techniques for the Compact Disc are basically similar to those used for vinyl LPs, the small dimensions and close tolerances needed demand extremely high standards of air cleanliness and quality control measures. For the user, however, the Compact Disc is an extremely robust medium. Dust or finger marks are ignored by the laser beam and the normal problems of stylus cleaning and careful pickup alignment are a thing of the past. Also, since there is no physical contact, there is no wear, of the recorded track or the scanning mechanism. The player itself can be quite small, yet the constant linear speed feature allows more flexible access and cueing facilities than the conventional LP. In technical terms, the Compact Disc uses a sixteen-bit format with a sampling frequency of 44.1kHz. This gives a claimed frequency response up to 20kHz, immeasurable wow-and-flutter, with dynamic range and channel separation of up to 90dB.

While the Philips Compact Disc uses the same basic principle of a pitted surface and laser-beam scanning as their 300mm diameter Laser Vision video disc system, the two media are in all other ways incompatible. Philips and their associated companies are convinced that separate players and different standards are preferable for digital audio and TV playback.

The Audio High-Density disc

In a quite different approach, JVC (Victor Company of Japan) have sought to develop a digital audio disc format which would be compatible with their video disc player design. Therefore they have developed alongside each other VHD (Video High-Density) and AHD (Audio High-Density) disc units, with a proposal that a single player can be used for discs of both types—perhaps with an external PCM adaptor for the digital audio application.

The AHD disc is 260mm (10.2in) in diameter and again contains the PCM signals in the form of a helical track of tiny pits or depressions in a conductive PVC plastic material (Fig 15.3). The track is scanned electro-mechanically rather than optically by means of a broad-tipped sapphire stylus carrying a

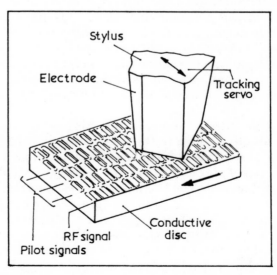

Fig. 15.3 The AHD system has pits in a conductive disc which are tracked by an electrode-carrying stylus

small electrode. The latter senses the differences in electrical capacitance which occur at each pit/blank space junction and so produces the required PCM output electrical signals. An adjoining track both guides the stylus so that it stays in line with the signal track and makes it possible to incorporate versatile access and cue facilities. The signal track includes provision for two or three sound channels as well as still colour pictures to be viewed on a standard TV set.

The AHD disc is double-sided, giving up to 60 minutes playing time per side. It runs at a fixed rotational speed (900rpm in Japan, 750rpm in Europe), has a sampling frequency of 47.25kHz and sixteen-bit quantisation. The disc is not proof against dust or fingermarks and so is kept in a protective case until loaded into the player.

The Mini-Disc

Telefunken in Germany have developed a digital audio disc as an extension of their earlier TED video disc which is no longer in production. The MD (Mini-Disc) is 135mm (5.3in) in diameter and carries grooves in which the digital signals are recorded as undulations (hill-and-dale) rather than laterally. The pickup device (Fig. 15.4) is a ceramic pressure transducer with a skid-shaped diamond stylus. The latter glides over several of the recorded undulations at a time and receives a mechanical 'shock' as each separate undulation passes the steep trailing edge. The disc has a constant groove velocity of 189cm/s, spins at between 278 and 695rpm and is supported on a cushion of air. A fine lubricating layer on the disc is said to give an extended life expectancy to both disc and stylus.

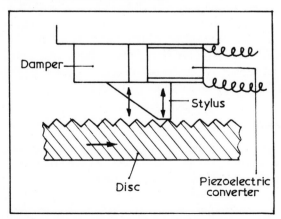

Fig. 15.4 The Telefunken Mini-Disc has hill-and-dale recorded grooves which are tracked by a skid-shaped stylus

The Mini-Disc gives up to 60 minutes stereo playing time per side and, like the AHD disc, must be kept in a protective case or 'caddy' until placed into the player. Manufacture is said to be no more expensive than for conventional LP records (the same vinyl material is used). The PCM system is fourteen-bit with a 48kHz sampling frequency, giving a signal-to-noise ratio of 85dB. Telefunken have also produced a smaller version, the Micro-Disc, measuring 75mm (3in) in diameter and giving up to 10 minutes per side stereo.

Digital tape in the home

The high cost and complexity of digital audio tape systems might suggest that their use would be confined to professional studios. However a number of manufacturers, particularly in Japan, have been quick to realise that the videocassette recorders now installed in many homes for use with the TV set (for recording and viewing at a later date or more convenient time) have the necessary bandwidth to make them into potentially competent storage systems for digital sound. There have already been demonstrated and marketed several digital processer units which can be connected between the normal stereo sound source (hi-fi set or microphones, etc) and a video recorder. In essence, the processer contains analogue-to-digital and digital-to-analogue converters in the record and replay chains respectively and generates PCM signals consistent with the TV video waveform.

Such adaptors, and the compact cassette integrated PCM recorders also being developed, give the amateur recording enthusiast a high-quality system with a specification and ease-of-use which he would find it difficult to match with the most expensive semi-professional analogue tape recorders available. Hopefully this equipment will encourage more people to take up creative 'live' recording and will not be used solely for the elementary (and distinctly uncreative) copying of disc records (analogue or digital) or off-air recording.

Surround sound

Ever since sound recording began, experimenters have tried to add a second and third acoustic dimension which would further enhance the ability of reproduced sound to recreate all the aural sensations of being present at a live concert. When stereophonic sound became a practical proposition in the late 1950s—after about eighty years of single-channel mono—discs, tape and broadcasts could recreate a limited arc of about

60° when reproduced through a matched pair of suitably spaced loudspeakers. This is enough to let listeners separate out the strands of music and locate orchestral players with acceptable naturalness.

Then in the 1970s we saw similar attempts made to launch a variety of 'quadraphonic' systems which used four channels and required the listener to sit at the centre of a square of four loudspeakers. The idea was to recreate in the domestic listening room the all-round bombardment of sound waves which is the normal (if only subconsciously appreciated) experience in the concert hall. After only two or three years, there was general agreement that quadraphony had failed to make any appreciable impact on the public's buying habits. Even though large sums of money had been spent by equipment manufacturers and record companies, they collectively decided to cut their losses and go back to stereo.

One major reason for the failure of quadraphony was the existence of several incompatible systems. The CD4 system used a complicated subcarrier tone to accommodate the third and fourth (rear) channels in a single record groove, while SQ and QS blended the extra signal information into two basic channels by different mixing (matrixing) of amplitude and phase-shifts. This by itself was enough to confuse the public, when the few people who bought one of the decoder units found that it would give a passable 'surround sound' effect from the few discs encoded in that particular format, but no other. In truth, each of the systems had some technical deficiency. Therefore the surround sound effect was more or less flawed and, in addition, the encoded discs could be recognised as giving inferior results to the best stereo-only discs when played in the stereo mode. The result was that they did not sell.

Despite this abortive exercise, it can hardly be doubted that some, hopefully trouble-free, technique for recording and reproducing the full acoustic ambience of a concert hall or music room will feature in sound installations of the future. One important ingredient missing from the early quad-raphonic systems was the directional information. To succeed fully in reproducing for the listener the sound field which would have surrounded him at a live concert, the system must capture and recreate in the listening room not only the time spread and phase dispersal, but also the directions of arrival of the reverberant sound waves.

Very effective results have already been demonstrated by the proponents of the Ambisonics UHJ system, though they have not yet been able to win the support of the major record companies or broadcasting organisations. Ambisonics UHJ is a British invention and is really a range or 'hierarchy' of systems. Depending on how much the record companies, broadcasters and consumers are prepared to pay, Ambisonics can offer several grades of directional fidelity. At the bottom of the list is surround sound in the horizontal plane, using two signal channels feeding a decoder connected to four loudspeakers. On the surface this looks very like the ill-fated quadraphonic systems, but the 'integrity' of the spatial effect produced is vastly superior. Also, as a bonus, discs encoded in this basic UHJ format can be played satisfactorily on a normal stereo system, so that no incompatibility problems arise. The Unicorn and Nimbus record companies, for example, encode many of their records even though they know that very few record buyers have an Ambisonics decoder.

Higher Ambisonics formats require a progressive increase in the number of recording/transmission channels. Adding one more channel of limited bandwidth, such as might be squeezed on to an existing stereo broadcasting system, is called '$2\frac{1}{2}$' and gives some improvement in surround sound. Adding one or two full bandwidth channels can introduce height information, with a suitable array of loudspeakers, to produce a so-called Periphonic full-sphere playback mode. One beauty of the system, which has been researched with support from the National Research and Development Corporation, is that the recording process captures the complete soundfield. Therefore this master recording is available for basic UHJ processing in the first instance but can be rendered in a higher format at any later date if required.

Though the Ambisonics recording process does make

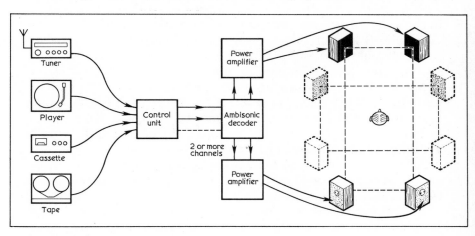

Fig. 15.5 Showing how an Ambisonic decoder can be introduced into a home hi-fi system

provision for mixing in extra spot microphones for special effects, its central feature is a cluster of four microphone capsules. These generate an omnidirectional signal W, as well as X, Y and Z signals representing the forward-, leftward- and upward-pointing components. At first an array of four standard microphones was used, but this was refined by the development of a special 'Soundfield' microphone. This has four capacitor microphone capsules in a tetrahedral grouping and a control box which allows the user to choose truly coincident stereo or ambisonic configurations, with remote control of tilt, rotation and polar diagram.

Future digital systems will be able to accommodate four discrete sound channels without difficulty, and it is noticeable that most of the home digital units so far announced make some reference to extra channel capability. If we can imagine flat, wall-mounted loudspeakers too, to get over the inconvenience of multiple speakers in the living-room, then surround sound may indeed stage a come-back.

Satellites and music-banks

Looking further into the future, we can glimpse even more spectacular hi-fi advances. The various digital disc and tape systems already in the pipeline may in their turn give way to a simple plastic card, like a credit card, containing several hours of music with each item accessible at a touch. Man-made satellites, which remain poised above a fixed point on the earth's surface, are already in space, and many more are planned. These carry radio receiving and transmitting equipment so that television and sound programmes can be relayed and beamed down to any country in the world. National boundaries will no longer limit our viewing or listening. Given the necessary dish-shaped aerial, we shall be able to choose from dozens of transmissions at will.

The glut of instant information and entertainment will be further multiplied if proposals for the setting up of 'music and literary banks' are put into effect. The storage capacity of computer data systems has already escalated so rapidly in recent years that we are told that it will soon be possible for readings of every worthwhile book, performances of every musical composition and copies of every film or TV programme to be located in centralised data banks. Consumers will be able to dial up any or all of these items in a moment. It seems that will-power and selectivity will be required human qualities, as they have always been, if the empty horrors of the 'Brave New World' predicted by Aldous Huxley are to be avoided.

APPENDIX 1: SUGGESTIONS FOR A BASIC RECORD COLLECTION

Chosen on the basis of both musical and technical excellence

Alain Organ Works. Marie-Claire Alain (Erato EDO 250–2)

Arnold Flute Concertos Nos 1 and 2, etc. John Solum (flute) and Philharmonia Orchestra conducted by Neville Dilkes (HMV ASD 3487)

Symphony No 1, etc. Bournemouth Symphony Orchestra conducted by Malcolm Arnold (HMV ASD 3828)

Bach, C. P. E. Symphonies Wq 182. English Concert directed by Trevor Pinnock (harpsichord) (Archiv 2533 449)

Bach, J. S. Organ Works, Vol 3. Peter Hurford (Argo D150D3)

Harpsichord Concertos (complete). Pinnock, Gilbert, Kraemer, Mortensen and English Concert (Archiv 2723 077)

Keyboard Works. Alfred Brendel (piano) (Philips 9500 353)

Bantock *Pierrot of the Minute*; **Bridge** Suite for strings, etc; **Butterworth** *The banks of green willow* Bournemouth Sinfonietta conducted by Norman Del Mar (RCA RL 25184)

Bartok Sonata for two pianos and percussion; **Debussy** *En blanc et noir*; **Mozart** Andante and Variations, K501. Martha Argerich and Stephen Bishop-Kovacevich (pianos), Willy Goudswaard and Michael de Roo (percussion) (Philips 9500 434)

String Quartets Nos 1–6. Tokyo Quartet (DG 2740 235)

Piano Concertos Nos 1 and 2. Maurizio Pollini (piano) and Chicago Symphony Orchestra conducted by Claudio Abbado (DG 2530 901)

Concerto for Orchestra. Chicago Symphony Orchestra conducted by Sir Georg Solti (Decca SXDL 7536)

Beethoven *Fidelio* Hildegard Behrens, Sona Ghazarian, Peter Hofmann, David Kuebler, Theo Adam, Hans Sotin, Gwynne Howell and Chicago Symphony Orchestra and Chorus conducted by Sir Georg Solti (Decca D178D3)

Piano Concerto No 5 *Emperor*. Rudolf Serkin and Boston Symphony Orchestra conducted by Seiji Ozawa (Telarc DG10065)

Violin Concerto. Itzhak Perlman and Philharmonia Orchestra conducted by Carlo Maria Giulini (HMV ASD 4059)

Symphonies Nos 1–9. Philharmonia Orchestra conducted by Kurt Sanderling; Sheila Armstrong, Linda Finney, Robert Tear, John Tomlinson and Philharmonia Chorus (HMV SLS 5239)

Piano Trio No 6 *Archduke*. Beaux Arts Trio (Philips 9500 895)

Piano Sonatas Nos 8–15. Bernard Roberts (Nimbus DC902)

Piano Sonatas Nos 27–32. Maurizio Pollini (DG 2740)

Bellini *Norma* Montserrat Caballé, Fiorenza Cossotto, Placido Domingo, Ambrosian Opera Chorus and London Philharmonic Orchestra conducted by Carlo Felice Cillario (RCA SER 5658–60)

Berlioz *Beatrice et Benedict* Dame Janet Baker, Christine Eda-Pierre, Helen Watts, Robert Tear, Thomas Allen, Robert Lloyd, John Alldis Choir and London Symphony Orchestra conducted by Sir Colin Davis (Philips 6700 121)

Requiem: *Grande Messe des Morts.* Robert Tear and London Philharmonic Choir and Orchestra conducted by André Previn (HMV SLS 5209)

Symphonie fantastique Berlin Philharmonic Orchestra conducted by Herbert von Karajan (DG 2530 597)

Bizet *Carmen* Leontyne Price, Mirella Freni, Franco Corelli, Robert Merrill, Vienna Boys' Choir, Vienna State Opera Chorus and Vienna Philharmonic Orchestra conducted by Herbert von Karajan (RCA SER 5600)

Symphony in C. French National Radio Orchestra conducted by Sir Thomas Beecham (HMV 30260)

Brahms Symphonies Nos 1–4, etc. Chicago Symphony Orchestra conducted by Sir Georg Solti (Decca D151D4)

Violin Concerto. Itzhak Perlman and Chicago Symphony Orchestra conducted by Carlo Maria Giulini (HMV ASD 3385)

Britten *Young Person's Guide to the Orchestra*; **Prokofiev** *Peter and the Wolf* Richard Baker (narrator) and New Philharmonia Orchestra conducted by Raymond Leppard (Classics for Pleasure CFP 185)

Canteloube *Chants d'Auvergne* Netania Davrath and orchestra conducted by Pierre de la Roche (Vanguard VSD 713–4)

Chopin Preludes Nos 1–26. Claudio Arrau (Philips 6527 091)

Piano Sonata No 3 etc. Vladimir Ashkenazy (Decca SXL 6810)

Debussy *Pelléas et Mélisande* Frederica von Stade, Richard Stilwell, José van Dam, Ruggero Raimondi, German Opera Chorus and Berlin Philharmonic Orchestra conducted by Herbert von Karajan (HMV SLS 5172)

Images, Prélude à l'après-midi d'un faune London Symphony Orchestra conducted by André Previn (HMV ASD 3804)

Nocturnes, Jeux Concertgebouw Orchestra conducted by Bernard Haitink (Philips 9500 674)

Delius *Appalachia, Sea Drift* John Shirley-Quirk, London Symphony Chorus and Royal Philharmonic Orchestra conducted by Richard Hickox (Argo ZRG 934)

Songs of Farewell, etc. Royal Philharmonic Orchestra conducted by Eric Fenby (Unicorn-Kanchana DPK 9008–9)

Donizetti *Lucia di Lammermoor* Montserrat Caballé, José Carreras, Claes H. Ahnsjö, Vicente Sardinero, Ambrosian Opera Chorus and New Philharmonia Orchestra conducted by Jesus Lopez Cobos (Philips 9500 183–5)

Dukas *Sorcerer's Apprentice*, etc. Rotterdam Philharmonic Orchestra conducted by David Zinman (Philips 9500 533)

Dvorak Symphony No 9 *From the New World.* Concertgebouw Orchestra conducted by Sir Colin Davis (Philips 9500 511)

Elgar Symphony No 1; **Vaughan Williams** *Fantasia on a theme of Thomas Tallis* London Philharmonic Orchestra conducted by Sir Adrian Boult (Lyrita REAM 1)

Symphony No 2. London Philharmonic Orchestra conducted by Vernon Handley (Classics for Pleasure CFP 40350)

Enigma Variations, Cello Concerto. Jacqueline du Pré and London Philharmonic Orchestra conducted by Daniel Barenboim (CBS 76529)

Violin Concerto. Kyung-Wha Chung and London Philharmonic Orchestra conducted by Sir Georg Solti (Decca SXL 6842)

Gershwin *Rhapsody in Blue, American in Paris* George Gershwin (piano-roll) and Columbia Jazz Band conducted by Michael Tilson Thomas (CBS 76509)

Gounod *Faust* Dame Joan Sutherland, Margreta Elkins, Franco Corelli, Nicolai Ghiaurov, Robert Massard, Ambrosian Opera Chorus, Choir of Highgate School and London Symphony Orchestra conducted by Richard Bonynge (Decca SET 327–30)

Handel *Acis and Galatea* Norma Burrowes, Anthony Rolfe-Johnson, Martyn Hill, Paul Elliott, Willard White and English Baroque Soloists conducted by John Eliot Gardiner (Archiv 2708 038)

Messiah Judith Nelson, Emma Kirkby, Carolyn Watkinson, Paul Elliott, David Thomas and Academy of Ancient Music conducted by Christopher Hogwood (Decca D189D3)

Haydn Symphony No 94 *Surprise*, Symphony No. 96 *Miracle.* Academy of St Martin-in-the-Fields conducted by Neville Marriner (Philips 9500 348)

Symphony No 103 *Drum Roll*, Symphony No 104 *London.* Philharmonia Hungarica conducted by Antal Dorati (Decca SDD 505)

Piano Trios. Beaux Arts Trio (Philips 6768 077)

The Seasons Edith Mathis, Siegfried Jerusalem, Dietrich Fischer-Dieskau, and Chorus and Academy of St Martin-in-the-Fields conducted by Neville Marriner (Philips 6769 068)

Holst *The Planets* Berlin Philharmonic Orchestra conducted by Herbert von Karajan (DG 2532)

Somerset Rhapsody, Brook Green Suite; **Vaughan Williams** *The Wasps* Bournemouth Sinfonietta conducted by Norman Del Mar (HMV ASD 3953)

Humperdinck *Hansel and Gretel* Frederica von Stade, Ileana Cotrubas, Christa Ludwig, Kiri Te Kanawa, Elisabeth Söderström, Siegmund Nimsgern, Children's Chorus of Cologne Opera and Gürzenich Orchestra conducted by John Pritchard (CBS 79217)

Janáček *Sinfonietta, Taras Bulba* Vienna Philharmonic Orchestra conducted by Charles Mackerras (Decca SXDL 7519)

Kodály *Háry János*, etc. London Philharmonic Orchestra conducted by Walter Susskind (Classics for Pleasure CFP 40292)

Lehár *The Merry Widow* Elizabeth Harwood, Teresa Stratas, Zoltan Kelemen, Rene Kollo, Werner Hollweg, Chorus of the German Opera and Berlin Philharmonic Orchestra conducted by Herbert von Karajan (DG 2707 070)

Leoncavallo *I Pagliacci* Renata Scotto, José Carreras, Kari Nurmela, Ugo Benelli, Thomas Allen, Southend Boys' Choir, Ambrosian Opera Chorus and Philharmonia Orchestra conducted by Riccardo Muti (HMV SLS 5187)

Liszt *Fugue on the theme BACH*, etc. Alfred Brendel (piano) (Philips 9500 286)

Mahler Symphony No. 8. Heather Harper, Lucia Popp, Arleen Auger, Yvonne Minton, Helen Watts, René Kollo, John Shirley-

Quirk, Martti Talvela, Vienna State Opera Chorus, Singverein Chorus, Vienna Boys' Choir and Chicago Symphony Orchestra conducted by Sir Georg Solti (Decca SET 534)

Symphony No 10 (ed Cooke). Bournemouth Symphony Orchestra conducted by Simon Rattle (HMV SLS 5206)

Mascagni *Cavalleria Rusticana* Montserrat Caballé, Julia Hamari, Astrid Varnay, José Carreras, Matteo Manuguerra, Ambrosian Opera Chorus and Philharmonia Orchestra conducted by Riccardo Muti (HMV SLS 5187)

Massenet *Werther* Frederica von Stade, Isobel Buchanan, José Carreras, Thomas Allen and Royal Opera House Orchestra, Covent Garden conducted by Sir Colin Davis (Philips 6769 051)

Le Roi de Lahore Dame Joan Sutherland, Huguette Tourangeau, Luis Lima, Sherill Milnes and National Philharmonic Orchestra conducted by Richard Bonynge (Decca SXL 6932)

Mendelssohn Symphony No 4 *Italian,* etc. London Symphony Orchestra conducted by André Previn (HMV ASD 3763)

Violin Concerto; **Bruch** Violin Concerto No 1. Itzhak Perlman and London Symphony Orchestra conducted by André Previn (HMV ASD 2926)

Monteverdi Sacred Vocal Music. Emma Kirkby, Ian Partridge, David Thomas, The Parley of Instruments and Roy Goodman (violin) (Hyperion A 66021)

Mozart *Don Giovanni* Dame Joan Sutherland, Elisabeth Schwarzkopf, Graziella Sciutti, Eberhard Waechter, Luigi Alva, Gottlob Frick, Giuseppe Taddei, Piero Cappuccilli and Philharmonia Orchestra conducted by Carlo Maria Giulini (HMV SLS 5083)

Die Zauberflöte Edita Gruberova, Lucia Popp, Brigitte Lindner, Siegfried Jerusalem, Roland Bracht, Wolfgang Brendel, Heinz Zednik, Bavarian Radio Chorus and Symphony Orchestra conducted by Bernard Haitink (HMV SLS 5223)

The Symphonies, Vol 5. Academy of Ancient Music directed by Jaap Schröder (violin) with Christopher Hogwood (harpsichord continuo) (L'Oiseaux-Lyre D171D4)

Symphonies Nos 25–41. Academy of St Martin-in-the-Fields conducted by Neville Marriner (Philips 6769 043)

Piano Concertos Nos 12 and 27. Murray Perahia (piano/conductor) and English Chamber Orchestra (CBS 76731)

Piano Concerto No 22 etc. Alfred Brendel (piano) and Academy of St Martin-in-the-Fields conducted by Neville Marriner (Philips 9500 145)

Horn Concertos. Dennis Brain and Philharmonia Orchestra conducted by Herbert von Karajan (HMV ASD 1140)

Mussorgsky *Pictures from an Exhibition, Khovantschina* (excerpts); **Borodin** *Prince Igor* (excerpts). Philharmonia Orchestra conducted by Herbert von Karajan (HMV SXLP 30445)

Offenbach *Tales of Hoffmann* Dame Joan Sutherland, Placido Domingo, Gabriel Bacquier, Ambrosian Singers and London Symphony Orchestra conducted by Richard Bonynge (Decca SET 545)

Poulenc *Les Biches* etc. Ambrosian Singers and Philharmonia Orchestra conducted by Georges Prêtre (HMV ASD 4067)

Prokofiev Piano Concerto No 1, etc; **Ravel** *Concerto for the left hand* etc. Andrei Gavrilov (piano) and London Symphony Orchestra conducted by Simon Rattle (HMV Melodiya ASD 3571)

Puccini *La Bohème* Victoria de los Angeles, Lucine Amara, Jussi Björling, Robert Merrill, John Reardon, Giorgio Tozzi, Fernando Corena and RCA Victor Orchestra and Chorus conducted by Sir Thomas Beecham (HMV SLS 896)

Madam Butterfly Mirella Freni, Luciano Pavarotti, Robert Kerns, Vienna State Opera Chorus and Vienna Philharmonic Orchestra conducted by Herbert von Karajan (Decca SET 584–6)

Tosca Montserrat Caballé, José Carreras, Ingvar Wixell, and Orchestra and Chorus of Royal Opera House, Covent Garden, conducted by Sir Colin Davis (Philips 6700 108)

Turandot Birgit Nilsson, Renata Scotto, Franco Corelli, Angelo Mercuriali, and Orchestra and Chorus of Rome Opera conducted by Francesco Molinari-Pradelli (HMV SLS 921)

Ravel *Daphnis et Chloé* Montreal Symphony Chorus and Orchestra conducted by Charles Dutoit (Decca SXDL 7526)

Bolero etc. Concertgebouw Orchestra conducted by Bernard Haitink (Philips 9500 314)

Rimsky-Korsakov *Scheherazade* Royal Philharmonic Orchestra conducted by Sir Thomas Beecham (HMV SXLP 30253)

Rodrigo *Concierto de Aranjuez, Concierto Andaluz* Angel Romero and Los Romeros (guitars) and Academy of St Martin-in-the-Fields conducted by Neville Marriner (Philips 9500 563)

Rossini *Barber of Seville* Maria Callas, Luigi Alva, Tito Gobbi and Philharmonia Orchestra conducted by Alceo Galliera (HMV SLS 853)

Saint-Saëns Symphony No 3. Chicago Symphony Orchestra and Gaston Litaize (organ) conducted by Daniel Barenboim (DG 2530 619)

Scarlatti, D. Sonatas. Trevor Pinnock (harpsichord) (CRD 1068)

Schubert Symphonies Nos 3 and 5. Royal Philharmonic Orchestra conducted by Sir Thomas Beecham (HMV SXLP 30204)

Piano Quintet, *The Trout*. Samuel Rhodes, Georg Hörtnagel and Beaux Arts Trio (Philips 6527 075)

String Quintet in C. Amadeus Quartet and William Pleeth (DG 2542 139)

Die Schöne Müllerin Dietrich Fischer-Dieskau (baritone) and Gerald Moore (piano) (DG 2530 544)

Song Recital. Dame Janet Baker (mezzo-soprano) and Geoffrey Parsons (piano) (HMV ASD 4054)

Schumann Symphonies Nos 1 and 4. Dresden State Orchestra conducted by Wolfgang Sawallisch (HMV SXLP 30526)

Kinderszenen, Kreisleriana Alfred Brendel (piano) (Philips 9500 964)

Shostakovich Symphonies Nos 1 and 9. London Philharmonic Orchestra conducted by Bernard Haitink (Decca SXDL 7515)

Symphony No 7, *Age of Gold* suite. London Philharmonic

Orchestra conducted by Bernard Haitink (Decca D213D2)

Sibelius *Finlandia, En Saga, Tapiola, Swan of Tuonela* Berlin Philharmonic Orchestra conducted by Herbert von Karajan (HMV ASD 3374)

Symphony No 4, *Luonnotar, Finlandia.* Elisabeth Söderström and the Philharmonia Orchestra conducted by Vladimir Ashkenazy (Decca SXDL 7517)

Strauss, Johann Jnr *Die Fledermaus* Anneliese Rothenberger, Renate Holm, Brigitte Fassbaender, Dietrich Fischer-Dieskau, Nicolai Gedda, Adolf Dallapozza, Walter Berry and Vienna Symphony Orchestra conducted by Willi Boskovsky (HMV SLS 964)

Waltzes, etc. Berlin Philharmonic Orchestra conducted by Herbert von Karajan (DG 2741 003)

Strauss, Richard *Till Eulenspiegel,* Also *Sprach Zarathustra, Salome* Dresden Staatskapelle conducted by Rudolph Kempe (HMV ESD 7026)

Stravinsky The *Firebird* Suite; **Mussorgsky** *Pictures from an Exhibition* Philadelphia Orchestra conducted by Riccardo Muti (HMV ASD 3645)

Petrushka (ballet). London Symphony Orchestra conducted by Claudio Abbado (DG 2532 010)

Tchaikovsky Symphonies Nos 1–6. Berlin Philharmonic Orchestra conducted by Herbert von Karajan (DG 2740 219)

Manfred Symphony New Philharmonia Orchestra conducted by Vladimir Ashkenazy (Decca SXL 6853)

Violin Concerto. Gidon Kremer and Berlin Philharmonic Orchestra conducted by Lorin Maazel (DG 2532 001)

1812 Overture, Marche Slave, Romeo and Juliet London Symphony Orchestra conducted by André Previn (HMV ASD 2894)

Vaughan Williams *Sea Symphony* Sheila Armstrong, John Carol Case and London Philharmonic Orchestra and Choir conducted by Sir Adrian Boult (HMV ESD 7104)

Symphony No 6, *The Lark Ascending.* Hugh Bean (violin) and New Philharmonia Orchestra conducted by Sir Adrian Boult (HMV ASD 2329)

Verdi *Aida* Mirella Freni, Agnes Baltsa, José Carreras, Piero Cappuccilli, Ruggero Raimondi, José van Dam, Vienna State Opera Chorus and Vienna Philharmonic Orchestra conducted by Herbert von Karajan (HMV SLS 5205)

Rigoletto Anna Moffo, Rosalind Elias, Robert Merrill, Alfredo Kraus, Ezio Flagello and RCA Italiana Orchestra and Chorus conducted by Sir Georg Solti (RCA RL 42865)

La Traviata Ileana Cotrubas, Placido Domingo, Sherill Milnes, Bavarian State Opera Orchestra conducted by Carlos Kleiber (DG 2707 103)

Wagner *Die Meistersinger* Hannelore Bode, Julia Hamari, Norman Bailey, Rene Kollo, Bernd Weikl, Kurt Moll, Vienna State Opera Chorus, and Vienna Philharmonic Orchestra conducted by Sir Georg Solti (Decca D13D5)

Parsifal Dunja Vejzovic, Peter Hofmann, José van Dam, Kurt

Moll, German Opera Chorus and Berlin Philharmonic Orchestra conducted by Herbert von Karajan (DG 2741 002)

Das Rheingold George London, Kirsten Flagstad, Gustav Neidlinger, Set Svanholm and Vienna Philharmonic Orchestra conducted by Sir Georg Solti (Decca SET 382)

Tristan und Isolde Linda Esther Gray, Anne Wilkens, John Mitchinson, Philip Joll, Gwynne Howell and Welsh National Opera Chorus and Orchestra conducted by Reginald Goodall (Decca D250D5)

Miscellaneous

It's a breeze André Previn (piano), Itzhak Perlman (violin) and rhythm players (HMV EMD 5537)

Sometimes when we touch Cleo Laine (vocal), James Galway (flute) and orchestra conducted by John Dankworth (RCA RL 25296)

Dmitri Tiomkin Western Film Music. Bob Saker (baritone), John McCarthy singers and London Studio Symphony Orchestra conducted by Laurie Johnson (Unicorn-Kanchana DKP 9002)

Songs my father taught me Robert White (tenor) and orchestra conducted by Ralph Mace (RCA RL 25345)

My own story Luciano Pavarotti (tenor) (Decca D253D2)

Digital Concert Orchestral pieces. Academy of St Martin-in-the-Fields conducted by Neville Marriner (HMV ASD 3943)

Together again Julian Bream and John Williams (guitars) (RCA ARL1 0456)

APPENDIX 2: SUGGESTIONS FOR FURTHER READING

Borwick, J. (Ed) *Sound Recording Practice* (London, 2nd ed 1980)

Culshaw, J. *Ring Resounding* (London, 1967)

Gelatt, R. *The Fabulous Phonograph* (London, 1956)

Marty, D. *An Illustrated History of Talking Machines* (Lausanne, 1979)

Olson, H. F. *Music, Physics and Engineering* (New York, 2nd ed 1967)

Read, O., and Welch, W. *From Tin Foil to Stereo* (New York, 1959)

Taylor, C. A. *Sounds of Music* (London, 1973)

Tombs, D. *Sound Recording: From Microphone to Master Tape* (Newton Abbot, 1980)

APPENDIX 3: GLOSSARY OF AUDIO TERMS

Absorption Attenuation of a sound wave on passing through a medium or striking a surface.

Acoustic feedback Fault condition in a sound reproducing system where signals from the loudspeaker can activate the input and so become re-amplified and cause instability. It can often be cured by mounting the loudspeakers on absorbent pads or otherwise breaking the physical return path from speakers to pickup cartridges.

Acoustic suspension Principle used in totally enclosed or **infinite baffle** loudspeakers. Making a virtue out of necessity, the stiffness of the enclosed air is used to provide the main restoring force to the speaker diaphragm which is deliberately designed with a slack mechanical suspension and **long-throw** coil assembly.

Alternating current (AC) See **Direct current.**

Ambience Acoustic environment. Increasingly used to mean the degree and character of the **reverberant** sound accompanying recordings.

Ambisonics System for recording and reproducing the full 360° soundfield.

Amplitude modulation (AM) Method of impressing sound signals on the much higher frequency currents of a radio transmitter, by making the amplitude of the radio 'carrier' vary according to the sound waveform.

Analogue Descriptive of a sound recording or transmission system where each stage retains the sound waveform in its original shape.

Anechoic Having no echo or reverberation. Anechoic rooms or enclosures are built to permit the testing of loudspeakers and microphones without interference from reflected sound waves and **standing wave** patterns.

Anti-skating device Attachment on pickup arm to compensate for the inward **sidethrust** or **bias** inherent in pivoted **offset** (cranked) arms. In the absence of such correction, the inward force causes the stylus to bear more heavily on the inner wall of the groove and may even make the pickup skate inwards.

Antistatic Fluid or impregnant used to disperse or render inert any static charges of electricity which might otherwise attract dust or discharge to give sparks or clicks. Gramophone records are prone to acquire and retain static charges caused, for example, by friction as the record is removed from its sleeve.

Automatic frequency control (AFC) Circuit arrangement in radio receivers which holds the tuning locked to a desired station and prevents drifting. AFC is an essential feature in push-button radios but can make accurate manual tuning to VHF/FM stations more difficult. The recommended procedure is therefore to tune with the AFC switched off and switch it on when the true setting (minimum background noise) has been found.

Automatic gain control (AGC) Circuit arrangement in radio receivers which maintains the reproduced signal at a steady volume irrespective of changes in the received signal strength, due to fading, etc. AGC, or **automatic volume control (AVC)**, is used in AM and FM receivers and has begun to have application in tape recorders. Here it amounts to automatic compression of the dynamic range and avoids the incidence of overload distortion or noisy reproduction (under-recording).

Azimuth Angle which the gap in a tape head makes with the horizontal (and the tape axis); should be exactly 90°. Accurate azimuth alignment is essential if tapes recorded on one machine are to be played on another with faithful reproduction of high frequencies. The alignment procedure is to reproduce a tape of high frequency tone and adjust the head base-plate screws for maximum output.

Balance control Twin variable resistor (potentiometer) fitted on most stereo amplifiers to enable the user to equalise the volume in left and right channels—which may be upset as a result of unequal sensitivity in the two halves of the stereo pickup cartridge or in the loudspeakers, etc. It is usually enough if the balance control can reduce the level in either channel by up to 10dB: but some controls can reduce either channel to zero.

Bandwidth Extent of the useful frequency range covered by a radio receiver or amplifier, etc. In audio it will generally be expressed as the upper and lower limit frequencies at which response falls to half power (-3dB). In radio it is given as so many kilohertz or megahertz.

Bass reflex Type of loudspeaker cabinet in which the back radiation emerges through a port in the front panel in phase with the frontal wave—and so reinforces it. Strictly, the phase inversion is accurate only at some selected resonant (low) frequency to which the compliance of the contained air and the mass of air in the port are tuned.

Bias (a) Signal at supersonic frequency (usually 40–100,000Hz) mixed with signal to be recorded on magnetic tape so as to give more linear transfer characteristic.

(b) DC voltage or current applied to valve or transistor to set operating point on linear portion of transfer characteristic.

(c) Sidethrust inherent in pivoted 'offset' pickup arms which may be neutralised by a sidethrust compensator or 'anti-skating device'.

Bit Contraction of the words 'binary digit' (1 or 0). Digital signals consist of binary words, with four-bit or eight-bit words sometimes referred to as **bytes**.

Capacitance Ability of components (capacitors) to store an electric charge; analogous to the **compliance** of a spring or contained volume of air (for example) to store mechanical energy. Capacitors are used in electronics for coupling, smoothing and tuning: the principle is also used in electrostatic microphones and loudspeakers.

Capstan Precision-turned spindle which drives a gramophone turntable (via idler wheels or belts) or magnetic tape (pinched between the capstan and a pressure roller). In turntables with fixed motor speed, the various playing speeds are generally selected by presenting the idler wheel or belt to a stepped diameter portion of the motor capstan. In tape drives, the capstan is usually mounted on the flywheel and is in turn driven via a stepped pulley arrangement from the motor.

Capture effect The ability of an FM receiver to reject the weaker of two signals at the same frequency.

Cardioid microphone Microphone with a heart-shaped (hence the name) directivity pattern: may also be called **uni-directional**, since it is sensitive over a wide frontal angle but 'dead' to sounds arriving at the back.

Carrier Continuous radio frequency signal on which the audio (or video) information is impressed as **modulation** of the carrier amplitude (AM) or frequency (FM).

Cartridge Gramophone pickup head. Confusion may sometimes arise since certain types of tape cassette are also referred to as 'cartridges'.

CCIR (International Radio Consultative Committee) Body responsible for drawing up recommended frequency correction characteristics for tape recording.

Channel separation Measure (in decibels) of the effective isolation between channels in a stereo system. Breakthrough of 'unwanted' signal into the 'wanted' channel is called **crosstalk** and should be at least -20dB at middle frequencies in a pickup and -40dB in amplifiers and tape recorders.

Clipping Excessive state of non-linear (overload) distortion in which waveform, viewed on an oscilloscope, is seen to flatten off on reaching the maximum amplitude of which the system is capable.

Coaxial Having the same centre line or axis. Thus **coaxial cable**, used in low-level audio connectors and aerial lead-ins, has one or more central 'live' wires insulated from and surrounded by an external metal braiding. The latter simultaneously provides the electrical return path and screens the central wire(s) from electrical interference. Again, a **coaxial loudspeaker** has one or more small drive units at the centre of the main cone.

Cocktail party effect Name given to our ability to listen selectively to one sound in the presence of other unwanted sounds, perhaps of equal intensity. This ability depends on the brain's analysis of the twin signals received by our two ears and is lost in monophonic (single-channel) reproduction. Twin-channel (stereophonic) reproduction restores part of our ability to separate the various strands of music, for example, in orchestral or vocal ensembles.

Compatible Consistent or able to co-exist with (literally 'to suffer with'!). Thus most developments in entertainment media have to be compatible with existing forms: colour TV transmissions must be compatible with—ie give a satisfactory picture on—monochrome sets; stereo gramophone pickups must play mono records satisfactorily; conversely, mono record players should be able to play stereo records—though, of course, producing only a mono output (this requirement is met only by those mono record players possessing 'mono compatible' or stereo cartridges); stereo tape machines should play mono tapes and vice versa (the latter requirement is met in the Philips Compact Cassette but not on most reel-to-reel recorders).

Compliance Ease with which a stylus, for example, can be displaced from its normal position, ie the reciprocal of **stiffness**. In a stereo pickup it is important that the cantilever holding the stylus and the cantilever's own termination or supports be designed to give reasonably high compliance in the vertical as well as the horizontal plane. The compliance unit (CU) equals 10^{-6}cm/dyne, ie a force of 1 dyne produces a displacement of .000001cm. (More recently, compliance is quoted in micrometres per milliNewton.) Unfortunately, there is no simple and universally applied method of measuring dynamic compliance (for an alternating force) which is more meaningful (and usually lower in value) than the static compliance.

Crossover distortion Non-linear distortion arising in Class B amplifiers, and often an important drawback in transistor amplifiers at low signal levels, because of discontinuity between the two halves of the push-pull output.

Crossover network Filter arrangement used in multiple-speaker systems to direct only the desired bands of frequencies to the various drive units—'tweeter', 'woofer', 'squawker', etc. Careful choice of the **crossover frequencies** is necessary and the degree of overlap between the units is determined by the slope of the crossover filter— 6dB or 12dB being the usual values.

Crosstalk Breakthrough between channels in a stereo system. (See **channel separation**.)

Cycle per second Unit of frequency: now superseded by **Hertz**.

Damping Reducing the sharpness of resonance in a tuned circuit (electrical or mechanical) by introducing resistance, air friction, etc.

Damping factor Ratio of the required (loudspeaker) load impedance of an amplifier to its effective source impedance. High damping factors, 30 and above, help to reduce speaker resonances.

Dead acoustic Environment with heavy absorption so that sounds die away rapidly with little reverberation.

Dead room Popular name for anechoic test chamber.

Decibel (dB) Logarithmic unit used to measure and compare sound intensities and the voltage or power levels in sound reproducing systems. Thus two intensities or powers differ by ten times the logarithm of their ratio and two sound pressures or voltages by twenty times the logarithm of their ratio. Again, doubling the power means a rise of 3dB: 1dB is about the smallest change detectable by the ear.

Decoder Receiver circuit designed to extract the separate signals in a transmission. Thus a stereo decoder separates out the left and right signals.

Decoupling Use of capacitors etc to prevent HT or unwanted alternating currents from reaching certain parts of a circuit. By analogy, compliance etc can be introduced in pickup arms and other mechanical systems to prevent transmission of unwanted acoustic energy.

De-emphasis Reduction of high frequencies in a receiver or record player to compensate for the original **pre-emphasis** and to achieve a lower level of background noise.

Defluxer (or demagnetiser). Device which will remove unwanted residual magnetisation in tape heads (or tapes) by the application of an AC field which is gradually reduced to zero.

Demodulator (or detector). Stage in a receiver which extracts the audio frequency signal from the modulated radio frequency carrier.

Deviation Extent to which the carrier frequency in a frequency modulated transmission is swung by the applied audio frequency signal. Maximum deviation is normally ± 75kHz.

Difference tone Low frequency (beat) tone produced when two tones are present together. Its frequency is the difference between the two original frequencies.

Diffraction Bending of waves round obstacles which are smaller than the wavelength. In audio, this accounts for irregularities in radiated response of loudspeakers, for example, as a result of longer wavelength sounds bending round the enclosure.

Digital Method of sound recording or transmission in which sound waveforms are encoded into streams of pulses representing binary words.

DIN (Deutsche Industrie Normen) Set of standards established, and enforced, in Germany and gradually adopted throughout Europe. It covers, for example, plugs and connectors, and includes DIN 45 500 which lays down minimum hi-fi standards and methods of measurement for tuners, turntables, tape recorders, microphones, amplifiers and integrated systems.

Diode Valve or semiconductor device which conducts current in one direction but not in the other: used in demodulators and power supplies where it 'rectifies' AC to produce DC.

Dipole Straight rod aerial effectively half a wavelength long at the required frequency.

Direct current (DC) Flow of electrons in one direction only due to application of a fixed voltage: as distinct from alternating current (AC) produced by an applied voltage which swings about zero or some fixed value.

Direct-cut Method of recording straight to disc without a tape stage.

Directivity pattern (or polar diagram). Graph showing the response of a loudspeaker, microphone or aerial at all angles in a given plane.

Distortion Any unwanted change in a reproduced signal affecting its frequency response or introducing new products.

Dolby system Noise-reducing circuitry used widely in cassette recorders.

Doppler effect Shift in frequency or pitch due to relative movement of source and observer, the whistle of a passing train, for example. It has some bearing on loudspeaker performance since the cone will normally move as a whole in response to low frequencies and act as a moving source during the radiation of simultaneous high notes.

Doublet Source of waves which radiates equally (but in anti-phase) to front and back, a speaker in flat baffle or free-standing electrostatic speaker, for example. Side radiation tends to cancel.

Drop-out Short-term fall in reproduced level from magnetic tape due to dust particle momentarily preventing intimate tape/head contact or imperfections in the tape coating.

Dubbing Copying a recording in the same medium: the record so obtained.

Dynamic microphone One using the moving-coil principle.

Dynamic range Ratio (in phons) between the loudest and softest sounds in a live performance (about 20 phons in speech and up to 70 phons in music). Ratio (in decibels) between the largest signal a system can handle without distortion to the smallest signal it can reproduce without masking by the inherent background noise.

Earth (or ground). Electrical connection to the mass of the earth: normally regarded as zero.

Earth loop Faulty interconnection between parts of an audio system in which more than one earth path exists: can result in trouble with induced mains hum.

Echo Discrete repetition of sound (or radio wave).

Efficiency Ratio of output to input, normally expressed as a percentage. Thus most loudspeakers are relatively inefficient transducers of electrical to acoustical power, having efficiencies of only about 1–10%.

Electromagnet Type of magnetic component which depends on current flowing in the vicinity of an iron core.

Electron Fundamental particle carrying negative electrical charge. An electric current consists of a flow of electrons: an electric charge (negative or positive) is an excess or deficiency of electrons respectively.

Electrostatic Using the principle of a fixed electric charge. Thus electrostatic loudspeakers and microphones have fixed and movable plates across which a fixed charge (polarisation) is applied.

Elliptical stylus Type of stylus whose tip has been formed with a bi-radial cross-section. The larger dimension (about 18μm radius) sits across the groove and the smaller (about 8μm radius) is better able to explore the waveform at high frequencies and so reduce tracing distortion.

Equalisation Process of frequency correction applied on replay to compensate for non-linear characteristic used in recording.

Erase head Electromagnet in advance of record tape head which erases any signal previously present on the tape by applying a strong field at supersonic frequency.

Farad Unit of capacitance, usually reduced to smaller sub-units: the microfarad (μF) or picofarad (pF).

$$1 \text{ Farad} = 10^6 \mu F = 10^{12} \text{ pF}$$

Feedback Return of signal to an earlier part in the chain, eg acoustic feedback from loudspeaker to microphone or pickup, and negative feedback used in amplifiers to reduce distortion, etc.

Ferrite Man-made material, iron based and used for compact aerials in radios etc.

Flutter Short-term speed fluctuations causing changes in musical pitch. Flutter frequencies are from 20Hz upwards, lower frequencies being classed as **wow**.

Frequency Rate of vibration in a mechanical system or alternating current, etc, being the number of complete cycles performed per second. Frequency was previously quoted in cycles per second (c/s) but is now internationally given in Hertz (Hz). Thus the frequency of concert pitch A is 440Hz.

Frequency doubling Production of second harmonic in a loud-speaker due to overloading and flexing of the cone.

Frequency modulation (FM) Method of impressing sound signals on the much higher frequency currents of a radio transmitter, by making the frequency of the radio 'carrier' vary according to the sound waveform. The audio frequency is represented by the rate of change of carrier frequency; audio volume governs the extent of frequency swing or deviation—with a maximum in the UK of 75kHz. FM has the advantage of reducing interference noise, which is further discriminated against by treble pre-emphasis.

Frequency response Range of frequencies over which equipment operates within stated decibel limits, eg 20–20,000Hz ±2dB.

Fundamental Frequency or musical note associated with the simplest form of vibration present, usually the first and lowest number of a harmonic series.

Gain Ratio of output to input, usually expressed in decibels; similar to amplification factor.

Handling capacity Maximum power (or voltage) which a loud-speaker, etc, can accept without serious distortion.

Harmonics Overtones or partials having frequencies which are exact multiples of the fundamental. The numbers and relative strengths of the harmonics determine the timbre or tonal quality of musical instruments.

Harmonic distortion Form of amplitude distortion in which spurious harmonics are generated.

Heat-sink Metal plate or chassis on which power transistors are fitted to give efficient conduction of heat and prevent excessively high temperatures.

Hertz (Hz) Unit of frequency, equalling one cycle per second.

High fidelity (Hi-fi) Reproduction of sounds with as much realism as present equipment can achieve.

High-pass filter Circuit which attenuates low frequencies.

Hill-and-dale Older system of disc recording in which the stylus moves up and down instead of from side-to-side as in modern mono (lateral) recording.

Hole-in-the-middle Descriptive of stereo reproduction where, perhaps due to speakers being too far apart, central images are faint or non-existent.

Horn loading Type of loudspeaker design in which the drive unit works into a tapered or flared pipe.

Hum Unwanted droning noise at the mains frequency and its harmonics.

Hum loop Condition liable to give hum troubles because of completion of a current path into which mains fields may induce hum. It is most often the result of earthing at more than one point.

Idler Wheel with rubber or plastic tyre which transmits drive from the motor capstan to a record turntable. It does not influence the speed of rotation, except that it will introduce wow or flutter if its surface is not completely uniform: it should be retracted in the 'off' position to avoid the formation of 'flats'.

Impedance (Z) Opposition to the flow of alternating current. It is measured in ohms and is the ratio of voltage to current. May have inductive, capacitive and resistive elements: an inductive impedance increases with frequency, a capacitive impedance decreases with frequency.

Infinite baffle Type of loudspeaker enclosure in which the wave from the back of the cone is prevented from reaching the front. This is commonly achieved by using a totally enclosed box (so-called **acoustic suspension**) but would also apply to a speaker mounted in a party wall.

Instability Undesirable tendency to break into oscillation and produce distortion or possible damage to components.

Insulator Material which does not pass electric currents, eg glass, porcelain and most plastics.

Integrated circuit (IC) Miniaturised electronic component which replaces complete networks of conventional transistors, capacitors, etc, and consists of microscopically small junctions and semi-conductor materials encapsulated in a plastic block.

Intensity Rate of flow of sound energy through unit area of a wavefront, measured in watts per square centimetre: the objective property associated with loudness.

Intermediate frequency (IF) The difference frequency produced in a superhet receiver by mixing the received and local oscillator signals. High amplification can then take place in several IF stages.

Intermodulation Production of sum and difference frequencies in any non-linear device: thus intermodulation distortion occurs as a result of non-linearity in amplifiers or transducers.

ips Abbreviation for inches per second, the unit of running speed for tape machines in UK and USA. For conversion to metric specifications, 1ips = 2.54 centimetres/second, e.g. $3\frac{3}{4}$ips = 9.5cm/sec.

Kilo Prefix for units which are 1,000 times the basic unit. Thus 1 Kilohertz (kHz) = 1,000Hz and we also have Kilohm, Kilovolt, Kilowatt, etc.

Künstkopf stereo Method of sound recording using twin microphones situated in the ears of a dummy head.

Labyrinth Type of loudspeaker enclosure in which folded channels apply a critical load on the drive unit and delay the emergence of the back wave.

Lateral recording System in which the stylus moves from side to side as opposed to the older hill-and-dale motion. Stereo disc recording can be considered to combine the two principles, though the planes of left and right channel motion are effectively at $+45°$ and $-45°$ to the record surface.

Limiting Automatic control of signal level by preventing signals exceeding a certain amplitude: essential feature of FM receivers to keep output amplitude constant.

Logarithmic (log) Refers to a scale in which equal divisions correspond to equal ratios instead of equal linear increments. The senses of hearing, sight and touch follow a logarithmic law and so scales of frequency and the loss introduced by volume controls, etc, are normally graduated logarithmically to correlate more closely with the ear's behaviour.

Long-throw Type of moving-coil loudspeaker construction in which high amplitudes of movement can be handled without undue distortion: a necessary feature of the compact 'infinite baffle' speakers now popular.

Loudness Subjective estimate of sound intensity.

Loudness control Type of volume control which attempts to take into account the ear's relatively poor response to low (and very high) frequencies at low listening levels. In fact, the effectiveness of such a control—which is often a simple bass boost network—can be only approximate and it is not often fitted on British amplifiers, though it is almost universal on American and Continental equipment.

Low-pass filter Network which cuts off above a predetermined frequency.

LP (long play) Applies to gramophone records designed to run at $33\frac{1}{3}$rpm and magnetic tapes of 35μm overall thickness (which give one and a half times the playing duration of Standard Play tapes).

Mains Source of domestic electricity supply. In UK and much of Europe it is 240 Volt, 50Hz AC: America generally uses 110 Volt, 60Hz.

Masking Effect in hearing, whereby the presence of one sound can raise the threshold of audibility of another, so making it more difficult to detect.

Matching Arranging the impedances of a signal source and its load for optimum transfer of signal.

Mega Prefix for units which are 1,000,000 times the basic unit. Thus 1 Megahertz (MHz) = 1,000,000Hz and we also have Megohm, Megavolt, Megawatt, etc.

Micro (μ) Prefix for units which are 1,000,000 times smaller than the basic unit. Thus 1 Farad = 1,000,000 microfarads (μF) and we also have microsecond (μs), microamp (μA), etc.

Microfarad (μF) Unit of capacitance.

Microphone Transducer which responds to sound waves and converts sound energy into electrical energy.

Milli Prefix for units which are 1,000 times smaller than the basic unit. Thus 1 Volt = 1,000 millivolts (mV) and we also have milligram, milliwatt, etc.

Modulation Superimposition of an audio (or video) signal on a high frequency 'carrier' signal by altering the amplitude or frequency of the latter. Also used to describe the impression of audio waveforms on a record groove. Maximum permissible level is referred to as 100% modulation.

Modulation noise Type of noise, for example in tape recording, which appears only when a signal is present and varies with signal amplitude.

Monaural Literally means 'with one ear' but is occasionally used as a misnomer for 'monophonic'.

Monitoring Checking programme quality either by ear or eye, using meters. The **monitor head** on a tape recorder is a playback head which scans the tape after the record head as an immediate check on recorded quality. A **monitoring loudspeaker** is one built to professional standards.

Monophonic (mono) Using a single channel of communication, as compared with 'stereophonic' which uses two separate channels.

Moving-coil Type of transducer (loudspeaker, microphone or pickup) which relies on vibrations of a coil of wire in a magnetic field.

Moving-iron Transducer in which one or more pieces of soft iron move in the magnetic field.

Moving-magnet Transducer in which one or more pieces of magnetised metal move in relation to fixed coils.

Multi-path distortion Interference condition in radio reception resulting from the desired signal reaching the aerial by paths of different effective length.

Multiplex Process by which several signals, for example left and right stereo channels, are combined for transmission on a single carrier and subsequently separated at the receiver.

Mu-metal Alloy of iron and nickel frequently used for screening.

Music power Rating used in some amplifier specifications which is based on the fact that musical signals are generally non-continuous and assumes that the standing voltage will not drop during the period of measurement. Genuine continuous or 'root-mean-square' power ratings give a better means of comparative measurement and are to be preferred.

Muting Making silent, as in some tuners which attenuate inter-station noise during tuning. Also used to describe the cut-out which operates during the auto-stop cycle on some record players.

NAB (National Association of Broadcasters) Body responsible in USA for drawing up recording standards (also NARTB). The NAB tape spool has a large centre hole and carries 730m (2,400ft) of standard tape.

Negative feedback Circuit technique in which part of an amplifier stage output is returned in anti-phase to an earlier point in the circuit. Gain is reduced but with advantages in reduced distortion and noise.

Neutral Side of the mains supply opposite the 'live' wire and effectively at or near earth potential. Was formerly colour-coded black but is now blue.

Noise By definition, any unwanted sound: in audio equipment it includes mains hum, resistor noise, tape hiss, record surface noise, etc.

Non-linearity Departure of transfer characteristics from the ideal straight line for all levels of input signals: results in non-linear distortion, ie generation of harmonics and intermodulation products.

Objective The measured value as opposed to the sensed or estimated (subjective) equivalent. Thus frequency is the objective property associated with musical pitch, intensity is allied to loudness, etc.

Obstacle effect Frequency disturbance due to the fact that objects in the path of a sound wave reflect only those sounds which have a shorter wavelength than their own dimensions. Longer wavelengths are not reflected but bend round the object. Thus low frequencies tend to ignore the obstacle while high frequencies are reflected, leaving a 'sound shadow' behind the obstacle.

Octave Musical pitch interval corresponding to a frequency ratio of 2:1.

Offset angle Extent to which the axis of a pickup cartridge is offset with respect to the line joining pivot and stylus, to minimise tracking error. (See also **overhang**.)

Ohm (Ω) Unit of electrical resistance, reactance or impedance.

Ohm's Law Formula which defines electrical resistance (ohms) in terms of the voltage applied (volts) and current flow (ampères). For any circuit, volts = amps × ohms or $V = I \times R$.

Omnidirectional Equally sensitive in all directions. An omnidirectional microphone or aerial picks up signals equally from all directions: an omnidirectional loudspeaker radiates equally in all directions.

Open circuit Condition of no-current resulting from discontinuity of the normal electrical path, for example when the switch is in 'off' position or a solder or screw contact has broken.

Oscillator Apparatus for producing sustained electrical oscillations, usually by means of positive feedback between the output and input at the required frequency.

Overhang Distance by which a pickup stylus overshoots the spindle centre. Combines with the calculated offset angle (qv) to give minimum tracking error distortion.

Overload (also over-modulation) Condition in which signal level has been allowed to exceed the 'safe' value so that the output can no longer rise in proportion to the input, ie non-linear distortion occurs.

Overload margin Extent to which input may exceed the nominal rating before causing serious distortion. This feature is now being given more prominence in amplifier design.

Parallel tracking Type of pickup arm which carries the stylus along the same radial path as was followed by the cutter-head during disc recording. Also called **linear tracking** or **radial tracking**.

PCM (Pulse Code Modulation) The most commonly used type of binary encoding in digital sound recording and transmission.

Phase Point reached in a cyclic motion, wave or electrical signal. Two loudspeakers, for example, are said to be in phase or correctly phased if their diaphragms move forward and back in synchronism on being fed with the same (mono) signal.

Phon A unit of loudness level related to the ear's subjective impression of signal strength. Equivalent to the decibel at 1,000Hz.

Pinch effect Type of disc-tracing distortion in which the stylus rides up and down twice in each recorded cycle due to the difference in shape between cutting and reproducing stylus tips.

Pitch (a) Aspect of auditory sensation which enables the listener to associate sounds on a subjective scale related to frequency.

(b) Number of disc grooves per inch.

Playing weight Another name for **tracking force**, measured in grammes, in a gramophone pickup.

Pre-echo Undesired transfer of a recorded signal from one disc groove to another. **Post-echo** can also occur.

Pre-emphasis Deliberate change in the frequency response during recording or transmission for the purpose of improving signal-to-noise ratio or reducing distortion. The opposite process on replay is **de-emphasis**.

Presence Degree of forwardness in a reproduced voice or instrument resulting from boosting in the frequency region 2–8kHz.

Print-through Undesired transfer of a recorded signal from one layer of tape to another.

Quadraphony System of sound recording and reproduction using four channels in an attempt to recreate a 360° soundfield around the listener. (See also **Ambisonics**.)

Quantisation Process in which the sampled values of a waveform are allocated values on a scale of levels in a digital system.

Quieting Reduction of background noise in a radio receiver when the aerial voltage reaches a stated value.

Rectifier Device for transforming an alternating current (AC) into a direct one (DC).

Resistance Property of a substance which restricts the flow of electric current through it. Measured in ohms.

Resonance Condition arising from the combination of mass and compliance (or inductance and capacitance) in a system, resulting in a maximum response to a particular frequency.

Reverberation Persistence of sound due to multiple reflections in a hall or enclosure.

RIAA (Record Industry Association of America) Refers to gramophone record equalisation curve.

RMS (Root mean square) The equivalent DC value of a varying quantity for power calculations, being the square root of the average value of the square of the instantaneous values.

Rumble Undesirable low-frequency vibration transmitted from a record-player or tape motor to the pickup or replay head. A **rumble filter** reduces its audibility.

Selectivity Ability of a receiver to discriminate between a wanted signal on one frequency and unwanted signals on other frequencies.

Sensitivity Measure of the signal level needed for a receiver, amplifier or transducer to deliver a stated output.

Side-bands Frequency bands on either side of the **carrier** containing the signal components produced by the process of modulation.

Signal-to-noise ratio Ratio of desired or reference signal magnitude to that of the noise, expressed in decibels.

Stereophony Method of recording or transmission using two or more channels to produce an illusion of spacial distribution of sound sources.

Stroboscope Pattern of dots or stripes which appears stationary when moving at the predetermined speed and illuminated by AC lighting.

Time constant Shorthand method of specifying the values of resistor and capacitor to be used in a frequency correction network: equals the product of R and C stated in microseconds (μs).

Tracing distortion Failure to reproduce the signal waveform recorded on disc due to the different shapes of the cutting and reproducing styli.

Tracking error Angular difference between the curved path followed by a pivoted gramophone pickup and the straight radial path of the cutter. Leads to tracking distortion.

Transducer Device designed to convert oscillatory energy from one form into another. Examples include microphones, loudspeakers, pickup cartridges and tape heads.

Transient Sudden change of state, for example in the signal from percussive musical instruments.

Tweeter Loudspeaker drive unit designed to reproduce high frequency sounds.

Velocity Distance travelled in unit time: for example, the velocity of sound in air at 20°C is 344m per second; the velocity of electromagnetic waves (light and radio) is 300,000,000m/s.

Vertical tracking angle Plane of stylus motion in a stereo pickup cartridge: should be about 20° in front of the true vertical to correspond with the angle taken up by the cutting stylus.

VHF (Very high frequency) Radio frequencies between 30 and 300MHz.

VU meter Volume unit meter having specified scale markings for monitoring the signal level during recording or playback.

Watt Unit of electrical power.

Waveband Band of wavelengths to be used for a stated purpose, for example the long, medium and short wavebands allocated for broadcasting.

Wavelength Distance measured along the path of a wave occupied by one cycle at the given frequency. Wave velocity = frequency × wavelength.

Weighting System of using agreed filters when measuring noise or wow-and-flutter to produce a measurement which accords more closely with the nuisance value to the human ear.

Woofer Loudspeaker drive unit designed to reproduce low frequency sounds.

Wow Slow fluctuations in the speed of a turntable or tape transport mechanism.

INDEX